The United States

Success for English Learners

www.harcourtschool.com

Copyright © by Harcourt, Inc.

All rights reserved. No part of this publication may be reproduced or transmitted in any form or by any means, electronic or mechanical, including photocopy, recording, or any information storage and retrieval system, without permission in writing from the publisher.

Permission is hereby granted to individuals using the corresponding student's textbook or kit as the major vehicle for regular classroom instruction to photocopy Copying Masters from this publication in classroom quantities for instructional use and not for resale. Requests for information on other matters regarding duplication of this work should be addressed to School Permissions and Copyrights, Harcourt, Inc., 6277 Sea Harbor Drive, Orlando, Florida 32887-6777. Fax: 407-345-2418.

HARCOURT and the Harcourt Logo are trademarks of Harcourt, Inc., registered in the United States of America and/or other jurisdictions.

Printed in the United States of America

ISBN-13: 978-0-15-349414-7
ISBN-10: 0-15-349414-X

If you have received these materials as examination copies free of charge, Harcourt School Publishers retains title to the materials and they may not be resold. Resale of examination copies is strictly prohibited and is illegal.

Possession of this publication in print format does not entitle users to convert this publication, or any portion of it, into electronic format.

4 5 6 7 8 9 10 1409 15 14 13 12 11 10

Contents

Introduction	v
Unit 1	
Unit Opener	1
Chapter 1	
Lesson 1	2
Lesson 2	6
Lesson 3	10
Lesson 4	14
Lesson 5	18
Chapter 2	
Lesson 1	22
Lesson 2	26
Lesson 3	30
Lesson 4	34
Lesson 5	38
Unit 2	
Unit Opener	42
Chapter 3	
Lesson 1	43
Lesson 2	47
Lesson 3	51
Lesson 4	55
Chapter 4	
Lesson 1	59
Lesson 2	63
Lesson 3	67
Lesson 4	71
Chapter 5	
Lesson 1	75
Lesson 2	79
Lesson 3	83
Unit 3	
Unit Opener	87
Chapter 6	
Lesson 1	88
Lesson 2	92
Lesson 3	96
Lesson 4	100
Lesson 5	104
Chapter 7	
Lesson 1	108
Lesson 2	112
Lesson 3	116
Lesson 4	120

Unit 4

Unit Opener **124**

Chapter 8
Lesson 1 .... **125**
Lesson 2 .... **129**
Lesson 3 .... **133**
Lesson 4 .... **137**

Chapter 9
Lesson 1 .... **141**
Lesson 2 .... **145**
Lesson 3 .... **149**
Lesson 4 .... **153**

Unit 5

Unit Opener **157**

Chapter 10
Lesson 1 .... **158**
Lesson 2 .... **162**
Lesson 3 .... **166**
Lesson 4 .... **170**
Lesson 5 .... **174**

Chapter 11
Lesson 1 .... **178**
Lesson 2 .... **182**
Lesson 3 .... **186**
Lesson 4 .... **190**

Unit 6

Unit Opener **194**

Chapter 12
Lesson 1 .... **195**
Lesson 2 .... **199**
Lesson 3 .... **203**
Lesson 4 .... **207**
Lesson 5 .... **211**

Chapter 13
Lesson 1 .... **215**
Lesson 2 .... **219**
Lesson 3 .... **223**
Lesson 4 .... **227**
Lesson 5 .... **231**

Chapter 14
Lesson 1 .... **235**
Lesson 2 .... **239**
Lesson 3 .... **243**
Lesson 4 .... **247**

Answer Key **251**

Introduction

One out of five students in classrooms today speaks a language other than English. When in content area classes, such as social studies, these English language learners are faced with the challenge of learning two aspects of the discipline at the same time. They must learn the specialized language and vocabulary of the content area, including unique grammatical structures, as well as the facts associated with the subject area.

Content area teachers may wonder why an English language learner functions successfully when using conversational English, yet he or she struggles to keep up academically with peers whose first language is English. The fact is that academic English is much more complex and abstract than conversational English. It is very important to understand that this is the normal course of second language development. Research shows that students can acquire high levels of proficiency in conversational English within one or two years. However, to attain proficiency in academic English that is equal to grade-level peers can take much longer.

Success for English Learners provides support for social studies teachers using *Harcourt Social Studies* who have English language learners in their classes. *Harcourt Social Studies* offers English Language Learner notes at point of use in the Teacher Edition. *Success for English Learners* can be used with English language learners who are at the beginning, intermediate, and advanced proficiency levels and who need additional support to be successful with each lesson in *Harcourt Social Studies*.

Challenges for English Learners in Social Studies

Since social studies concepts are abstract, they are particularly language-dependent. In addition, social studies requires prior knowledge that is culture-specific, unlike other subjects. American cultural references that English speakers may recognize automatically will be foreign to English language learners from other countries. The vocabulary and social studies concepts present specific challenges to the English language learner.

The following are examples of vocabulary, grammar, word usage, and syntax challenges that should be considered when planning social studies instruction for English language learners.

SOCIAL STUDIES CHALLENGES	EXAMPLES
Vocabulary	
Abstract concepts	democracy, representation
Specialized vocabulary	monarchy, revolution, liberty
Culture-specific vocabulary	pioneer, frontier, colonists
Sentence Structures	
Embedded clauses	He explored a large area of what was to become the Southeastern United States, including present-day Florida . . .
Unclear references	Would it be difficult for you to move to a new place? What might you like about it?
Unreal past conditions	What might have happened to the colonists on Roanoke Island?
Verb tenses	How might his experiences as a backwoodsman have helped him become a successful leader?
Clauses and factual sequence do not match	This backwoodsman surprised many people when he was elected a Tennessee congressman.
Recognition of Signal Words	
Sequence	First, initially, next, subsequently, after that, then, finally, ultimately
Cause/Effect	As a result, because, consequently, leads to, causes, therefore, in order to, to make
Comparison/Contrast	Like, as, similarly, equally, whereas, on the other hand, unlike, however, although
Rhetorical Patterns	
Generalization/Examples	Their traditional lifestyle has disappeared; they live in modern homes, their food comes from the store, and most communities have television.
Definition/Classification	An island is a landform that is surrounded by water. (Identify class, then add defining characteristics.)
Comparison/Contrast	This is because the land is flat, not hilly and rocky like land in the Northeast.
Time Relationships	"I found Rome a city of bricks and left it a city of marble." Augustus is supposed to have spoken these words as he lay dying. He was Rome's first emperor, and started the first of its great building programs.
Cause/Effect	As president, he doubled the size of the United States when he purchased the Louisiana Territory from France.

Classroom Strategies for English Learners

We know from research that students learn best when they feel that they are in a safe learning environment. Classroom teachers create that environment in different ways, based on their own unique situations. *Success for English Learners* provides a wide array of instructional suggestions designed to help you help every student experience academic success while reading and learning from *Harcourt Social Studies*. Unit by unit, lesson by lesson, you can find the tools you need to ensure that these important things happen:

- inclusion of and respect for students' cultural backgrounds and life experiences by building bridges to prior knowledge
- accessible, varied vocabulary instruction for all key words
- cognates for appropriate lesson vocabulary
- oral language development through content-based chants
- creative, engaging scaffolding of lessons
- student-generated visuals and graphic organizers that serve as home involvement tools
- sheltered writing experiences

Success for English Learners is designed to help you help students toward their goals: to achieve academic success that is equivalent to their native English speaking classmates.

Identify Proficiency Levels

The ability levels of English learners in any classroom might be similar or mixed. Whatever the situation, the following information is designed to support teachers who have English learners in their classes.

Among English learners, there are many different levels of proficiency. The Proficiency Levels chart shows student traits and research-based "best practices" responding appropriately to all student levels. Remember, too, that most English learners comprehend more information than they are able to communicate. The strategies suggested in the Proficiency Levels chart will help teachers reach all learners on any given day.

PROFICIENCY LEVELS

Student Traits	Best Practice
BEGINNING • Students are new to English. • Students respond by pointing, nodding, or using other nonverbal communication, leading to one-word or short-phrase responses. • Students create incomplete meanings from non-print features of text. • Students write very simple texts with many errors.	• Use visuals and real objects as much as possible. • Gesture and dramatize to reinforce meaning. • Provide opportunities for active listening. • Present new vocabulary before each lesson. • Ask only the types of questions which students can respond to nonverbally or verbally (yes, no, list generators, either/or).
INTERMEDIATE • Students understand concepts in concrete contexts. • Students begin to speak in phrases and short sentences. • Students share more freely through spoken and written language. • Students create meaning from text through the use of background knowledge. • Students write using more variety, with fewer errors.	• Keep lessons focused on key concepts; limit details. • Check students' comprehension frequently. • Ask open-ended questions (the five Ws, cloze, descriptions). • Provide corrective feedback on academic language. • Assess students' background knowledge and fill gaps when necessary. • Provide models for students' writing.
ADVANCED • Students join discussions with increased level of grammatical accuracy and language complexity. • Students may still struggle with understanding the language of abstract topics, orally or in text. • Students read and write as ways of learning new information. • Writing is more accurate, with errors that don't affect comprehensibility.	• Encourage students' responses both verbally and in writing. • Challenge students to synthesize information through structural higher-order activities. • Teach and model strategies within a communicative context. • Use graphic organizers to help make the abstract more concrete. • Use guided writing and self- and peer-editing.

Planning and Grouping Strategies

Once English learners' proficiency levels have been determined, that information can be used for a variety of planning purposes, including forming learning groups and tasks. Research suggests that opportunities for English learners to engage in language use within meaningful contexts are essential to developing high-levels of language proficiency. Cooperative learning and small group tasks offer opportunities for focused interaction and for developing meaningful contexts.

Students need to be in mixed groups for many learning tasks, including grouping English learners with native English speakers. This is important, because a group of learners at similar levels will not be equipped to provide one another the necessary modeling or corrective feedback required for English learning to occur. Beginning students learn from those who are more advanced. More advanced students increase their proficiency when they have leadership roles in groups.

Evidence has shown that carefully designed cooperative learning tasks provided students more practice in speaking and listening than did tasks that were teacher directed. When teachers are planning learning experiences, they should create contextual scenarios that are focused and deliberate in both content-area goals and language goals. The learning task should be highly structured so that students practice using new language skills in a safe environment. Students who are aware of the instructional goals of the task have been shown to make significant gains in learning. Also critical to students' success is corrective feedback, regarding students' progress toward those goals. Productive corrective feedback is more than a casual or conversational "recast" of students' speech, writing, spelling and grammatical errors. Teachers must provide explicit feedback about each dimension of language use.

Whether you are pairing students or having them work cooperatively in larger numbers, choose the groupings carefully. Also be sure that the tasks assigned to pairs or groups are purposeful and allow for natural language to flourish.

Reminders for Social Studies Classrooms with English Learners

- **Beware of Tricky Vocabulary** Beyond the high concept load and assumptions of prior knowledge that present challenges for English learners in social studies, several vocabulary issues must be addressed. As in all texts, multiple-meaning words exist in social studies curricula. Additionally, social studies texts present many culture-specific terms *(pioneer, Congress, Gulf Coast)*. Students are most successful when teachers are vigilant about the different usages, both in texts and in the language they use during instruction. Idioms are noticed and explained, as is colloquial language, such as "ace in the hole" or "agree to disagree." Furthermore, once vocabulary is taught, the best teachers work hard to ensure students practice it repeatedly through reading, listening, and in written form.

- **Present Models for All Expected Tasks** Whoever said, "A picture is worth a thousand words" could have been speaking directly to teachers of English learners. Making word meanings concrete for English learners is essential when dealing with abstract social studies concepts. Use pictures, gestures, demonstrations, and realia, or real objects. If possible, similarly engage students in acting out concepts or showing their comprehension in ways that are not language dependent.

   For teachers of English learners, another cliché is especially true: "Actions speak louder than words." Instead of using many verbal instructions to explain tasks, show students what you want them to do. Good modeling will result in positive experiences and lower frustration levels for all.

- **Respect All Participation** Remember that the main goal of social studies instruction for English learners is the mastery of academic content and achieving an appropriate level of class participation. The goal is not grammatical perfection, eloquent speech or writing, or error-free interactions. Build a safe, trusting environment where all feel free to contribute. Praise all efforts and tactfully model correct grammar and structures.

Using *Success for English Learners*

The information that follows introduces you to the specific parts of each lesson plan in *Success for English Learners*.

Unit Openers

The Unit Opener lesson plans in this guide are designed to help teachers prepare English learners for the academic language they will encounter throughout the *Harcourt Social Studies* unit. A Reading Focus Skill is taught in the Student Edition and reinforced and practiced at the chapter and lesson levels of *Harcourt Social Studies*.

Success for English Learners provides teachers with a plan for pre-teaching the Reading Focus Skill. Teachers introduce the skill and give several examples that demonstrate it. Vocabulary commonly associated with the skill is defined and made concrete for English learners. Practice and apply scenarios suggest appropriate activities for English learners, including using the same graphic organizer featured in the Student Edition of *Harcourt Social Studies*. Having prior experiences with academic language, English learners are now prepared to participate in the *Harcourt Social Studies* lessons.

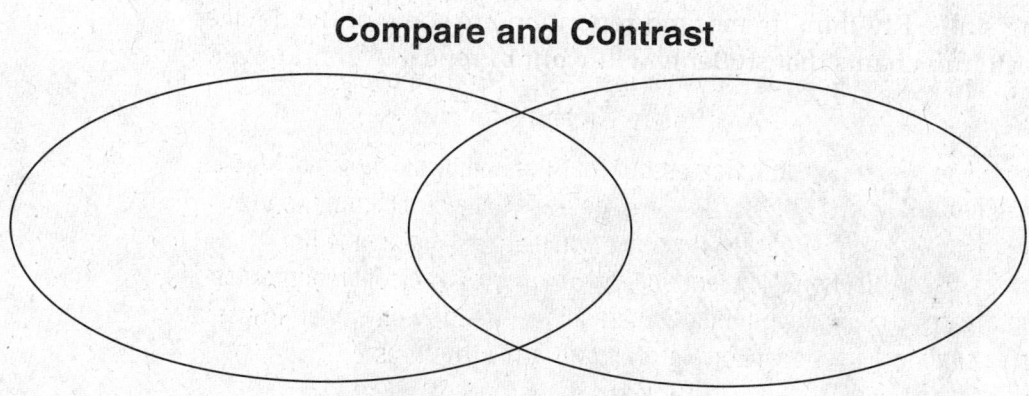

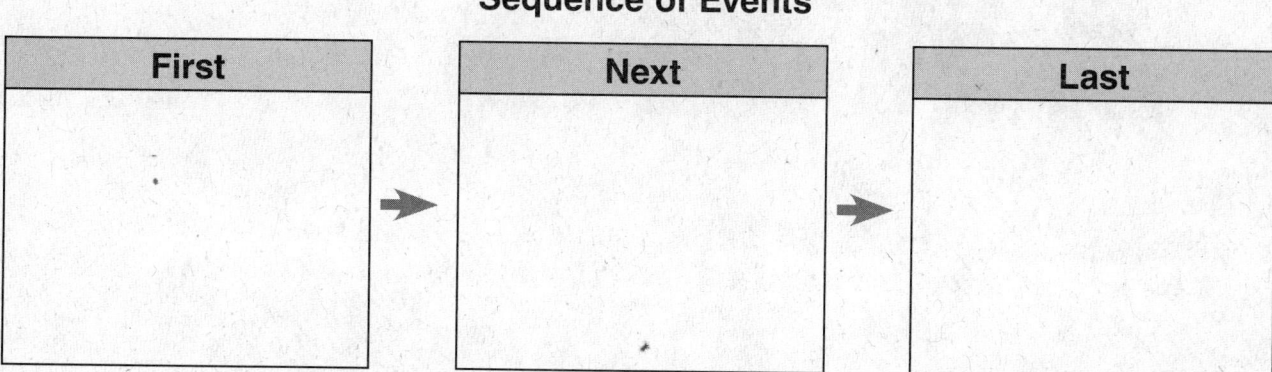

Build Background

Each Lesson Plan begins with Build Background, designed to prepare English learners to study the content of the lesson. **Access Prior Knowledge** helps teachers tap into students' existing knowledge. *Success for English Learners* creates a "common hook" to the students' own experiences about the lesson concepts. When no hook was obvious for a very important concept, a short, simple explanation is provided.

Next, the **Lesson Vocabulary** is introduced. Students are asked to read, write, and define the words in grade-appropriate ways. Engaging vocabulary activities are suggested. Additional program resources are available, including the glossary from the Student Edition of *Harcourt Social Studies* and Word Card blackline masters. In this section, troublesome words from the lesson are called out in the sidebar. These include multiple-meaning words or idiomatic expressions, for example. In addition, cognates are provided. There are many words in Spanish and English that look alike and have almost the same meaning. By listing cognates teachers are able to connect the lesson vocabulary to students' existing knowledge. Teachers can instruct students to add these words to vocabulary notebooks or challenge them to find additional cognates in the lessons.

Then, students are given an opportunity to **Build Fluency.** A chant related to the lesson content provides practice and application of vocabulary and reading skills. Rhythm, rhyme, and repetition are some of the devices used to create fun chants that students will want to repeat over and over.

Scaffolding the Content

Scaffolding the Content is for use during *Harcourt Social Studies* lesson instruction. Critical points of the lesson that English learners should understand are addressed in this section of the Lesson Plan. In **Preview the Lesson,** *Success for English Learners* focuses on key visuals, headings, or other content indicators for students to examine as they scan the text. Vocabulary words taught in Build Background might also be readdressed.

Modify Instruction has suggestions for how to ensure the accessibility and comprehensibility of the content for English learners. The point is to clarify the content and not to simplify it. The Modify Instruction section breaks the lesson content into manageable chunks. The teacher may work directly with small groups of English learners, using the suggestions to bring the content alive and make it more concrete for students.

A critical part of the Lesson Plan is a **blackline master** for students to complete. These pages are designed to help students internalize the main ideas of the lesson. Most often, the page features a graphic organizer that allows students to see concrete connections between ideas. In addition, this page is designed for students to take home and share with family members. A meaningful **School-Home Connection** provides students further opportunities to talk about the social studies content they are learning. In doing so, English learners practice their language skills in a meaningful context.

Suggestions for how to **Extend** the lesson end the Scaffolding the Content section. You will find that these activities review main lesson concepts while giving English learners a new way to synthesize the information.

Apply and Assess

The last part of the lesson plan is called Apply and Assess. It serves two distinct purposes. The Apply section matches the writing or performance activity in the Lesson Review section of the Student Edition. *Success for English Learners* offers sheltered-writing experiences. These activities are designed to help English learners produce a very similar product to that produced by their native-speaking peers.

The Assess section provides a rubric that suggests ways to informally assess students' comprehension of lesson concepts. This rubric includes carefully articulated tasks for students to do. The rubric also gives possible responses expected from students with beginning, intermediate, and advanced language proficiencies.

Conclusion

Throughout the Lesson Plans, *Success for English Learners* has been designed to suggest when to use each section in relation to *Harcourt Social Studies* lesson plans. In addition, estimates are given for how long each section might take. This information is found as a sidebar at point of use in the Lesson Plan.

This guide provides a useful toolbox for teachers to use with English learners in the social studies classroom. From Developing Academic Language to Apply and Assess, *Success for English Learners* is full of strategies and methods that have been proven to increase English learners' language proficiency and their acquisition of content knowledge. Each activity in this guide is designed to help teachers solve students' particular problems or meet a specific need.

When Minutes Count

Success for English Learners is a comprehensive guide for explicit language and content instruction. When time is short, there are some important concepts that can be integrated into lesson plans that will support English language learners. Consider the following ten tips:

For All English Language Learners

1. Provide a low-anxiety environment.
2. Keep your expectations high. Differentiate instructional strategies while teaching the same standards to all students.

Beginning Level

3. Ask questions that can be answered with a single word or by pointing to pictures.
4. Utilize photos, paintings, drawings, and maps as much as possible.

Intermediate Level

5. Frontload vocabulary and language structures.
6. Introduce graphic organizers, and then allow students to use them as a prewriting tool.
7. Use writing frames to scaffold written responses.

Advanced Level

8. Maximize the teachable moments to accelerate the learning of new language forms and to expand vocabulary.
9. Provide ample opportunities to practice, apply, and use language purposefully.
10. Allow students time to reflect on language forms and processes.

Rebecca Valbuena
Language Development Specialist
Stanton Elementary School
Glendora Unified School District

Unit 1 Opener

Developing Academic Language

Throughout this unit, students will be asked to look for comparisons and contrasts. When students know the words that signal these relationships and can recognize the sentence structures that introduce and present them, they can better understand what they read.

Introduce Compare and Contrast

Explain that when you compare, you tell how two or more things are alike. The result is called a **comparison.** Write and say *comparison* and *compare*. Write the word *alike* above them. Hold up common classroom objects, like a piece of chalk and a pen. Tell how they are alike. Explain that you have just made a comparison. Explain that when you contrast, you tell how two or more things are different. The result is called a **contrast.** Write and say the word *contrast,* and write the word *different* above it. Hold up the classroom objects again. Tell how they are different. Explain that you have just made a contrast.

- Before **Compare and Contrast**, p. 6
- 15 minutes

List some common words and phrases that signal comparisons: *both, and, alike, also, too, like,* and *similar.* Write and say this context sentence: *We use both chalk and a pen to write.* Circle *both* and *and.* Explain that these words show comparison. List some common words and phrases that signal contrasts: *but, instead, unlike, however,* and *different.* Write and say this context sentence: *I write on the board with chalk, but I write on paper with a pen.* Circle *but.* Explain that this word shows contrast. Encourage students to say other compare and contrast sentences as they are able.

Practice

To help students recognize the structure of sentences that compare and contrast, write the following sentence frames on the board. Have the class fill in the remaining blanks with appropriate signal words.

1) Sam and James are _____ because they _____ have brown eyes.
2) John is a boy, _____ Sarah is a girl. _____ Sarah and John have brown hair.
3) A soccer ball is _____ a baseball, because they are _____ balls.

Apply

Draw the following chart. Say the headings as you point to them. For each topic, write any two familiar items, such as two classroom pets. Point out the objects. Have students work in small groups to complete the organizer.

Topic 1:	
Topic 2:	
Similar	Different

Success for English Learners • 1

Use with Chapter 1, Lesson 1

Build Background

Access Prior Knowledge

Post this diagram of terms: *continent—country—region—state—city*. Use the maps on pages 20–21 to explain that continents are large masses of land. Further explain that countries are divisions, or parts, of continents, and regions are divisions, or parts, of countries. Explain that the United States divides its regions into states, but other countries divide regions differently. For example, Canada has provinces rather than states. Ask students to compare and contrast how the United States and their home countries divide land into regions. Discuss a second point of comparison related to a cultural topic, such as language or food.

- Before **Introduce**, p. 14
- 15 minutes

Lesson Vocabulary

Explain the vocabulary words by posting brief definitions and using examples from the maps on page 15 and 20–21. Have students work in pairs to create vocabulary cards, with one vocabulary word on one side and a brief definition on the other side. Have them use the cards to quiz each other. One student may begin by reading a definition, while the other student names the corresponding word. Increase the level of difficulty by having a student read the words while the partner provides the definitions or key words.

Additional Vocabulary Explain the meanings and uses of the words in the margin. Point out that the word *fewer* means less. Explain that the word fewer is used with things that can be counted, like people and states. Less is used with things that cannot be counted, like land and mass.

border	measure
features	ranks
fewer	spread out
land mass	

Cognates As students read the lesson you may wish to point out cognates such as: **continent/continente, different/diferente, population/población, region/región.**

Build Fluency

Read aloud the following rhyme, and point out the words that sound alike. Have students repeat it several times to develop oral language skills. Return to the rhyme throughout the lesson to help develop vocabulary, compare and contrast skills, and lesson content.

> Fifty states make up our nation.
> They are split into five **regions** in different locations.
> What is a region? Several states there
> Have land, culture, and history they share.
> In separate regions, far away
> People live and work in different ways.

Scaffolding the Content

Preview the Lesson

Read the "What to Know" question on page 14: *How are the 50 states alike, and how are they different?* Ask students to use the illustrations and text on pages 15–17 to note a few possible answers. Next, read the names of countries under "Places" on page 14. Talk about what the United States, Canada, and Mexico have in common.

• During **Teach**, pp. 14–19
• 30 minutes

Modify Instruction

Read the following information to students. Help them take notes by writing key phrases on the board or overhead. Have students use their notes to complete the blackline master on the next page.

1. The United States has 50 states; 48 are contiguous, or next to each other. Alaska and Hawaii are not contiguous.

2. There are five regions in the United States: the West, the Southwest, the Midwest, the South, and the Northeast. The relative location of these regions is where the region is compared to the others. A region is an area with similar features.

3. States in each region are alike. They have similar land, history, and culture. People live in each region in similar ways. States in different regions have different land, history, and culture. People in different regions live differently.

4. The Earth has seven continents, or very large chunks of land. These are Asia, Africa, North America, South America, Antarctica, Europe, and Australia.

5. North America has three nations. These are Canada, the United States, and Mexico. The United States is one of the largest nations on North America. Nations can be measured by the size of the land, or by population, or by the number of people. Canada is the largest nation in North America by land area. The United States is the largest nation in North America by population.

6. Canada is north of the United States. The British and French explored both Canada and the United States. The British ruled both countries at one time. Some of Canada is cold much of the year. Most Canadians live near the southern border. Fewer people live in Canada than in the United States or Mexico.

7. Mexico is south of the United States. Mexico City is one of the largest capital cities in the world. Mexico has less land than the United States and Canada. Mexico has more people than Canada. Mexico and the United States have a similar history because Spain sent settlers to both countries.

Extend

Ask students to think of statements that highlight similarities and differences between the United States, Canada, and Mexico. For example: *These countries are on the continent of North America* or *This country has the largest population in North America*. Write statements on the board. Have students copy each statement onto the front of an index card. On the back of the card, have students write the name of any countries that the statement describes. Have students take turns drawing cards and identifying the correct countries.

• After **Teach**, pp. 14–19
• 10 minutes

Name _____ Date _____

DIRECTIONS Listen as your teacher reads. Use your notes to write or draw ways the 50 states are similar and different.

Things that are true of all 50 states:	Things that differ from state to state:

 School-Home Connection Encourage students to take this page home to share with family members. They can use their notes to tell about regions in the United States and countries in North America. They may also explain the concept of comparing and contrasting.

4 ▪ Success for English Learners

Unit 1, Chapter 1, Lesson 1

Apply and Assess

Draw a Map

Refer students to maps on pages 15 and 20. Tell them they may use the maps to help them draw the form of North America and the borders between Canada, the United States, and Mexico.

• During **Close**, p. 19
• 30 minutes

When students have completed their maps, give them practice identifying such geographical terms as *continent, state, contiguous state, region,* and *country.* Call out a term and have students show comprehension by pointing to their maps. Give beginning students questions that require only pointing to the correct location on the map, such as: *Show where Canada is located.* Give intermediate students questions that require pointing and verbalization of specific places, such as: *Show North America and name the three countries on this continent.* Give advanced students questions involving regions and contiguous states that require them to point and explain verbally. For example: *Show me two states that are not contiguous and explain how you identified them.*

Informal Lesson Assessment

	Beginning	**Intermediate**	**Advanced**
Task	Have students list ways states are similar to and different from each other using key words, phrases, and sketches.	Have students describe ways states are similar to and different from each other using phrases and sentences.	Have students write several sentences describing ways states are similar to and different from each other.
Below Expectations	• no answer is comprehensible and/or correct	• no answer is comprehensible and/or correct	• inappropriate ideas • no complete sentences • many errors
Meets Expectations	• some answers are comprehensible and/or correct	• some answers are comprehensible and/or correct	• appropriate ideas • some incomplete sentences • some errors
Above Expectations	• all answers are comprehensible and correct	• all answers are comprehensible and correct	• appropriate ideas • complete sentences • few errors

Success for English Learners

Use with Chapter 1, Lesson 2

Build Background

Access Prior Knowledge

Remind students that they live in one of fifty states. Ask them to name their state. Have students name other states they know. Tell students they also live in one of many landform regions. Explain that landforms are features of the earth like lakes, rivers, mountains, and flat areas called plains. Ask students to name a landform they have seen, and tell where they saw it.

- Before **Introduce**, p. 22
- 20 minutes

Lesson Vocabulary

Explain the vocabulary words from this lesson by using pictures from pages 25–29 and flashcards that accompany the lesson. Play a vocabulary game to help students practice the words by associating them with images. Divide the class in half. Choose one student from each side to come to the board. Show them a vocabulary word so no one else can see it. Allow students to sketch pictures so their team members can guess the word. A team member must raise his or her hand before guessing. If the team member guesses the word, the team gets another turn. If not, the other team gets a turn. Give beginning students words that require concrete sketches, like **mountain range**. Give advanced students less concrete words, such as **landform** and **environment**.

Additional Vocabulary Explain the meanings and uses of the words in the margin. Explain that the compound terms *wear away* and *worn down* are related. Tell students that wear away means to take parts from a physical feature, like the top of a mountain. Once many parts have been taken, the feature is worn down. Explain that *jagged* is similar to *rocky* when used to describe mountains in this chapter.

basin	rocky
jagged	rolling
peak	strip of land
plains	wear away
plateau	worn down

Cognates As students read the lesson, you may wish to point out cognates such as: **climate/clima, coast/costa, diverse/diverso, valley/valle.**

Build Fluency

Read aloud the following rhyme, and point out words that sound alike. Have students repeat it several times to develop oral language skills. Return to the rhyme throughout the lesson to help develop vocabulary, compare and contrast skills, and lesson content.

> **Landforms** vary from place to place.
> **Climates** change from hot to cold and wet to dry.
> The Great Plains are very flat.
> The Rocky Mountains seem to reach the sky.
> The Mississippi River divides the plains.
> The Great Basin is flat and low.
> From the Coastal Plain to the Sierra Nevada,
> **Environments** are different everywhere you go.
> Fifty states make up our nation.
> We have lakes, plains, and mountains, too.
> All these wonderful places
> Help give us many points of view.

Scaffolding the Content

Preview the Lesson

Point out the map on page 24. Read and explain the key. Ask volunteers to use the key to name a few landforms in the United States. Next, have students name landforms they see in photographs on pages 25 to 29 of the text. Have students use captions to find the location of each landform and point to the location on the map. Explain that this lesson will describe different landforms across the country.

- During **Teach**, pp. 22–29
- 30 minutes

Modify Instruction

Teach the lesson region by region using the map on page 24. After each region, ask students to work in pairs to complete the corresponding box on the blackline master page.

1. **Landform Regions** Landforms are physical features like plains, mountains, plateaus, hills, and valleys. A landform region is an area where there is a lot of a particular landform.

2. **The Coastal Plain** Find the Atlantic Coast. Using your finger trace it from Maine to Florida. Then find the coast of the Gulf of Mexico. Trace it from Florida to Mexico. This is the Coastal Plain. The land there is flat and low.

3. **The Appalachians** Find New Jersey on the map. Trace a line to Alabama. This is where the Piedmont is. It is higher than the Coastal Plain and has hills and valleys. Find the mountains that are just west of the Piedmont. These are the Appalachian Mountains.

4. **The Interior Plains** Put your finger on the Great Lakes. Now run your finger along the Mississippi River from the north part of the country to the Gulf of Mexico. Find the Central Plains east of the river. The land here is flat or rolling and covered with grass. Now find the Great Plains to the west. The land here is flatter, and there are few rivers and trees.

5. **The Rocky Mountains and Beyond** Find Alaska. Trace the mountain range from there to Mexico. These are called the Rocky Mountains. Find the Great Basin west of the Rocky Mountains. It is a low, bowl-shaped area with higher land all around it. A desert is there.

6. **More Mountains and Valleys** Find the Sierra Nevada. Between it and the Rocky Mountains is a large valley called the Central Valley which has thick grass and many streams. Along the Pacific Ocean is the Coast Range. These mountains are rocky and rugged.

Extend

Invite students to make Venn diagrams to compare and contrast pairs of regions, or areas within regions. Students may also use information from the map on page 24 to make their comparisons. Have students explain to a partner what their diagrams show.

- After **Teach**, pp. 22–29
- 20 minutes

Success for English Learners

Name _____ Date _____

DIRECTIONS In each box, read the name of the region. Write about its location and describe it.

Landform Regions
Location:
Description:

The Coastal Plain
Location:
Description:

The Appalachians
Location:
Description:

The Interior Plains
Location:
Description:

The Rocky Mountains and Beyond
Location:
Description:

More Mountains and Valleys
Location:
Description:

School-Home Connection Have students take this page home to share with family members. They should tell which landform region they live in, and explain how it is different from other regions.

8 ■ Success for English Learners

Unit 1, Chapter 1, Lesson 2

Apply and Assess
Make Flashcards

Review information about landforms. Ask students to work in groups to note several landforms they found in the chapter. Then have each group share their list. Record the landforms on the board as column headings. As a class, write brief descriptions about each landform.

Ask students to copy the names of the landforms and their descriptions onto individual cards. Have them use their notes to find the regions that contain these landforms. Write the names of these regions on the back of the corresponding cards.

Have students use the cards to practice in pairs. One student will name landform regions, and the partner will name corresponding landforms. Students should take turns naming landform regions and describing various landforms.

- During **Close**, p. 29
- 15 minutes

Informal Lesson Assessment

	Beginning	Intermediate	Advanced
Task	Provide a list of locations from the lesson. Have students list landforms and features in each location using key words and sketches.	Provide a list of locations from the lesson. Have students describe landforms in each location using phrases or sentences.	Provide a list of locations from the lesson. Have students write a paragraph that compares and contrasts landforms and features in each location.
Below Expectations	• responses are not comprehensible or correct	• no answer is comprehensible or correct	• incorrect ideas • incorrect paragraph form • many errors
Meets Expectations	• responses are partially comprehensible and/or correct	• most of the answers are comprehensible and correct	• appropriate ideas • correct paragraph form • some errors
Above Expectations	• responses are comprehensible and correct	• all answers are comprehensible and correct	• appropriate ideas • correct paragraph form • few errors

Use with Chapter 1, Lesson 3

Build Background

Access Prior Knowledge

- Before **Introduce**, p. 30
- 15 minutes

First, remind students that rivers, lakes, and oceans are all bodies of water. Then divide the class into small groups. Write the following questions on the board, and assign each group one of the questions by number: *1) What bodies of water have you seen or heard about? 2) What types of land are close to bodies of water? 3) How do you think bodies of water help people who live around them?* Ask each group to share their responses.

Lesson Vocabulary

Explain the vocabulary words using the Glossary and sketches. Have students work in mixed-proficiency groups to create illustrations of the words. Have each student write the corresponding vocabulary word on the back of the pictures. Collect all of the pictures and use them to play a game. Hold up a picture. Call on a group to respond with the word and definition. Give the group about 15 seconds to figure out the answer. If the group is right, let it go again. If not, the next group gets a turn. When the students become comfortable with the words, decrease the amount of time they have to guess the answer to make the game more exciting.

Additional Vocabulary Explain the meanings and uses of the words in the margin. Tell students that in this lesson, *salty* is the opposite of *freshwater*, which describes a body of water such as a lake, which does not have salty ocean water. Explain that *mouth* is often used to describe part of a face. However, in this lesson the word describes the part of a river that empties into an ocean.

bay	salty
bodies	source
drain	transport
freshwater	waterfall
lie	waterway
mouth	

Cognates As students read the lesson you may wish to point out cognates such as: **ocean/océano, rapids/rápidos, salt/sal, transport/transportar.**

Build Fluency

Read aloud the following rhyme, and point out the words that sound alike. Have students repeat it several times to develop oral language skills. Return to the rhyme throughout the lesson to help develop vocabulary, compare and contrast skills, and lesson content.

> In the United States today,
> There are many **inlets, river systems,** and bays.
> Some cities are built where oceans meet rivers
> Where goods are easy to ship and deliver.
> In some bodies of water, ships come and go
> Like the gulfs of Alaska and Mexico.

Scaffolding the Content

Preview the Lesson

Read the "Reading Check" questions on pages 31–34, and have students skim the text around boldface words to predict responses. Write the questions on the board, and allow volunteers to post their responses there as well.

- During **Teach**, pp. 30–34
- 30 minutes

Modify Instruction

Read the following summaries with students. Write key phrases on the board or overhead. Have students use their notes to complete the blackline master page.

Gulfs and Inlets An inlet is an area of water that reaches into land from a larger body of water. A gulf is a large inlet. The Gulf of Mexico and the Gulf of Alaska are the biggest gulfs in the United States. Bays and sounds are found along the coast. A sound is a long inlet that separates islands from the mainland. There are harbors in large bays and sounds where ships can dock.

Lakes The largest lakes in the United States are called the Great Lakes. They are Lake Superior, Lake Michigan, Lake Huron, Lake Erie, and Lake Ontario. Most United States lakes have fresh water, but the Great Salt Lake in Utah has salt water.

Rivers Rivers are bodies of moving water. Rivers begin at a source and end at a mouth, where they empty into a larger body of water. A tributary is a stream or river that flows into a larger stream or river. A river and its tributaries make up a river system. The land drained, or emptied, by a river system is called a drainage basin. The Mississippi River is the largest United States river system. The Mississippi flows from Minnesota to the Gulf of Mexico.

Population Many cities were built where rivers flow into oceans. New York City was built where the Hudson River flows into the Atlantic Ocean. This helped people travel and transport goods. Other cities were built where the water flows to lower land, creating waterfalls. In the past, people used fast-moving water to give machines power.

Continental Divide The Continental Divide is an imaginary line along the Rocky Mountains that divides river systems of North America. The Continental Divide separates river systems that flow to the Gulf of Mexico and the Atlantic Ocean, from those that flow into the Pacific Ocean. Rivers east of the Continental Divide, like the Missouri and Rio Grande, flow into the Atlantic Ocean. Rivers west of the Continental Divide, like the Sacramento, Columbia, and Colorado, flow into the Pacific.

Extend

Revisit the questions asked during "Preview the Lesson." Have students use their notes to check their predictions. Ask students to name two facts that they learned that were not covered in the "Preview" activity.

- After **Teach**, pp. 30–34
- 10 minutes

Name _____   Date _____

DIRECTIONS Take notes as your teacher reads. Use your notes to check which body of water is described in the sentences below.

	Inlet	Gulf	Lake	River
1 A _____ is a body of moving water.				
2 _____s provide good harbors.				
3 A sound is a long _____ that separates islands from the mainland.				
4 A stream or _____ that flows into a larger one is called a tributary.				
5 The Missouri and Rio Grand are _____s that are east of the Continental Divide.				
6 Superior, Michigan, Huron, Erie, and Ontario are part of the Great _____s.				
7 The largest _____ system in the United States is the Mississippi River.				
8 The Great Salt _____ in Utah has salt water.				
9 An _____ is an area of water that reaches into land from a larger body of water.				
10 The population is large where the Hudson _____ flows into the Atlantic Ocean.				
11 The Continental Divide is a line that divides _____ systems of North America.				
12 The _____ of Mexico and the _____ of Alaska are the largest in the United States.				
13 The Sacramento, Columbia, and Colorado _____s are west of the Continental Divide.				
14 A _____ is a large inlet.				

School-Home Connection Have students take this page home to share with family members. They can use their notes to tell about bodies of water in the United States, where they are located, and why they have been useful over time.

Apply and Assess

Draw a Poster

Refer students to the map on page 32. Ask them to point to the location of the state and city where your school is located. Have students use the map to identify landforms and bodies of water near this location. Then ask them to find the closest river.

• During **Close**, p. 34
• 30 minutes

Put students in mixed-proficiency pairs to make a poster of the river. Write the following directions on the board or overhead:

Draw a river near your city and state.
Write the name of the river.
Label any nearby cities, landforms, and tributaries.
Use color to make your drawings stand out.
Explain your poster to another pair of students.

Informal Lesson Assessment

	Beginning	Intermediate	Advanced
Task	Provide a blank map of the United States or a map with labeled states. Have students label bodies of water on the map using key vocabulary words and names of bodies of water they learned in this lesson.	Provide a blank map of the United States or a map with labeled states. Have students identify bodies of water on the map. On a separate piece of paper, have them write definitions of each type of body of water using words or phrases.	Provide a blank map of the United States or a map with labeled states. Have students identify famous bodies of water on the map. On a separate piece of paper, have them write definitions of each type of body of water using complete sentences.
Below Expectations	• no answer is comprehensible and/or correct	• no answer is comprehensible and/or correct	• incorrect ideas • no complete sentences • many errors
Meets Expectations	• some answers are comprehensible and/or correct	• some of the answers are comprehensible and/or correct	• appropriate ideas • some incomplete sentences • some errors
Above Expectations	• all answers are comprehensible and correct	• all of the answers are comprehensible and correct	• appropriate ideas • complete sentences • few errors

Use with Chapter 1, Lesson 4

Build Background

Access Prior Knowledge

Have students work in pairs to ask each other questions and note responses: 1) *Name or describe two to three plants in your home country that you have not seen in the United States.* 2) *Is weather in your home country the same or different from the weather you have seen in the United States?* 3) *In your home country, do you have summer, fall, winter, and spring, or only one or two seasons?* Post several responses on the board.

• Before **Introduce**, p. 36
• 15 minutes

Lesson Vocabulary

Explain the vocabulary word definitions using the Glossary. Draw pictures to help students understand **elevation** and **tundra**. Use the photograph on page 39 to describe the words **arid** and **natural vegetation**. Ask students to write paraphrased definitions. Explain that students must shorten the definition and change some words. Then, have them play a game with a partner. Have the first partner think of a word. The second partner can ask yes and no questions to try to figure out the word. For example: "Does the word mean dry?" Students play until each partner guesses all four words correctly.

Additional Vocabulary Explain the meanings and uses of the words in the margin. Explain to students that the suffix *-er* is used to compare two things, so the word *farther* means "more far," and *drier* means "more dry." Specify that a *season* is a period during the year when the temperature and weather are different from other times.

axis	orbit
drier	season
equator	soil
farther	survive
grassland	tilted

Cognates As students read the lesson you may wish to point out cognates such as: **cactus/cacto, elevation/elevación, equator/ecuador, precipitation/precipitación, vegetation/vegetación.**

Build Fluency

Read aloud the following rhyme, and point out the words that sound alike. Have students repeat it several times to develop oral language skills. Return to the rhyme throughout the lesson to help develop vocabulary, compare and contrast skills, and lesson content.

> The climate changes in certain locations,
> Like near the equator or at high **elevations**.
>
> The climate controls which **natural vegetation**
> Grows in an area, region, or nation.
>
> Summer, spring, winter and fall seasons—
> All four happen in some of our regions.
>
> Some places are dry or cold all year round,
> Like hot deserts and **tundra** on frozen ground.

Scaffolding the Content

Preview the Lesson

Post the chapter headings and subheadings in the lesson: 1) *Climate—Factor Affecting Climate and Earth and the Sun: This section teaches how the equator, oceans and large bodies of water, elevation, and the sun affect climate.* 2) *Climate and Vegetation—Vegetation Regions and Dry Climates: This section describes four regions in the United States where different types of vegetation grow.* Ask students to paraphrase the descriptions, and to identify illustrations on pages 37–39 that relate to the topics.

- During **Teach**, pp. 36–39
- 20 minutes

Modify Instruction

Read the following outline with students. Write key phrases on the board as you read. Have students complete the blackline master page using their notes.

I. Climate

A. Factors Affecting Climate
The equator is an imaginary line around the center of the earth. Southern states like Florida and Texas are usually warm because they are close to the equator. Northern states like Michigan and Montana are usually cool because they are farther from the equator.
Oceans, or large bodies of water affect climate. In the winter, nearby water warms places. In the summer, nearby water cools places. Elevation is the height of the land from sea level. Elevation also affects climate. The temperature drops three degrees Fahrenheit every 1,000 feet above sea level.

B. The Earth and Sun
Seasons include summer, fall, winter, and spring. The seasons change because of the earth's orbit, or travel, around the sun.

II. Climate and Vegetation

A. Natural Vegetation: plant life that grows naturally in a place
Natural vegetation depends on soil, temperature, precipitation. Different places have different natural vegetation.

B. Vegetation Regions: places with similar vegetation
Vegetation regions in the United States are forest, grassland, desert, and tundra. The forest region has trees and is in the eastern and northwestern United States.

C. Dry Climates: trees cannot grow, but some vegetation can
Grassland: grasses grow in part of Central Plains and all of the Great Plains
Deserts: have plants that can live without much water (grasses, bushes, cactuses)
Tundra: cold, dry region where trees cannot grow, but mosses and herbs can

Extend

Copy the names of three cities from the map on page 38 on sheets of paper. Use different cities on each paper. Put students in pairs and give each pair a paper. Using the map and key, have students find the cities, identify their climate regions, and name one or two climate traits.

- After **Teach**, pp. 36–39
- 15 minutes

Success for English Learners ■ 15

Name _____ Date _____

DIRECTIONS Take notes as your teacher reads the outline. Use your notes to compare and contrast the following ideas from the lesson.

Places Close to the Equator	Places Far from the Equator

Places Close to the Ocean or Large Bodies of Water	Places Far from the Ocean or Large Bodies of Water

Grassland Vegetation Region	Forest Vegetation Region

Tundra Vegetation Region	Desert Vegetation Region

School-Home Connection Have students take this page home to share with family members. They can use their notes to tell about climate regions in the United States, where they are located, and types of natural vegetation that grow there.

Apply and Assess
Write a Poem

Ask students to volunteer phrases that describe the climate and region where they live. Note their suggestions on the board. Write a model poem on the board, adding words and ideas as necessary. For example:

• During **Close**, p. 39
• 30 minutes

> Rocky mountains
> all around,
> In this region
> sun shines down.

Ask students to use the phrases and words on the board, along with new, original ones to form a poem. Have beginning students write a descriptive poem, but tell them the lines do not have to rhyme. Allow intermediate students to use phrases and ask them to make at least two or four of the lines rhyme. Have advanced students use sentences that rhyme.

Informal Lesson Assessment

	Beginning	Intermediate	Advanced
Task	Ask students to list different climate regions in the United States. Then ask them to point to a few locations where they can find these regions on a map.	Ask students to list different climate regions and describe them using words and phrases. Ask them to show you where they can find the regions on a map.	Ask students to list different climate regions in the United States, and compare and contrast them using sentences. Have them write locations of the regions using names of cities and states.
Below Expectations	• no answer is comprehensible and/or correct	• no answer is comprehensible and/or correct	• incorrect ideas • no complete sentences • many errors
Meets Expectations	• some answers are comprehensible and/or correct	• some of the answers are comprehensible and/or correct	• appropriate ideas • some incomplete sentences • some errors
Above Expectations	• all answers are comprehensible and correct	• all of the answers are comprehensible and correct	• appropriate ideas • complete sentences • few errors

Build Background

Use with Chapter 1, Lesson 5

Access Prior Knowledge

Explain the concept of resources and products using the example of trees and pencils. For example, explain that people need trees and other resources for the wood to make pencils. Give students a few minutes to list five resources and products they use every day, including two resources and products they used today before or during class. Review the answers, naming both the resources and the products. Explain that this lesson will teach them about different types of resources, their uses, and how they affect people's lives.

- Before **Introduce**, p. 40
- 15 minutes

Lesson Vocabulary

Explain the words using sketches, examples, and brief definitions. Have students write which vocabulary words correspond with the following phrases: *1) school 2) corn 3) farming 4) mountains 5) water 6) oil 7) to change land to get water by digging a well 8) using a pipe to move water 9) cars that use little gas.* Provide the correct responses. Ask students to think of one additional example that represents each vocabulary word and see if the class can identify the word correctly.

Additional Vocabulary Explain the meanings and uses of the words in the margin. Demonstrate how to use the words by clustering them into sentences, such as: "Some resources take thousands of years to *replace*. We *conserve* them so they do not *run out*."

alter	raft
conserve	replace
dams	reservoirs
fuel	run out
mining	wells
ores	

Cognates As students read the lesson you may wish to point out cognates such as: **canal/canal, conserve/conservar, electricity/electricidad, minerals/minerales, plastic/plástico.**

Build Fluency

Read aloud the following rhyme, and point out the words that sound alike. Have students repeat it several times to develop oral language skills. Return to the rhyme throughout the lesson to help develop vocabulary, compare and contrast skills, and lesson content.

> Where did people settle before?
> Where they could farm, build shelter, and more!
> Rivers and coasts were near routes that could
> Help people travel simply and carry goods.
>
> But people wanted to settle more lands
> They built **human features** so they could expand.
> People built wells and dams for irrigation.
> They changed harbors or dug channels for transportation.
>
> They found uses for **renewable resources** like water and trees
> Knowing they can grow and replace what they need.
> But **nonrenewable resources** like minerals can
> Be made only by nature, not by woman or man.

Success for English Learners

Scaffolding the Content

Preview the Lesson

Write the "What to Know" question from page 40 on the board. Review the words *adapt, change,* and *environment* as needed. Put students into groups. Ask each group member to note possible responses to the focus question using one of the following parts of the text: the story on page 40, the summary on page 45, and the map on page 43. Suggest that beginning students use the map, intermediate students use the summary, and advanced students use the story to generate responses.

• During **Teach**, pp. 40–45
• 30 minutes

Modify Instruction

Read the following questions and answers with students. Summarize key phrases on the board. Discuss the headings on the blackline master page and help students complete it.

Q: Why do some areas in the United States have many people and others do not?

A. A long time ago, people settled where there was farmland. They looked for physical features like good climate, soil, water, and landforms that made it possible to travel and to build shelter. In desert, tundra, and mountains, building shelter and finding food was difficult. Later, inventions helped people settle other areas. Now most people live near cities, by coasts, or near transportation routes.

Q: How do people use land to meet their needs?

A. People build transportation systems and communities. They use natural resources from the land. In the United States, people use half the land for farming. In mountains, people use the land for mining.

Q: How do people change land to meet their needs?

A. To get water to areas far from lakes or rivers, people build pipes or canals for irrigation, or moving water. Across streams and rivers, people build dams to collect the water, and use it for drinking water and to create electricity. People change land for other products too. They cut down trees for paper products. They dig wells to get oil and water from the ground.

Q: What types of natural resources exist?

A. A natural resource is something in nature that people can use. Renewable resources, like water and trees, can be made again. People cannot make nonrenewable resources, like oil and gas. We use these resources to heat homes, fuel cars, and make plastic products. Many people conserve these resources so they do not run out, or come to an end.

Extend

Have students use the lists they made during "Access Prior Knowledge." Ask them to add a few resources to the list that they use occasionally. Then ask them to classify each resource as renewable or nonrenewable.

• After **Teach**, pp. 40–45
• 10 minutes

Name _____ Date _____

DIRECTIONS Take notes as your teacher reads. Use your notes to fill in the missing information on the chart.

Physical Features and Human Features	
Examples of each feature:	How they are different:

Uses of Land and Uses of Natural Resources	
Examples of each use:	How they are different:

Renewable Resources and Nonrenewable Resources	
Examples of each resource:	How they are different:

School-Home Connection Encourage students to take this page home to share with family members. They can use their notes to tell about ways people in the United States use the land and natural resources.

Apply and Assess

Write a Paragraph

Write a paragraph on the board about different types of natural resources. Explain the purpose of the topic sentence, supporting details, and conclusion sentence. Have students write a paragraph about ways to conserve natural resources using these steps:

- During **Close**, p. 45
- 30 minutes

1. Brainstorm resources we use that may run out if we are not careful. Write responses on the board using correct spelling and syntax. Add ideas if necessary.
2. Have students think of ways we can begin conserving resources. Write these ideas on the board.

Give beginning students a paragraph with sentence starters or blanks to be filled in with vocabulary that reflects their understanding of resources and ways to conserve them. Allow intermediate students to use some words and phrases from the board in writing their paragraph, but ask them to use some original examples. Ask advanced students to write their paragraph using original examples and words.

Informal Lesson Assessment

	Beginning	Intermediate	Advanced
Task	Ask students to show different ways people adapt to and change the environment by drawing before and after sketches of land and resources. Ask them to label their pictures using key words.	Ask students to list different ways people adapt to and change the environment using words and phrases. They should describe the environment before and after changes people make to land and resources.	Ask students to list different ways people adapt to and change the environment using complete sentences. They should describe the environment before and after changes people make to land and resources.
Below Expectations	• no answer is comprehensible and/or correct	• no answer is comprehensible and/or correct	• incorrect ideas • no complete sentences • many errors
Meets Expectations	• some answers are comprehensible and/or correct	• some of the answers are comprehensible and/or correct	• appropriate ideas • some incomplete sentences • some errors
Above Expectations	• all answers are comprehensible and correct	• all of the answers are comprehensible and correct	• appropriate ideas • complete sentences • few errors

Success for English Learners

Use with Chapter 2, Lesson 1

Build Background

Access Prior Knowledge

Tell students that many, many people live in North America. Ask students for ideas about how people in North America live today. Elicit details about holidays, traditions, schools, writing, and art. List students' ideas. Point out that all of these things make up a civilization. Tell students that a civilization is a group of people who live together and share the same government, religion, and schools. Explain that long ago, people started the first civilizations.

- Before **Introduce**, p. 52
- 15 minutes

Lesson Vocabulary

Write and say each vocabulary word. Have students write each word on a card. Then discuss their meanings. Use gestures, pictures, or words to provide real-world examples of the words. For example, for **achievement**, hold up an example of excellent work by a student. Have students write words or draw pictures on the back of each card that will help them with its meaning. Use each word in a sentence that gives context clues, such as: *The civilization had a government, writing, and schools;* or, *Scientists have an idea, or theory, about how people came to the Americas.* Have children hold up the correct card when they hear the meaning.

Additional Vocabulary Define the words and phrases, and provide examples of their use. For example, make a statement to the class that you cannot prove is true: *It will rain/be sunny after school.* Explain that your statement is a *theory*, an idea that is based on facts you know, such as the weather right now. Also, tell students that a *land bridge* is a piece of land that connects two bigger pieces of land. Tell students that the abbreviation "B.C." means "before the year 0" or "before the Common Era." Before, it had a religious meaning of "before Christ." A.D. stands for "anno Domini," which is Latin for "year of our Lord." It means "after the year 0."

A.D.	glacier
achievement	Ice Age
B.C.	land bridge
burial	mammoth
counting system	origin
extinct	writing system

Cognates As students read the lesson you may wish to point out cognates such as: **theory/teoría, civilization/civilización, calendar/calendario, culture/cultura, family/familia.**

Build Fluency

Read aloud the following rhyme, and point out the words that sound alike. Have students repeat it several times to develop oral language skills. Return to the rhyme throughout the lesson to help develop vocabulary, compare and contrast skills, and lesson content.

> After hundreds of years of **migration**
> Early people formed **civilizations**.
> How did people first arrive?
> Did they cross a land bridge, or did boats bring the tribes?
> Or did Native Americans always live here?
> These are some of the **theories** that people have shared.
> First people were nomads, traveling day after day.
> Then they began farming, creating new **traditions** and ways.

Scaffolding the Content

Preview the Lesson

Have students look at the four main headings of the chapter. Tell students they will learn about how civilizations started in the Americas. Show students the picture on page 55. Ask: *Is life different now than it was a long time ago?* Brainstorm a list of examples with students.

- During **Teach**, pp. 52-59
- 30 minutes

Modify Instruction

Read aloud the following summaries. Guide students as they take notes on the blackline master page.

I. The Land Bridge Story

1. Around 14,000 B.C., the first people came to North America. Scientists do not know for sure how these people got here. Some scientists think people walked over a bridge of land that connects Asia and North America.

II. Other Theories

1. Some scientists think people have been in the Americas much longer. They think people arrived on North America by boat.
2. Native Americans have stories about their history. Native Americans believe that their people always lived in the Americas.

III. Early Ways of Life

1. Early people hunted giant animals for food. They were nomads because they did not live in one place. They followed the animals that they hunted.
2. Around 8,000 B.C., the climate was warmer. They learned to farm, so they began to stay in one place. They developed farming, or agriculture.

IV. The Olmec and the Maya

1. The Olmec was one of the first civilizations in the Americas. They ruled what is now southern Mexico from about 1500 B.C. to A.D. 300. The Olmec also used rivers to travel and trade. They had a writing system and a number system. They had a 365-day calendar. The Olmecs fell from power. No one knows why.
2. From A.D. 300 to A.D. 1500, the Maya ruled what are now southern Mexico, Guatemala, and northern Belize. The Maya had a writing system based on hieroglyphs, or picture symbols. Religious people were the social leaders. The Mayans were ruled by a king.

V. Other Civilizations

1. The Mound Builders lived east and west of the Mississippi River from 1000 B.C. to A.D. 200. They are famous for mounds they used to bury their dead.
2. The Puebloans lived in the place where Utah, Colorado, Arizona, and New Mexico meet. Their houses were built against canyon walls, or in caves.

Extend

Have pairs of mixed-proficiency students choose one aspect of civilization, such as government, schools, or writing. They should create a Venn Diagram to compare it as it was long ago and as it is today.

- After **Teach**, p. 59
- 20 minutes

Success for English Learners ▪ 23

Name _____ Date _____

DIRECTIONS Listen to the summaries. Write details in the chart about early people and civilizations of the Americas. Then look at your chart and think about how the groups of people are the same and how they are different.

	Early People	Olmec	Maya	Mound Builders	Puebloans
Time Period					
Location					
Achievements and Other Facts					

 School-Home Connection Encourage students to draw pictures in each box showing what happens. Have them take this page home to share with family members. They can use their drawings and the captions to tell about early civilizations in North America.

24 ■ Success for English Learners

Unit 1, Chapter 2, Lesson 1

Apply and Assess

Write a Paragraph

First, help students review by asking volunteers for examples of theories. Tell students they will write a paragraph about theories about how early people came to the Americas.

- During **Close**, p. 59
- 20 minutes

Write a short paragraph about early civilizations on the board. Explain the purpose of the topic sentence, supporting details, and conclusion. Then model the prewriting process for students. Write: *Three Theories About How People Arrived in the Americas.* Ask for volunteers as you guide students through a review of each theory. Write one-word summaries of each theory below the first phrase: *Land Bridge, Boats,* or *Always There.* Circle the phrase and the summaries together. Tell students that the circle shows the main idea of the paragraph they will write. Help students brainstorm details about one theory, and write them below its one-word summary. Circle the list of details, and draw a line to connect it to the main idea circle. Tell students that the second circle shows details that support the main idea.

Have students copy your web. Encourage them to complete the web by adding details for the other two theories. Check students' work, and help as needed as they write their paragraphs.

- Give beginning students a paragraph with sentence starters or blanks to be filled in with vocabulary that will reflect their comprehension of key facts.
- Allow intermediate students to use some sentences from your paragraph.
- Consider pairing advanced students with beginning students during the writing process.

Informal Lesson Assessment

	Beginning	Intermediate	Advanced
Task	Ask students to draw and label pictures about how civilizations developed in the Americas.	Ask students to use short phrases to list details about how civilizations developed in the Americas.	Ask students to write a short paragraph describing how civilizations developed in the Americas.
Below Expectations	• no correct pictures or labels	• few or no phrases given, or phrases are incomprehensible • 2 to 4 phrases, but none are correct	• no correct details described • no complete sentences • many errors
Meets Expectations	• some correct pictures or labels	• 2 to 4 comprehensible phrases • most are correct	• some details are correct • some incomplete sentences • some errors
Above Expectations	• all pictures and labels are correct	• phrases and some complete sentences • all of the responses are correct	• all details described are correct • complete sentences • few errors

Use with Lesson 2 · Chapter 2

Build Background

Access Prior Knowledge

Have students examine the illustrations on pages 62–67 that show life in the Eastern Woodlands long ago. Ask students to try to guess from what the structures, tools, and weapons in the illustrations are made. Ask them to guess how the people traveled and what kinds of foods they ate.

• Before **Introduce**, p. 62
• 15 minutes

Lesson Vocabulary

Explain the terms **palisade** and **longhouse** by pointing to illustrations of these objects on pages 64 and 65 of the text. Draw a dome-shaped shelter and tell students that it is called a **wigwam**. Explain **wampum** by sketching a string of beads and a seashell. Define **division of labor** as "giving everyone the same amount of work," and show students the different jobs that are being done on pages 64 and 65. Explain **confederation** as "many tribes or groups making decisions together." Next, divide the class in half. Choose one student from each side to come to the board. Show them a flashcard with a word so other students cannot see. Have them sketch pictures so their team members can guess the vocabulary word. A team member must raise his or her hand before guessing. If the team member is right, the team gets a point. Record the points on the board. Challenge advanced students by giving them abstract terms like *confederation*.

Additional Vocabulary Define the words and provide examples of their use. For example, explain that the word *bank* can mean a business where people keep their money, but in this lesson, it means "land near water." Explain that the word *bark* can mean the sound a dog makes, but in this lesson it means "the outside layer of a tree."

bank	peacemaker
bark	rely on
canoe	shelter
fertile	stretched
inland	woodlands
league	

Cognates As students read the lesson you may wish to point out cognates such as: **canoe/canoa, climate/clima, division/división, peace/paz.**

Build Fluency

Read aloud the following rhyme, and point out the words that sound alike. Have students repeat it several times to develop oral language skills. Return to the rhyme throughout the lesson to help develop vocabulary, compare and contrast skills, and lesson content.

> The Eastern Woodlands people
> Were people of the woods.
> The forests had many animals
> People hunted when they could.
> The forests gave them shelter.
> They built houses out of trees.
> They all lived near the Great Lakes
> But the Iroquois lived further east.
> The Iroquois ate crops and traded **wampum**
> And built **longhouses** that fit twenty.
> The Algonquin ate fish and lived in **wigwams**.
> The Eastern Woodlands gave everyone plenty!

Scaffolding the Content

Preview the Lesson

Read the lesson title aloud. Refer students to the map on page 56. Show them the east coast, pointing first to Florida and drawing an imaginary line up to Canada. Describe this area as the Eastern Woodlands. Tell students they will learn about the geography and climate of the area. They will also learn how these things influenced the lives of the Native Americans who lived there long ago.

- During **Teach**, pp. 62–67
- 20 minutes

Modify Instruction

Read the summary aloud. Tell students to listen for information about the landforms, resources, and weather of the Eastern Woodlands. Have them underline details that show how these things influenced different Native American groups. They will use the information to fill out the cause and effect chart on the next page.

Life in the Eastern Woodlands

The Eastern Woodlands were east of the Mississippi River. They had thick forests and flowing rivers and streams. People lived in villages. They farmed, hunted, and gathered food. Trees were important resources. People used them for canoes, weapons, tools, and fruits. The northern and southern parts were different. The north had rocky soil, so people there hunted and gathered more than they farmed. The south had good soil, so people farmed crops like corn, beans, and squash. People used division of labor. This means they divided the work between men, women and children. In the north, women made food and made clothes from animal skins, and men hunted and fished. In the south, men cleared land, and women and children grew crops.

The Iroquois

The Iroquois lived near Pennsylvania, New York, and Canada. They lived far from the coast. Animals were an important source of food. The Iroquois lived near rivers and streams so they could have fresh water. They farmed more than they fished. The Iroquois used trees to build wooden walls called palisades. They also used trees to construct long buildings called longhouses. The Iroquois traded wampum, strings of beads made from shells. Iroquois groups included the Mohawk, Oneida, Onondaga, Cayuga, and Seneca, or the Five Nations. The Iroquois formed a league and council that solved arguments.

The Algonquians

They lived near the Great Lakes, so they fished more than they farmed. Fish was an important source of food. People lived in longhouses and wigwams, or dome-shaped shelters. Winters were cold, so women made clothes from deer skin. The Algonquians had one chief for war and another chief for times of peace. Algonquian groups included the Delaware, Wampanoag, Powhatan, Ottawa, Chippewa, and Miami.

Extend

Have children create a Venn diagram to compare and contrast the ways of life of the Iroquois and Algonquian peoples.

- After **Teach**, pp. 62–67
- 15 minutes

Name _____ Date _____

DIRECTIONS The left column shows facts about the geography and climate of the Eastern Woodlands. Write "Cause" above it. The right column shows details about Native American ways of life. Write "Effect" above it. Draw arrows to show how geography and climate (cause) influenced the Native Americans of the Eastern Woodlands (effect). Causes may have more than one effect.

_____	_____
1 The Eastern Woodlands had thick forests with many trees.	1 Iroquois men hunted. Iroquois women made food, clothing and moccasins.
2 The Eastern Woodlands had many rivers and streams.	2 Algonquians built canoes for fishing.
3 The northeastern part had rocky soil.	3 The Iroquois farmed, hunted, and gathered more than they fished.
4 The southern part had good soil.	4 The Iroquois built villages where they could get fresh water.
5 The Eastern Woodlands had coastal areas.	5 The Iroquois used trees to build longhouses and palisades.
6 The Eastern Woodlands had cold winters.	6 The Algonquians used wood to build longhouses and wigwams.
7 Much of the Eastern Woodlands was far away from the coast.	7 People planted corn, bean, squash and other plants.
	8 Men cleared land. Women and children gathered crops.
	9 The Iroquois used wood to build palisades and longhouses.
	10 The Algonquians fished more than they farmed.

School-Home Connection Have students take this page home to share with family members. Ask them to read it aloud and explain what it says about the Eastern Woodlands.

28 ■ Success for English Learners   Unit 1, Chapter 2, Lesson 2

Apply and Assess

Give a Speech

Start by writing "Iroquois League" on the board, saying the words, and asking students to tell what it was. Repeat and write their ideas. Then present this sentence starter and complete it as a class:

• During **Close**, p. 67
• 20 minutes

The purpose of the Iroquois League was _____.

Move on to another sentence starter and work with students to complete it.

Before there was a league, the Five Nations _____.

Help students elaborate on what life might have been like before the league. Record some reasons for joining the league.

Ask students to write a draft of their speech, and then to work with a partner to make it better and practice it. You may want to pair advanced or intermediate students with beginning students. Consider reading one or two of the speeches aloud to the class.

When students are ready to give their speech, have them switch to a new partner and deliver their speeches to a new listener.

Informal Lesson Assessment

	Beginning	**Intermediate**	**Advanced**
Task	On the board, write: Many Trees, Rocky Soil, Rivers and Coasts, Cold Winters. Ask students to draw and label pictures to show how people in the Eastern Woodlands lived with each fact.	On the board, write: Many Trees, Rocky Soil, Rivers and Coasts, Cold Winters. Ask students to list details that show how people in the Eastern Woodlands lived with each fact.	On the board, write: Many Trees, Rocky Soil, Rivers and Coasts, Cold Winters. Have students write sentences describing how people in the Eastern Woodlands lived with each fact.
Below Expectations	• no correct pictures or labels	• few or no correct responses	• incorrect ideas • very few details named • unclear expression
Meets Expectations	• some correct pictures and labels	• some correct responses	• appropriate ideas • several details named • some errors in expression
Above Expectations	• all pictures and labels correct	• all responses are correct	• appropriate details • many details named • clear expression

Success for English Learners

Use with Chapter 2, Lesson 3

Build Background

Access Prior Knowledge

As they look at the illustration on page 70, have students imagine people long ago on the plains. Some of these people stayed in one area, and others moved from place to place. Ask students to predict how the homes and lives of these two groups of people were the same and different. Explain that students will soon learn whether their predictions are correct.

- Before **Introduce**, p. 70
- 30 minutes

Lesson Vocabulary

Have students work in mixed-proficiency pairs to make a crossword puzzle with the words **lodge, sod, scarce, tepee, travois, council,** and **ceremony.** Ask them to write definitions for the words on the crossword puzzle. Explain the words using sketches, illustrations in the text, and brief definitions. Distribute the lesson vocabulary cards so that students can compare their definitions with those on the cards. Have pairs exchange and complete the puzzles.

Additional Vocabulary Remind students that many words have more than one meaning. As you encounter the words at the right in the reading, explain the common meanings and the text meaning. For example, *hide* can be used as a verb. However, point out that on page 70, the word means "skin."

earth
hide
lodge
pipe
oil

Cognates As student read the lesson, you may wish to point out cognates such as: **ceremony/ceremonia, buffalo/búfalo, valley/valle, society/sociedad.**

Build Fluency

Read aloud the following rhyme, and point out words that sound alike. Have students read the part of either *The Nomads* or *Central Plains Indians*, and repeat their part several times to develop oral language skills. Return to the rhyme throughout the lesson to help develop vocabulary, compare and contrast skills, and lesson content.

Central Plains Indians:
The Earth has many resources to give.
These resources influence how we live.

The great buffalo gives us food to eat,
Clothes, and moccasins for our feet.

But from the grasslands to the flat plains,
Our ways of life are not the same.

Nomads:
"We will travel where the buffalo go!"
Said the Cheyenne, the Kiowa, and the Crow.

"We will pack up the **tepee** and the animal hide."
Said each member of the tribe.

Central Plains Indians:
"We will farm the land and hunt buffalo too,"
Said the Pawnee and the Sioux.

"We build **lodges** with **sod** and stay on our land,"
Said the people who were called Mandan.

Scaffolding the Content

Preview the Lesson

Preview the headings, and have students study the illustrations. For each heading, focus attention on the illustration on the same page, and ask how it helps explain or give details about the heading. For example, for "Life on the Plains" on page 71, ask students what animal was very important for life on the plains.

• During **Teach**, pp. 70–75
• 30 minutes

Modify Instruction

To teach the content, read the following summary aloud. Stop after each major heading so students can find and complete the chart on the blackline master page. Remind students what the words *geography, climate* and *resources* mean. Help them with group, or tribe, names. Review answers for each section before proceeding to the next.

1. **Life on the Plains** The Plains people lived on the Interior Plains between the Mississippi River and the Rocky Mountains. Plains are large, flat lands with few trees. They hunted buffalo. They used the buffalo for food, clothing, bags, and for cord or rope, needles, and other tools. Buffalo were the Plains people's main resource.

2. **Farmers and Hunters** Some people lived in the eastern part of the Plains. These are the Central Plains. They included the Mandan, Pawnee, and Sioux. They gathered plants, hunted deer, elk, and buffalo. They farmed the good soil in the valleys of the Missouri River and Platte River. They lived in villages made up of large, circular homes called lodges. Several families lived in one lodge. The lodges were made of dirt. On the northern prairies, lodges were covered with sod, a layer of soil held together by roots and grasses. On the southern prairies, lodges were covered with animal skins.

3. **Nomadic Society** Nomadic peoples lived in the western part of the Interior Plains called the Great Plains. They moved from place to place. They included the Kiowa the Cheyenne, and the Crow. They built cone-shaped shelters called tepees that were easy to move. They used buffalo droppings to light fires during the cold winters. They used a kind of carrier called a travois that was pulled by a dog. They did not farm. They ate meat from buffalo.

4. **Plains Cultures** Plains peoples had different customs and governments. The Lakota people formed seven groups, and all made their own choices. The Cheyenne had a council of chiefs with representatives from ten groups. The council made decisions together. The Plains people shared some traditions and beliefs. Each group had a story that described the beginning of their people. The Blackfoot, for example, believed that a spirit called Old Man created them. Many Plains people performed the Sun Dance ceremony to help keep the buffalo strong.

Extend

Write this topic sentence for a paragraph: *Plains groups had some similar and some different ways of life.* Have mixed-proficiency pairs write a detail sentence that could support that topic sentence. Put them together to form a paragraph. Add transitions and edits as needed for sense and clarity. Have students in each pair take turns reading the paragraph aloud.

• After **Teach**, pp. 70–75
• 10 minutes

Name _____ Date _____

DIRECTIONS Listen to the information. Then fill in sections of the chart.

Life on the Plains

Location: _____
_____

Importance of Buffalo: _____
_____

Farmers and Hunters

Location: _____
_____

Names of Tribes: _____
_____

Homes: _____
_____

A Nomadic Society

Location: _____
_____

Names of Tribes: _____
_____

Homes: _____
_____

Plains Cultures

Government: _____
_____

Beliefs and Traditions: _____
_____

School-Home Connection Encourage students to draw pictures to illustrate some facts in the chart. Have students take this page home to share with family members. They can use their chart to explain what they have learned about ways of life among the Plains people.

32 ■ Success for English Learners

Unit 1, Chapter 2, Lesson 3

Apply and Assess

Draw a Building Plan

Start by pointing out the illustrations on pages 72–73. On page 72, point out the poles and write *poles* on the board. Point out that the poles form a circle at the bottom. Write *circle* on the board. Show how the poles are tied at the top. Write *tied* on the board.

• During **Close**, p. 75
• 20 minutes

Have students focus on page 73. Explain that the poles were covered with buffalo skins. Write *buffalo skins* on the board. Also note that there was a hole at the top of the tepee. This let out smoke from fires that burned inside the tepee. Write *hole* on the board.

Tell students that a building plan is a list of jobs to do. They will create a building plan for making a tepee.

Ask students what they think the Plains people did first. A reasonable guess is cut or make the poles. Write the following example of a numbered step:

1) They cut poles for the tepee.

Ask students to name the next step. Have students continue writing the steps.

- You may want to group all the beginning students for support when they write or draw.
- Intermediate and advanced students may work independently.

When all students have finished, ask them to read or act out their plans to a partner.

Informal Lesson Assessment

	Beginning	Intermediate	Advanced
Task	Ask students to draw and label pictures showing how Plains peoples lived. Tell them to show the land, weather, and resources they had.	Ask students to make a list of how Plains people lived with the region's land, weather, and resources.	Have students write at least three sentences describing how Plains people lived with the region's land, weather, and resources.
Below Expectations	• no correct pictures or labels	• few or no correct responses	• incorrect ideas • no complete sentences • many errors
Meets Expectations	• some correct pictures and/or labels	• some correct responses	• appropriate ideas • some incomplete sentences • some errors
Above Expectations	• all pictures and labels correct	• many correct responses are given	• appropriate ideas • complete sentences • few errors

Success for English Learners ■ 33

Use with Lesson 4, Chapter 2

Build Background

Access Prior Knowledge

Make a two-column chart with the headings "Hot and Dry" and "Cool with Streams." Write side headings for homes, food, and ways of life. Invite students to pantomime or volunteer words, phrases, or sentences to describe how people might live in each type of place.

- Before **Introduce**, p. 76
- 30 minutes

Lesson Vocabulary

Use the vocabulary cards to explain words to students, and discuss the definitions as a class. Instruct students to make vocabulary squares for each of the vocabulary words. Ask students to draw three squares in a horizontal row to represent each word. In the first square, they write a brief definition. In the second square, they write a sentence using the word. (Allow beginning students to use words or phrases instead of sentences.) In the third square, they draw a picture or symbol of the word. For the abstract term **adapt**, for example, students could draw a picture of sunglasses to show one way they would adapt to a hot, sunny environment. Have them repeat this process for each word. Ask them to show their sketches to a partner, and have the partner guess the word.

Additional Vocabulary Explain the words listed in the margin, and provide examples of their uses. Point out that the word *mesa* means "table" in Spanish, but in English it is "a flatland with steep sides."

canyon	dry
cliff	environment
cotton	mesa
drought	

Cognates As students read the lesson you may wish to point out cognates such as: **adapt/adaptar, desert/desierto, mountain/montaña, tribe/tribu.**

Build Fluency

Read aloud the following rhyme, and point out the words that sound alike. Have students repeat it several times to develop oral language skills. Return to the rhyme throughout the lesson to help develop vocabulary, compare and contrast skills, and lesson content.

> In climates mild or hot and dry,
> Western peoples **adapted** to survive.
> Some said mesas were good places to live.
> They ate all the food the earth could give.
>
> In climates mild or hot and dry,
> Western peoples adapted to survive.
> Some built with **adobe,** sun-dried clay.
> Medicine people sang illness away.
>
> In climates mild or hot and dry,
> Western peoples adapted to survive.
> They stored **surplus** food for times of drought
> And traded for things they couldn't live without.

Scaffolding the Content

Preview the Lesson

Ask students to work in small groups to note the differences in the environments shown on pages 77 and 79. Use the illustrations to point out major differences in life for groups in the West and the Southwest.

• During **Teach**, pp. 76–80
• 20 minutes

Modify Instruction

Explain the following points to students using simple language, and help them take brief notes. Ask questions to check student comprehension.

I. The Southwest

1. Geography: desert, hot, dry, mountains, mesas, cliffs, few trees
2. Climate: hot summers, bitter cold winters
3. Pueblo Cultures
   - The Hopi lived in present-day Arizona; Zuni lived in present-day New Mexico
   - Homes: close together, pueblos, made of stones, mud, or adobe bricks of clay
   - Food: corn, beans, squash grew in the dry environment
   - Other resources: clay (for bricks and pottery), cotton (for clothing and blankets)
   - Traded: pottery made of clay, and baskets
4. Navajo: in the Four Corners (where Utah, Colorado, Arizona, and New Mexico meet)
   - Homes: far apart hogans (cone-shaped shelters of wood, covered by adobe)
   - Traded: pottery made of clay, baskets, and later grew cotton

II. The West

1. Geography: deserts, valleys, forests, coastal lands
2. Climate: dry, mild, rainy, sometimes extreme temperature changes
3. Shoshone: hunters in the Great Basin (little food and water)
   - Homes: made of dry brush
   - Food: hunted small animals in the Great Basin; hunted buffalo in the mountains of present-day Wyoming
4. Nez Perce: lived near streams in the mountains in the Columbia Plateau
   - Homes: made movable shelters to use while fishing
   - Food: hunted salmon with long spears

Extend

Present several true and false statements about Native Americans who lived in the West and Southwest. Have beginning students identify the statements as true or false. Ask more advanced students to correct false statements.

• After **Teach**, p. 80
• 15 minutes

Success for English Learners ■ 35

Name _____ Date _____

DIRECTIONS Use your notes to write details about the people who lived in different environments in the West and the Southwest.

Group and Environment	How People Used Resources

Southwest
Example

Group: Hopi and Zuni
Environment: desert, dry, hot

1. cotton → blankets, clothes
2. clay → bricks for homes
3. corn → food

Group:
Environment:

1. →
2. →
3. →

West

Group:
Environment:

1. →
2. →
3. →

Group:
Environment:

1. →
2. →
3. →

Group:
Environment:

1. →
2. →
3. →

School-Home Connection Encourage students to draw pictures in each box showing what happens. Have them take this page home to share with family members. They can use their drawings and the captions to tell about Native Americans who lived in the West and Southwest.

36 ■ Success for English Learners   Unit 1, Chapter 2, Lesson 4

Apply and Assess

Draw a Map

Refer students to the map on page 61. The map shows borders of states as they are today. Labels tell the Native American groups who lived in each state. On a separate sheet of paper, have students trace or copy an outline of the United States. Ask students to lightly color the West in one color and the Southwest in another color. Write the names of Native American groups from this lesson: *Hopi, Zuni, Navajo, Shoshone, Nez Perce,* and *Chumash.* Using page 61 as a reference, ask students to write the names of the Native American groups on the map in the approximate area of where they lived. When they are finished, practice calling the name of a Native American group and having students respond "West" or "Southwest" to indicate where the group lived.

• During **Close**, p. 80
• 40 minutes

Informal Lesson Assessment

	Beginning	Intermediate	Advanced
Task	Provide a list of Native American groups from the lesson. Have students write or draw details that show how the groups adapted to the region's geography and climate.	Provide a list of Native American groups from the lesson. Have students write short sentences about how the groups adapted to the region's geography and climate.	Provide a list of Native American groups from the lesson. Have students write a paragraph about how the groups adapted to the region's geography and climate.
Below Expectations	• no response correctly identified	• few or no responses are comprehensible • 2 to 4 responses, but none are correct	• no correct resource or use described • no complete sentences • many errors
Meets Expectations	• some responses correctly identified	• 2 to 4 comprehensible phrases • most responses are correct	• some resources and uses described are correct • some incomplete sentences • some errors
Above Expectations	• all responses correctly identified	• phrases and some complete sentences • all of the responses are correct	• all resources and uses described are correct • complete sentences • few errors

Use with Chapter 2, Lesson 5

Build Background

Access Prior Knowledge

Have students imagine people living in a land of snow and ice a long time ago. Ask students to predict what their houses and tools are made of. Ask them to predict how the people travel and what kind of food they eat. Encourage students to draw pictures. Do the same for a land of thick forests and heavy rains. Explain that in this lesson, student will learn whether their predictions are correct.

- Before **Introduce**, p. 82
- 35 minutes

Lesson Vocabulary

Explain the new vocabulary words, and ask questions to check student comprehension. Tell students that when learning new words and ideas, it helps to connect what they already know with what they are learning. To demonstrate, ask students to create a small word web for each vocabulary word. Students should fill out the web using words or ideas that they connect to the vocabulary word. For example, the word **clan** may be associated with words like *family, group,* or *many*. Finally, invite students to make their own webs for each vocabulary word.

Additional Vocabulary Explain the words listed in the margin, and give examples of how they are used in the lesson. Mention that the word *fat* is commonly used as an adjective. However, in this lesson, it is used as a noun. Explain that *speech* can mean "speaking." However, in this lesson, it refers to a talk given by one person to a group of people. Help students use context clues to figure out the meanings of *seal, mouth,* and other unfamiliar words.

at sea	seal
fat	speech
mouth	stranded
potlatch	totem pole
rank	

Cognates As students read the lesson you may wish to point out cognates such as: **capture/capturar, clan/clan, kayak/kayak, lamp/lámpara.**

Build Fluency

Read aloud the following rhyme, and point out the words that sound alike. Have students repeat it several times to develop oral language skills. Return to the rhyme throughout the lesson to help develop vocabulary, compare and contrast skills, and lesson content.

> Trees and plants and fish they had.
> Trees and plants and fish they had.
> In the Northwest, people lived by the coast
> With plenty of wood.
> The fishing and farming were good!
>
> Foxes and **kayaks** and seals they had.
> Foxes and kayaks and seals they had.
> In the Arctic, the land was frozen.
> Plants and trees did not grow.
> Some people lived in **igloos,** houses made of snow.

Scaffolding the Content

Preview the Lesson

Point out the illustrations on pages 83–86. Ask students what they can tell about where Arctic, Northwest, and Sub-Arctic peoples lived and some of their activities. As students study illustrations, return to the rhyme and see if students can match the words and images for igloos and kayaks.

- During **Teach**, pp. 82–87
- 30 minutes

Modify Instruction

Remind students that geography is made up of landforms and resources of a region. Climate is the weather of a region over a long time. Explain that the ways of life for people of the Northwest and Arctic regions depended on geography and climate. Explain the following points to students using simple language, and help them take brief notes.

A Region of Plenty

The Northwest included parts of Oregon, Washington, and Canada. This region is near the ocean and had much rain. People did not farm. People of the Northwest Coast included the Kwakiutl, Makah, and the Chinook. They fished, hunted, and gathered plants and nuts. Salmon and whale were staple foods. Whale was an important resource. Some people used harpoons to kill whales. Harpoons are long spears.

Resources and Trade

People used wood from trees for houses, tools, boats, and totem poles. These were carvings that told stories. Makah houses were like Iroquois longhouses, but much bigger. Many members of a family made up a clan. Trading was an important part of the Northwest economy. The Chinook used a special language for trading. So they could barter, or trade, with people who spoke different languages. Many Northwest groups became rich. They celebrated in a potlatch. It had dancing, food, and speeches.

Lands of the North

The Arctic is a frozen place near the North Pole. The Aleut lived there along the coast of the Aleutian Islands. Another group was the Inuit. They lived in what is now Alaska and Canada. Plants and trees did not grow well in the Arctic. So people hunted foxes, caribou, polar bears, seals, walruses, and whales. They used boats called kayaks. The land gave the people few resources; they did not waste anything. They used seal meat for food. They used seal skins for clothes and tents. They used seal bones to make tools. The Inuit lived in igloos, houses made of ice. The Aleut built their houses with whalebone and dirt.

The sub-Arctic is south of the Arctic. It stretches from eastern Canada to Alaska. People there hunted and gathered food. The Cree lived in a large part of what is now Canada. They could not farm during the long winters.

Extend

Draw a table with columns labeled "Northwest Coast" and "Arctic and Sub-Arctic." Label side heads "geography," "climate," "resources," "houses," and "food." Have students write details from the summary for each region.

- After **Teach**, p. 87
- 10 minutes

Name _____ Date _____

DIRECTIONS Check the column that shows which area each phrase describes. Use your notes to remember details about people from different environments in the Northwest, Arctic, and Sub-Arctic regions.

Phrase	Northwest	Artic	Sub-Artic
____ The Makah people there lived in wooden longhouses like the Iroquois', but much larger.			
____ The Inuits lived in homes of ice there during winter.			
____ The food staples there were mainly salmon and whales.			
____ The Aleut and Inuit there hunted whales, polar bears, and seals.			
____ The people there had very few plants, so they wasted no resources.			
____ Wood was a very important resource there because there were many trees.			
____ The Cree developed a special language for trading there.			
____ People there hunted, gathered, and fished for food there.			
____ People there did not farm there.			
____ People used special boats called kayaks there.			

School-Home Connection Encourage students to draw pictures in each box showing what happens. Have them take this page home to share with family members. They can use their drawings and the captions to tell about people who lived in the Northwest, Arctic, and Sub-Arctic regions.

Apply and Assess

Write a Poem

Remind students that a poem does not have to rhyme. It can be a list, a few short phrases, or a group of sentences.

• During **Close**, p. 87
• 30 minutes

Begin gathering ideas by making a cluster on the board. In the center, write "Arctic Ways of Life." Elicit ideas about what Arctic people hunted, ate, used, built, and believed.

Provide these starters. The first two lines can be completed with a series of action words, such as *build* and *fish;* the last three lines are sentence completion frames.

On land, we _____.
On sea, we _____.

In the morning, we _____.
At midday, we _____.
At night, we _____.

Allow beginning students to use illustrations instead of words.

Informal Lesson Assessment

	Beginning	Intermediate	Advanced
Task	Write some details about Northwest people on sentence strips. For example: *The Aleut could not farm.* Have students read them aloud, and sort them to show whether they are related to geography or climate.	Have students name three facts about the Northwest geography and climate. Then have them tell how these facts affected people who lived there.	Have students write a paragraph telling how the Northwest geography and climate affected people who lived there.
Below Expectations	• language is not comprehensible or correct • incorrect groupings	• few or no facts given, or statements are incomprehensible • 2–4 facts, but none are correct	• no correct facts or are given • no complete sentences • many errors
Meets Expectations	• language is partially comprehensible and/or correct • half of groupings are correct	• 2–4 comprehensible phrases • most are correct	• some correct details are given • most complete sentences • a few errors
Above Expectations	• groupings are correct	• drawings show aspects of a suburb • labels or phrases correspond with the drawings • spelling is correct	• paragraph includes correct details about Northwest geography, climate, and how they affected people.

Developing Academic Language

To understand what they read, students need to be able to identify the main idea and distinguish it from the details that support and explain it. One strategy for finding the main idea is recognizing placement: the main idea is often—but not always—stated near or at the beginning of a paragraph. Students can occasionally also use signal words to help them understand which ideas in a paragraph are subordinate or explanatory.

Introduce Main Idea and Details

Explain to students that every paragraph has a topic. The topic is what the whole paragraph is about. Some topics include winter, basketball, and dogs. The **main idea** is usually a sentence that states the topic and says something about it. In a paragraph, **details** usually follow the main idea. A detail can be a fact about the topic, an example, or words to help explain the topic.

- Before **Main Idea and Details**, p. 102
- 20 minutes

Write this example in paragraph form: *Dogs are a lot of work. For example, you have to train them. You have to walk them. You also have to feed them, and take them to the vet.* Circle and label the topic *dogs*. Double underline and label the main idea sentence, the first sentence. Then underline and label the detail sentences.

Practice

Write the following main idea and details. Have students write the paragraph that might result:

   Main Idea: Spring vacation was fun.
   Details: My dad took me to the zoo.
   My friend Dino came to visit.
   I played outside in the park.

Now post and read the details below. Have students work in pairs to name the topic for a paragraph about these details *(new camera)*. Then work with students as a class to write the topic sentence *(I got a new camera.)*.

   It is a digital camera. I took 20 pictures the first day I had it!

Apply

Draw the following chart, and have partners copy it onto a piece of paper. Then read this paragraph: *Baseball is fun! Many people go to baseball games. They hope their favorite team wins.* Work with students to write the sentences in the chart. Then ask them to tell what their organizers show.

Main Idea

↑

Details

42 ■ Success for English Learners

Use with Chapter 3, Lesson 1

Build Background

Access Prior Knowledge

Write the word *expedition*. Break it into syllables (ex·pe·di·tion), say them, and repeat the word. Explain that an expedition is a long trip in search of something. Make a chart with four "Ws" that correspond to these questions: *Who* goes on an expedition? *Where* do people on an expedition go? *Why* do people plan expeditions? *What* are some things expeditions search for? Discuss and record answers.

• Before **Introduce**, p. 108
• 10 minutes

Lesson Vocabulary

Draw the following symbols on the board, find pictures of them, or bring in the objects: ship, dollar sign (or dollar bill), king's crown, compass. Name them and be sure students understand what they show. If any of them are objects, pass them around. Next, distribute the word cards to partners and have them read and discuss each definition. Ask students to choose which symbols each word goes with.

Note that some word cards may go with more than one symbol and answers may vary (**technology:** compass, dollar sign; **navigation:** all; **expedition:** all; **empire:** dollar sign, crown; **entrepreneur:** dollar sign, compass; **cost:** dollar sign; **benefit:** dollar sign; **Reconquista:** crown).

When students have finished, discuss their choices with them.

Additional Vocabulary Explain the words and provide examples of their use. Point out words with multiple-meanings. Point out that the word *movement* can refer to a physical motion as well as a new way of thinking.

Cognates As students read the lesson, you may wish to point out cognates such as: **exploration/exploración, technology/tecnología, conquer/conquistar, route/ruta.**

entrepreneur
invent
movement
Renaissance
rush
supplies

Build Fluency

Read aloud the following rhyme, and point out words that sound alike. Have students repeat it several times to develop oral language skills. Return to the rhyme throughout the lesson to help develop vocabulary, main idea and details skills, and lesson content.

When Europeans first sailed the sea,
They did not have much **technology**.
Compasses and astrolabes were the tools of the day,
But **expeditions** didn't always find their way.
Entrepreneurs wanted to explore and paid the **cost**
But received no **benefit** if ships were lost.
For the promise of riches, out they set,
Which led to a place where two worlds met.

Success for English Learners ■ 43

Scaffolding the Content

Preview the Lesson

Post the question *What did Europeans need from Asia?* Have students look at page 109 to find responses (spices, silk, and riches). Next, have students work in pairs to identify differences in the maps on pages 112 and 122. Explain that traveling to Asia by going west over land was long and difficult, so Europeans tried to go east by sea.

- During **Teach**, pp. 108–115
- 30 minutes

Modify Instruction

Outline the main ideas and details of the chapter for students. As you read, have students write key words, phrases, and details on the blackline master page.

I. A Rush of New Ideas

During the Renaissance, Johannes Gutenberg invented the printing press. This helped people share new ideas. A book by Marco Polo described China and riches there. Europeans read this book and wanted Asian silks and spices, but travel was difficult. People did not have correct maps, the right technology, or scientific tools to help them.

II. The World Awaits

A. Prince Henry and Navigation—Prince Henry of Portugal opened a school of navigation. Sailors there learned to sail a new kind of ship, called the caravel. People also improved maps and tools, like the compass. They went on expeditions, or trips, for exploration.

B. Limited Knowledge—The Europeans traded with people in Asia and Africa. They did not know that other continents existed or that the Vikings had explored present-day North America 500 years earlier.

III. The Business of Exploring

A. Christopher Columbus—The Italian sailor Columbus wanted to reach Asia and its riches by sailing west. Explorers were also entrepreneurs. Columbus persuaded King Ferdinand and Queen Isabella of Spain to pay for his ship and supplies.

B. The Reconquista—The king and queen wanted all of Spain to be Catholic. During the Reconquista, Muslims had to become Catholic or leave Spain. Many Jews also had to leave. After the Reconquista, Spain paid for Columbus' voyage.

IV. Two Worlds Meet

In 1492, Columbus and his crew sailed on three ships—the Niña, the Pinta, and the Santa María. In time, they reached land they believed to be Asia.

Extend

Work with students to make a time line or sequence chain that shows the order of key events and developments discussed in this chapter. Discuss what the completed time line or chain shows.

- After **Teach**, pp. 108–115
- 10 minutes

Name _____ Date _____

DIRECTIONS Listen to the chapter summary. Complete the outline.

Exploration and Technology

I. A Rush of New Ideas

_____
_____
_____

II. The World Awaits

   A. Prince Henry and Navigation

_____
_____

   B. Limited Knowledge

_____
_____

III. The Business of Exploring

   A. Christopher Columbus

_____
_____

   B. The Reconquista

_____
_____

IV. Two Worlds Meet

_____
_____
_____

School-Home Connection Have students take this page home to share with their families. They can use the information in the outline to tell a family member about the age of exploration and technology.

Unit 2, Chapter 3, Lesson 1

Apply and Assess

Draw a Chart

Before you begin, review the vocabulary related to charts. Draw an outline of a two-column chart with three rows on the board. Use it to teach or reteach the words *column*, *row*, and *heading*. You may also want to introduce or reteach the multiple-meaning word *cell*.

• During **Close**, p. 115
• 20 minutes

Read the directions for this activity aloud. Ask students how many columns they think their chart should have (two). On the chart on the board, ask students to tell you what headings to write (Costs, Benefits). Suggest that their chart have three rows. Work with students to complete the first row, for example, Cost/new tools for navigation; Benefits/help to find their way.

- Support beginning students as they work in a group to draw pictures and write key words.
- Intermediate students may work in pairs to write phrases.
- Advanced students may complete the remainder of the chart on their own.

When students are finished, discuss what their completed charts show.

Informal Lesson Assessment

	Beginning	Intermediate	Advanced
Task	Have students copy and complete these frames: *Columbus set out to find _____. He needed _____ before he could go.*	Ask: *Why did Columbus travel? What did he need before he could go?*	Have students write a paragraph telling why Columbus traveled and what made his journey possible.
Below Expectations	• neither answer is comprehensible or correct	• no part of the answer is comprehensible or correct	• incorrect ideas • the answer is not in paragraph form • many errors
Meets Expectations	• one answer is comprehensible and correct	• one part of the answer is comprehensible and correct	• most ideas are correct • the answer is in paragraph form • some errors
Above Expectations	• both answers are comprehensible and correct	• both answers are comprehensible and correct	• clear, correct ideas • the answer is in paragraph form • few errors

Use with Chapter 3, Lesson 2

Build Background

Access Prior Knowledge

Write the multiple-meaning, multiple-part-of-speech word *claim* on the board. Tell students you are an explorer, and, if possible, use a flagpole to demonstrate "planting the flag" and *claiming* land, or making a *claim*. Announce that you claim this classroom, this whole school, this whole state, and even this whole country, for your leader. In other words, all of these are your *claim*. Then ask what happens if someone in the next classroom plants a flag there and claims the classroom, the same school, the same state, or the same country.

- Before **Introduce**, p. 118
- 10 minutes

Lesson Vocabulary

Discuss the definitions of the words **isthmus** and **treaty**. Use body language, sketches, and examples to help students understand the meanings of the words. Explain to students that you will ask several questions in a row. They should respond using one of these two words. Ask a question aloud and call on different students. Repeat the questions until the students clearly understand them:

1) Which is a piece of land that connects North and South America? 2) Which is a formal agreement between countries? 3) Which can you see on a map? 4) Which can you find in a museum? 5) Which stopped the success of explorers who tried to reach Asia from Europe? 6) Which is necessary when two or more countries want one thing?

Additional Vocabulary Explain the words and provide examples of their use. Explain that the word *claim* is often used as a verb, but in this chapter it is used as a noun that means "something a person or country calls its own."

claim
goal
inspire
success

Cognates As students read the lesson, you may wish to point out cognates such as: **leader/líder, coast/costa, describe/describir, published/publicado, ocean/océano.**

Build Fluency

Read aloud the following rhyme, and point out words that sound alike. Have students repeat it several times to develop oral language skills. Return to the rhyme throughout the lesson to help develop vocabulary, main idea and details skills, and lesson content.

> Explorers traveled across the seas
> Trying to solve some mysteries
> Because the map of the world changed.
> Explorers made many faraway claims
> And gave old lands new names.
> And so the map of the world changed.
> When Spain and Portugal claimed the same lands,
> A **treaty** settled their demands.
> And, again, the map of the world changed.

Success for English Learners

Scaffolding the Content

Preview the Lesson

Have students look at the illustration on page 118 and relate it to a word they have just learned. Ask students to turn to page 121 and explain that it shows the explorer Vasco Núñez de Balboa. He is shown crossing the isthmus between North and South America. Then point out the isthmus on the map on page 122. Ask what ocean Balboa crossed into.

• During **Teach**, pp. 118–123
• 30 minutes

Modify Instruction

To teach the content, read the following summary aloud. Have students follow explorers' routes on the map on page 122. Point out the chart on the blackline master page and review the words *goals*, *problems*, and *results*. Stop after each explorer to give students time to write details on the chart. Discuss the information on the chart.

1. **John Cabot:** This explorer's Italian name was Giovanni Caboto, but the English called him John Cabot. The king of England paid him to lead an expedition. The king wanted land and money. After a long, slow journey, Cabot reached a land he thought was Asia. He claimed it for England. Many people today think this land was Newfoundland in Canada.

2. **Amerigo Vespucci:** The Italian explorer Vespucci sailed along the coast of South America to find out if Cabot and Columbus reached Asia. He found no signs that this land was Asia. Vespucci discovered that he and the earlier explorers found a new continent. As a result, a new map of the world was published with America on it. The name of the continent came from Amerigo Vespucci's name.

3. **Vasco Núñez de Balboa:** The Spanish explorer Balboa searched for gold in what is now Panama. He had little money for a voyage. Native Americans told him about an ocean to the west. He found it beyond the Isthmus of Panama and called it the Pacific Ocean. He proved that the land Columbus and Cabot reached was not Asia.

4. **Ferdinand Magellan:** The Portuguese explorer Magellan wanted to find a trade route to Asia. He sailed west from Spain, around the tip of South America, and across the Pacific Ocean. There were many problems. Many sailors died of hunger and illness. Magellan died in a battle in the Philippine Islands. Some of his sailors went all the way around the world. Sometimes Spain and Portugal claimed the same lands. They made a treaty in 1494. The treaty gave Portugal the land that is now Brazil. The treaty gave Spain most other lands claimed in the Americas.

Extend

Write this main idea: *The desire to find a new trade route to Asia led to claims, problems, and changes.*

• After **Teach**, pp. 118–123
• 10 minutes

- Ask pairs of students to write a detailed sentence for a paragraph about a claim, a change, or a problem.
- Then put the sentences together, editing and revising as needed, to form a main idea and detail paragraph.
- Read the paragraph aloud. Have partners read it aloud to each other.

Name _____ Date _____

DIRECTIONS Listen for details. Write them in the chart.

Explorer	Goals	Problems	Results
John Cabot			
Amerigo Vespucci			
Vasco Núñez de Balboa			
Ferdinand Magellan			

School-Home Connection Have students take this page home to share with their families. They can use the information in the chart to tell about early explorations that affected the Americas.

Apply and Assess
Make a Table of Explorers

Tell students that they can use a chart like the one they just completed to do this activity. They need to change some information and headings.

• During **Close**, p. 123
• 20 minutes

Have students begin by figuring out the number of rows and columns they need. Ask students to name the explorers they will cover. Explain that these names will be the headings for each column. Explain that students will also need the heading "Area Explored" for the row. Draw a table like this to demonstrate:

	Cabot	Vespucci	Balboa	Magellan
Area Explored				

Have students work in mixed-proficiency pairs to complete the table and to trace the routes on the map on page 122.

Informal Lesson Assessment

	Beginning	Intermediate	Advanced
Task	Read these sentence starters and have students complete them: *The goal of early explorers was to find ____. Instead, they found ____.*	Have students write two or more phrases or sentences telling what early explorers were searching for and what they found instead.	Ask: *How did early explorers change the map of the world?* Have students first write their answers, and then read them aloud.
Below Expectations	• neither answer is correct	• incorrect ideas • no correct phrases or complete sentences • many errors	• no correct answer is given • many errors
Meets Expectations	• one answer is correct	• appropriate ideas • some correct phrases or complete sentences • some errors	• one correct answer is given in incomplete sentences
Above Expectations	• both answers are correct	• appropriate ideas • correct phrases or complete sentences • few errors	• more than one correct answer is given in complete sentences

Use with Chapter 3, Lesson 3

Build Background

Access Prior Knowledge

Ask students what they think are the most important things in life for all people. Make a list. Ask for big concepts, such as love and faith. When you have finished, circle whatever comes closest to religion/faith/belief/God, and whatever comes closest to wealth/money. Explain that these were Spain's two main reasons for exploring the Americas. Add that some explorers also wanted fame or glory.

• Before **Introduce**, p. 126
• 10 minutes

Lesson Vocabulary

Distribute vocabulary word cards to each student. Have them work in mixed-proficiency pairs to talk about each definition. Then ask students to sort the vocabulary words into these three categories: people (**conquistador, missionary**); movements (**Reformation, Counter-Reformation**); and things (**grants, reforms**). Have students give reasons for their groupings.

Additional Vocabulary Define the words for students. Explain how the words relate to the lesson.

Cognates As students read the lesson, you may wish to point out cognates such as: **attack/atacar, adventure/aventura, convert/convertir, conqueror/conquistador, protest/protestar.**

empire	prisoner
expedition	protest
claimed	punished
glory	set foot on
priest	

Build Fluency

Read aloud each verse of the following chant, and point out words that sound alike. Have students repeat each verse several times to develop oral language skills. Return to the chant throughout the lesson to help develop vocabulary, main idea and details skills, and lesson content.

> Brave Spaniards received **grants** to explore
> For riches, for God, for glory.
> They crossed the Atlantic and came ashore
> For riches, for God, for glory.
> Each dreamed of being a **conquistador**
> For riches, for God, for glory.
> They explored Florida, the Southwest, and more
> For riches, for God, for glory.

Scaffolding the Content

Preview the Lesson

Have students turn to the map on page 129. Write three brief statements about the map, and have students label them *true* or *false:* 1) This map shows cities in South America. 2) This map shows the routes of five explorers. 3) This map shows where the Aztec Empire was. [Answers: *false–North America, true, true*] When you complete the activity, explain to students that they will now learn why the explorers went to the areas shown on the map and what happened on their voyages.

• During **Teach**, pp. 126–132
• 30 minutes

Modify Instruction

Read the following summaries aloud. After each major heading, stop to have students complete the matching row of information on the blackline master page. Have students use their charts to tell what the explorers' goals were and what happened when they came to the Americas.

1. **Juan Ponce de León:** Juan Ponce de León, like other explorers, received a grant, or large sum of money, from the Spanish king for leading an expedition. He landed in what is now Florida. He claimed this and many other lands for Spain.

2. **Hernando Cortés:** Cortés and his men landed in Mexico looking for gold. They went to the Aztec capital, Tenochtitlán. Cortés was a conquistador, or conqueror, who took the emperor Motecuhzoma prisoner, conquered Tenochtitlán, and built Mexico City in its place for Spain.

3. **Francisco Vásquez de Coronado:** Coronado heard about cities of gold. He wanted to find them. He and his men claimed many lands in the southwestern United States for Spain. He did not find gold.

4. **Hernando de Soto:** De Soto wanted wealth and glory, so he and his men searched for rich empires throughout the Southeast. Here, they claimed land for Spain and fought many Native Americans. They were the first Europeans to see the Mississippi River.

5. **Missionaries:** Some people disagreed with the Church. They wanted change, or reforms. Martin Luther was the leader of a movement called the Reformation that started new Protestant churches. The Catholic Church reacted by making changes through efforts called the Counter-Reformation. During this movement religious teachers called missionaries were sent to convert Native Americans to the Catholic religion. As a result, some Native Americans changed the way they lived and worshipped.

Extend

Write this sentence: *In general, Spanish explorers did not find what they were looking for in the Americas.*

• After **Teach**, pp. 126–132
• 10 minutes

- Ask partners to create sentences that support this main idea.
- Write their sentences where all the students can see them. Then join the sentences, using transitions and other necessary edits, to form a paragraph.
- Read the paragraph aloud. Then have students read it.

Success for English Learners

Name _____ Date _____

DIRECTIONS Listen to the summaries. Complete the chart.

Explorer or Settler	Goal	Area Claimed or Other Result
Juan Ponce de León		
Hernando Cortés		
Francisco Vásquez de Coronado		
Hernando de Soto		
Missionaries		

School-Home Connection Have students take this page home to share with their families. They can use the information in the chart to tell a family member about Spanish explorers and missionaries.

Unit 2, Chapter 3, Lesson 3

Apply and Assess

Write a Travelogue

Help students understand the activity by modeling the prewriting stage. Explain that the first step is to choose an explorer, for example, de Soto. Then create a tree diagram with two branches. Put "Hernando de Soto" at the top. On the first branch, write "Places I Saw." On the second, write "People I Met." Ask students for ideas to record on each branch. Elicit speculations beyond the text, such as encounters with Native Americans, and endless days crossing the desert Southwest without much water.

- During **Close**, p. 132
- 20 minutes

Hernando de Soto

Places I Saw   People I Met

- Have beginning students use this organizer to create a travelogue in words and pictures.
- Have intermediate students work with a partner to create an organizer like this for another explorer, and to write a travelogue.
- Have advanced students develop a different organizer about another explorer, and write a travelogue.

Informal Lesson Assessment

	Beginning	**Intermediate**	**Advanced**
Task	Have students copy this sentence frame on paper and fill in the blank. *Columbus set out to find ____. He needed ____ before he could go.*	Ask: *Why did Columbus travel? What did he need before he went?*	Ask students to write a few sentences or a paragraph telling why Columbus traveled and what made his journey possible.
Below Expectations	• neither part of the answer is comprehensible and/or correct	• neither answer is comprehensible and/or correct	• incorrect ideas • no complete sentences • many errors
Meets Expectations	• one part of the answer is comprehensible and/or correct	• one answer is comprehensible and/or correct	• appropriate ideas • some incomplete sentences • some errors
Above Expectations	• both parts of the answers are comprehensible and correct	• both answers are comprehensible and correct	• appropriate ideas • complete sentences • few errors

Use with Chapter 3, Lesson 4

Build Background

Access Prior Knowledge

Ask students to name reasons explorers went on voyages. Have them work in pairs to make four flashcards each by writing names of these explorers on the front and hints on the back: *Columbus*—found a new continent sailing west for Asia; *Balboa*—found the Pacific Ocean looking for gold; *Cabot*—wanted land and wealth for the king of England and found land in present-day Canada; *Vespucci*—a continent was named after him; *Magellan*—his crew sailed around the world. Have students use the flashcards to review each explorer. Tell them they will now learn about explorers who looked for the Northwest Passage to Asia.

- Before **Introduce**, p. 136
- 10 minutes

Lesson Vocabulary

Write the two vocabulary words and their meanings. Discuss the meanings. Then have partners complete the following sentences with the correct words.

Many explorers hoped to find the _____ for sailing from the Atlantic Ocean to the Pacific Ocean.

When sailors are angry with their captain, they sometimes have a _____.

Discuss the context clues that helped partners make their choice.

Additional Vocabulary Explain the words and provide examples of their use.

Cognates As students read the lesson, you may wish to point out cognates such as: **company/compañía, difficult/difícil, metal/metal, nation/nación, expedition/expedición.**

bay
big business
shortcut
trade route

Build Fluency

Read aloud each verse of the following chant, and point out words that sound alike. Have students repeat each verse several times to develop oral language skills. Return to the chant throughout the lesson to help develop vocabulary, main idea and details skills, and lesson content.

> Verrazano looked far and wide
> With many sailors at his side
> Looking for the **Northwest Passage**.
>
> Cartier made three long trips
> In search of a new route for ships
> Looking for the Northwest Passage.
>
> Hudson made four trips across the sea.
> His searches led to ice and **mutiny**
> Looking for the Northwest Passage.
>
> Although explorers tried and tried
> All of them failed, and some of them died
> Looking for the Northwest Passage.

Success for English Learners

Scaffolding the Content

Preview the Lesson

Read the summary of the lesson on page 141 with the students. Next, direct them to the illustrations on pages 140 and 141. Work with them to use the summary, map, and illustrations to answer the following questions: 1) Name three explorers from this lesson and the places they explored. 2) Name three things they found. 3) Name one thing they did not find.

• During **Teach**, pp. 136–141
• 30 minutes

Modify Instruction

Post notes on the board or overhead as you review the following content summary with students. Ask students to record details about where each explorer traveled and what happened on the trip. Have volunteers tell what they learned about each explorer.

1. **Verrazano:** Giovanni da Verrazano was an Italian explorer who hoped to find the Northwest Passage, a waterway across North America that would take sailors from the Atlantic Ocean to the Pacific Ocean. Like other kings, the king of France knew that finding the Northwest Passage would mean a good trade route and riches. He sent Verrazano to find it. Verrazano found what is now North Carolina, and he sailed north along the Atlantic Coast to Newfoundland. He did not find the Northwest Passage.

2. **Cartier:** The king of France also sent Jacques Cartier to find the Northwest Passage, as well as gold and other valuable metals. Cartier made three trips. He sailed to the mouth of the St. Lawrence River and into what is now Quebec. He claimed an area of present-day Canada for France. His voyages taught Europeans more about North America, but he never found gold or the Northwest Passage.

3. **Hudson:** Henry Hudson made four voyages to North America, paid for by English and Dutch companies including the Dutch East India Company, a trading company, in Holland. Hudson sailed up the Hudson River near what is now New York, and claimed the whole Hudson River valley for the Dutch. He claimed the area around the Hudson Bay for the English. On Hudson's last difficult voyage, his crew mutinied, or rebelled. The men put Hudson and eight other men in a small boat. No one ever saw them again.

Extend

Ask: *Who else besides the Spanish explored North America?*

• After **Teach**, pp. 136–141
• 10 minutes

- Make a chart and write as headings the countries or businesses that students name, such as the French, the Dutch, the English, and the Dutch East India Company.

- Then ask students for details about the explorers and explorations, including the claims they made for different countries.

56 ■ Success for English Learners

Name _____ Date _____

DIRECTIONS Listen to the summaries. Then fill in the chart.

Who?	Where?	What Happened?
Giovanni da Verrazano		
Jacques Cartier		
Henry Hudson		

School-Home Connection Have students take this page home to share with their families. They can use their notes to talk about explorers who searched for the Northwest Passage.

Apply and Assess

Draw a Picture

Begin by explaining that Netherlands is another name for Holland, and that people from the Netherlands are the Dutch. Write *Netherlands = Holland*.

• During **Close**, p. 141
• 20 minutes

Ask students to tell how they could find out what, for example, the flag of Spain looked like in 1600. Guide them to name search terms, such as "historical flags of Spain." Write and say the search terms.

Suggest that beginning and intermediate students work in pairs to do the research and to create their drawings. Advanced learners may work independently.

Suggest that students use rulers to create neat flags, stripes, and geometric designs. Explain that if designs are difficult to draw (such as coats of arms) students can use stick figures and other simple drawings. Ask students to color and label their flags. Have individuals or pairs discuss their drawings with each other and show how and where they found their information.

Informal Lesson Assessment

	Beginning	**Intermediate**	**Advanced**
Task	Ask: *Why did Europeans explore North America?* Provide a list of the three explorers in this lesson and a list of the reasons they explored North America. Have students match them by drawing lines.	Provide students with a list of the three explorers in the lesson. Ask them to list the reasons they explored North America.	Ask students to write a paragraph naming the explorers in this lesson who traveled to North America and telling why they explored.
Below Expectations	• no items correctly identified	• few or no phrases, or phrases are incomprehensible • 2 to 4 phrases, but none are correct	• no correct items described • no complete sentences • many errors
Meets Expectations	• some items correctly identified	• 2 to 4 comprehensible phrases • most of the items are correct	• some items described are correct • some incomplete sentences • some errors
Above Expectations	• all items correctly identified	• phrases and some complete sentences • all of the items are correct	• all items described are correct • complete sentences • few errors

Use with Chapter 4, Lesson 1

Build Background

Access Prior Knowledge

Ask students to imagine that they need to control a huge area of land in a faraway place. This land is mostly undeveloped, though Native Americans have homes and farms there. What do they need to do? Ask students for ideas about what they would build or create. Elicit key concepts such as food supply, protection (forts), roads, and a growing population.

- Before **Introduce**, p. 146
- 10 minutes

Lesson Vocabulary

Write the vocabulary words on the board as you say them, and tell their meanings. Ask students to repeat them. Read the following paragraphs aloud. Then read them again, but leave out the bracketed words. Work with the class to complete the paragraphs as cloze exercises. As students supply words, discuss the context clues that determined their choices.

> Spain wanted to protect its claims, so it created [**colonies**]. The people who lived in them were colonists. Some started large farms called [**plantations**] in New Spain. The colonists needed many workers for these large farms, and they forced people to work for them. This is called [**slavery**].

> New Spain was very large. Lands on the edge of it were called [**borderlands**]. These lands stretched into what is now the southern United States. Religious leaders started settlements called [**missions**]. Some ranchers built [**haciendas**], huge ranches where they raised animals and farmed.

Additional Vocabulary Explain the words and provide examples of their use. Explain that the word "mine" has two meanings in this lesson. As a verb it means to collect metals from the ground, and as a noun it is a place where metals are collected from the ground.

Cognates As students read the lesson, you may wish to point out cognates such as: **condition/condición, animal/animal, fort/fortaleza, protect/proteger, mission/misión.**

disease
govern
landowner
mine
rights
treatment

Build Fluency

Read aloud the following rhyme, and point out words that sound alike. Have students repeat it several times to develop oral language skills. Return to the rhyme throughout the lesson to help develop vocabulary, main idea and details skills, and lesson content.

> The Spanish had to defend their claims
> And sent people to settle land for Spain.
> They formed New Spain and new **colonies**
> And settled them with people from across the seas.
> Native Americans were used as slaves,
> Forced to farm and mine all day
> They wanted money and personal gain.
> America changed with the growth of New Spain!

Success for English Learners

Scaffolding the Content

Preview the Lesson

Use the illustrations to preview content and reinforce vocabulary. Have students look at the illustration on page 147 and note that it shows the inside of a fort. Note the picture of a Brazilian sugarmill on page 148. Have students predict how sugarmills affected Native Americans. Point out the missions and the borderlands on the map on page 149. Ask students to predict how Spanish movement into these areas would have affected Native Americans.

- During **Teach**, pp. 146–150
- 30 minutes

Modify Instruction

Outline the chapter with students. Read the heads below, and have students find the matching headings on the blackline master page. As you read the information, have students write key words, phrases, and details in their outline.

I. New Spain
Often, European countries claimed the same land in the Americas. Native Americans also thought the land was theirs. To control the land, Spain needed to set up colonies, or areas it would rule from far away. Spain set up colonies north of the Isthmus of Panama and on many islands in the Caribbean.

II. Slavery in the Americas
When the first settlers came, some started large farms called plantations. They needed workers to grow crops and mine gold and silver. They made Native Americans work as slaves. Many died from hunger, disease, and overwork. Then colonists like Bartolomé de Las Casas spoke out for better treatment of the Native Americans. Soon, however, other colonists began bringing slaves from Africa to work in New Spain. These slaves worked under the same terrible conditions.

III. Settling the Borderlands
- **A.** Forts—Spain wanted to protect lands on the northern edges of New Spain, or borderlands. Soldiers built forts there. In St. Augustine, Florida, they built the first permanent, or long-lasting, European colony in what is now the United States. The king of Spain chose leaders to rule these areas.
- **B.** Missions—Spain also built religious settlements called missions to spread its power. Missions were for making the Native Americans become Christians. Some Native Americans learned new ways of life from missions. Some fought against the missions, because they were forced to work on them.
- **C.** Haciendas—Ranchers in the borderlands built haciendas. These were houses on huge areas for raising animals and crops. The Spanish, and the animals they brought with them, changed ways of life for many Native Americans.

Extend

Write and say this main idea sentence: *Spain protected its claims in the Americas in many ways.* Have students name details that support and explain this sentence. Repeat them, and record them below the sentence.

- After **Teach**, pp. 146–150
- 10 minutes

60 ■ Success for English Learners

Name _____ Date _____

DIRECTIONS Listen to the summaries. Then complete the outline with main ideas and details.

The Spanish Colonies

I. New Spain

_____
_____
_____
_____
_____

II. Slavery in the Americas

_____
_____
_____
_____
_____

III. Settling the Borderlands

   A. Forts

_____
_____

   B. Missions

_____
_____

   C. Haciendas

_____
_____

School-Home Connection Have students take this page home to share with their families. They can use the information in the outline to tell a family member about how the Americas changed as Spain built colonies and settled New Spain.

Apply and Assess
Build a Model

Remind students that there is an illustration of a fort on page 147. Have them turn to page 147 and help them name some things they see. Guide students to see that the fort has high walls. The walls have places for guards to stand so they can see over them. Some buildings are built right into the fort and are protected by it. These buildings have support beams that cross the length and width of the building and stick out beyond the building's walls.

- During **Close**, p. 150
- 20 minutes

Supply clay, and if you want, toothpicks and craft sticks. You might suggest the use of a large piece of cardboard as a foundation for the fort.

Put students into small, mixed-proficiency groups. Ask each group to discuss what it will build and to draw a simple sketch. When groups have finished, invite them to tell other groups about its fort. Beginners can point to objects and name them, and intermediate and advanced students can speak in complete sentences.

Informal Lesson Assessment

	Beginning	Intermediate	Advanced
Task	Say: *Name two reasons that the Spanish set up colonies in North America.* Students may respond *with single words, gestures, or by pointing to pictures.*	Have students list two ideas to complete this frame: *The Spanish set up colonies in North America to ____ and ____.*	Ask students to write two sentences that tell why the Spanish set up colonies in North America.
Below Expectations	• no comprehensible or correct answer is given	• no part of the answer is comprehensible or correct	• no correct details • no complete sentences • many errors
Meets Expectations	• one comprehensible or correct answer is given	• part of the answer is comprehensible or correct	• some details are correct • some incomplete sentences • some errors
Above Expectations	• two correct, comprehensible answers are given	• the answer is comprehensible and correct	• all details are correct • complete sentences • few errors

Use with Chapter 4, Lesson 2

Build Background

Access Prior Knowledge

Write the words *gold, silver, control, glory, fame,* and *riches* as reasons countries wanted to claim lands in the Americas. Remind students that they learned about Spanish colonies in the last chapter, and in this chapter they will learn about English colonies.

- Before **Introduce**, p. 152
- 10 minutes

Lesson Vocabulary

Display the following sentences. Have pairs of students say or write a definition for each vocabulary word based on context clues. Students can look up the vocabulary words in the Glossary to verify their meanings.

1. The colonists could turn **raw materials** like trees into products like lumber.
2. Some English merchants bought **stock**, or a share of the ownership, in the Virginia Company.
3. Many colonists grew food for their own families to eat, but they grew tobacco as a **cash crop**.
4. Some farmers needed help with farming. They paid for people's trips to Virginia, and these people worked for them as **indentured servants**.
5. The colonists in Virginia set up a **legislature** to make laws.
6. The colonists elected people to **represent**, or speak for, them.
7. The king of England took over Virginia. Virginia became a **royal colony**.

Additional Vocabulary Define the words listed in the margin for students. Explain how the words relate to the lesson.

lumber
merchant
ownership
swamp

Cognates As students read the lesson, you may wish to point out cognates such as: **attack/atacar, mystery/misterio, represent/representar, servant/sirviente.**

Build Fluency

Read aloud each verse of the following chant, and point out words that sound alike. Have students repeat each verse several times to develop oral language skills. Return to the chant throughout the lesson to help develop vocabulary, main idea and details skills, and lesson content.

The first English colonists went to Roanoke.
This happened in Virginia.

Tobacco was a **cash crop** and brought wealth.
This happened in Virginia.

Indentured servants and slaves worked the farms.
This happened in Virginia.

A **legislature** was formed to make laws.
This happened in Virginia.

Success for English Learners ■ 63

Scaffolding the Content

Preview the Lesson

Tell a picture story to students: Queen Elizabeth of England (page 152) wanted to start an English colony. The first English settlers went to Roanoke Island (page 153) but they did not stay. The first successful English colony was Jamestown (page 154). Virginians bought the first slaves in America (page 155). They fought against the Powhatans (page 156).

- During **Teach**, pp. 152–156
- 30 minutes

Modify Instruction

To teach the content, read the following paragraphs aloud. Stop after each numbered item so students can locate the matching box on the black line master page. Have students write the number of the paragraph in the box. When they have finished, ask partners to retell the events using phrases in the boxes.

1. Queen Elizabeth of England wanted a colony in North America. She thought a colony would bring England riches and raw materials—resources that can be turned into products.

2. A group of settlers went to Roanoke Island in an area the English called Virginia. They did not remain there. No one knows what happened to them.

3. Merchants formed the Virginia Company, and set up a colony in Jamestown. Almost half of the first colonists died. John Smith helped them by encouraging them to farm. They also had conflicts with the Native Americans.

4. John Rolfe brought tobacco plants to the colonies. People began to grow tobacco. It became a cash crop that the colonists could sell, and brought Virginia wealth.

5. Tobacco led to the need for many workers, and soon farmers paid for people to come to Virginia in return for work. These workers became indentured servants who worked and were later given freedom. Farmers also used slaves. Slaves were rarely freed.

6. The colonists took steps toward a democratic government. They created a legislature, or lawmaking group called the House of Burgesses. Its members spoke for, or represented, the people.

7. As more and more colonists spread out over Native American lands, the Powhatan people became angry. They attacked. A war followed. The Native Americans were defeated.

8. The king of England took control of Virginia. He made it a royal colony. He chose a governor to share power with the House of Burgesses.

Extend

Use the sequence of events in the lesson to create a sequence chain.

- After **Teach**, pp. 152–156
- 10 minutes

- Have students tell you what to write first, next, and so on.
- Write their ideas on the board or on an overhead.
- Have pairs of beginning and intermediate students read the steps in the chain aloud to one another. Advanced learners can produce a written summary of the chain.

Name _____ Date _____

DIRECTIONS Listen to your teacher. Read the phrase in each box. Write the number of each paragraph in the correct box.

The king of England makes Virginia a royal colony.	Captain John Smith helps Jamestown survive.
Settlers go to Roanoke Island.	Tobacco brings wealth to Virginia.
The Powhatan War takes place.	England wants a colony in North America.
The colonists set up a legislature.	Virginia had indentured servants, and slaves.

School-Home Connection Have students take this page home to share with their families. They can use the page to tell their families about what happened in the early days of the Virginia Colony.

Apply and Assess

Write a Persuasive Letter

Write this sentence starter on the board and read it aloud:

> You should move to the Virginia Colony because _____.

- During **Close**, p. 156
- 20 minutes

Ask students for suggestions for completing the sentence. List their ideas, saying each one as you write it. Elicit ideas about opportunities for land and wealth, including how growing tobacco is making some people rich.

Review letter form, including the correct way to state the date. Write and say a sample date, such as July 1637. Also, review the salutation and the closing, writing more samples and saying them.

Have beginners copy the words and phrases from the board as they construct sentences. Beginners may also illustrate parts of the letter to show what they mean. Provide sentence frames as needed for intermediate students. Allow advanced students to use the information that you listed, but tell them that they must use their own words.

When students finish writing, invite them to read their letters aloud to another student.

Informal Lesson Assessment

	Beginning	Intermediate	Advanced
Task	Ask: *What was the first successful English colony?*	Ask: *What was the first successful English colony? Why did people there survive and do well?*	Have students write a paragraph to explain how Virginia was settled and why some people did well there.
Below Expectations	• the answer is not comprehensible or correct	• no part of the answer is comprehensible or correct	• incorrect ideas • incorrect paragraph form • many errors
Meets Expectations	• answer is partially comprehensible and/or correct	• most of the answer is comprehensible and correct	• appropriate ideas • correct paragraph form • some errors
Above Expectations	• answer is comprehensible and correct	• the answer is complete, comprehensible, and correct	• appropriate ideas • correct paragraph form • few errors

Use with Chapter 4, Lesson 3

Build Background

Access Prior Knowledge

Write the multiple-meaning word **pilgrim** on the board. Say it one syllable at a time, framing each syllable as you say it. Explain that a pilgrim is anyone who goes on a journey related to his or her religion. Then write **Pilgrim** with a capital **P**. Explain that this word names a person who settled in a place called Plymouth. Point out pictures of these Pilgrims on pages 159 and 160.

- Before **Introduce**, p. 158
- 10 minutes

Lesson Vocabulary

Explain the lesson vocabulary words by reading the definitions aloud and using sketches, synonyms, and visuals. Next, have students number a sheet of paper from one to eight. Call out the following hints, and have students write the corresponding vocabulary word. Check answers together. Write this question on the board, and read the hints that follow aloud: *Which vocabulary word is . . . ?* 1) a person 2) an agreement 3) a way to control 4) a way to vote 5) a way to make a decision 6) connected to religion 7) a promise or contract 8) a way to be independent (pilgrim, compact, self-government, majority rule, majority rule, pilgrim, compact, self-government).

Additional Vocabulary Explain the words and provide examples of their use. Explain that the word *follow* can mean "to go after or behind," but in this lesson it is used in the phrase *follow the law*, which means "to obey the law."

Cognates As students read the lesson, you may wish to point out cognates such as: **decision/decisión, document/documento, majority/mayoría, region/región, passage/pasaje.**

fair
follow
for the good of
freedom
journey
order

Build Fluency

Read aloud the following rhyme, and point out words that sound alike. Have students repeat it several times to develop oral language skills. Return to the rhyme throughout the lesson to help develop vocabulary, main idea and details skills, and lesson content.

> The **Pilgrims** sailed across the sea
> And created their own colony.
>
> They made a **compact** called the Mayflower.
> In their government, each person had some power.
>
> **Majority rule** was part of their plan
> For getting along in a new land.

Success for English Learners

Scaffolding the Content

Preview the Lesson

Post and explain the main idea behind each heading in the lesson: *The Pilgrims' Journey*—The Pilgrims were people who traveled from England to the Americas on a ship called the *Mayflower* for religious freedom; *The Mayflower Compact*—The Mayflower Compact was the Pilgrims' agreement to make fair laws; *Building a Colony*—The Pilgrim's colony was Plymouth, and their leader was William Bradford. They had many problems, but Native Americans helped them trade and farm better; *Plymouth Grows*—More people came to Plymouth and had problems with Native Americans.

- During **Teach**, pp. 158–163
- 30 minutes

Modify Instruction

To teach the content, read the following events in order. Stop after each paragraph and have students write main ideas in the matching section of the chart on the blackline master page. To complete the chart, students may use single words, phrases, and drawings to express key concepts. Have volunteers show or tell what they wrote in each box.

1. **The Pilgrims' Journey:** People in England became interested in the region called New England after John Smith went there and wrote a book about it. Some people wanted to go there to make money. A group of people called the Pilgrims wanted to go there in order to have religious freedom. In England they did not have religious freedom. They left England in 1620 aboard a ship called the *Mayflower*.

2. **The Mayflower Compact:** The settlers signed a compact, or agreement, called the Mayflower Compact. They agreed to make fair laws for the good of all the people in the colony. In other words, they would govern themselves. This idea of self-government was very new because at that time, Europe was ruled by kings. The Pilgrims also decided to follow majority rule, which meant that if half the people agreed to a law, then everyone had to follow it. Their new home was Plymouth. Their leader was William Bradford.

3. **Building a Colony:** After a long and hard first winter, the Pilgrims got help from the Native Americans. A Wampanoag named Tisquantum showed them where to fish and how to plant vegetables such as squash, corn, and pumpkins. For a while, the Pilgrims lived in peace with their Native American neighbors and benefited from trading with them.

4. **Plymouth Grows:** The people worked hard and the colony grew. As more people arrived, problems started between the Native Americans and the colonists. Over time, these problems grew into terrible wars. Meanwhile, William Bradford continued to lead the colony.

Extend

Make a word web with the words "Plymouth Colony" in the middle. Ask students for words and phrases to add to the word web. Record their ideas, showing relationships with related circles. Have volunteers expand on different parts of the word web.

- After **Teach**, pp. 158–163
- 10 minutes

Name _____ Date _____

DIRECTIONS Listen as your teacher reads. Write the most important ideas you hear.

1.

2.

3.

4.

School-Home Connection Have students take this page home to share with their families. They can use the chart to tell about the early days of Plymouth Colony.

Unit 2, Chapter 4, Lesson 3

Success for English Learners ■ 69

Apply and Assess

Write a Speech

Ask: *If you were a Native American, what would you like to say to the Pilgrims?*

• During **Close**, p. 163
• 20 minutes

Record students' ideas. Elicit a variety of comments from "Welcome," to "This is our land." If students have trouble coming up with ideas, ask them how they would feel if unknown people built houses and grew crops on lands where they liked to go hunting and fishing.

Work with students to use details to develop two or three main ideas, such as the following:

> I welcome you to this land.
> I hope you will remember that these lands are where we hunt and fish.
> We would like to trade with you.

Once you develop main ideas, help students make a list of details that would support each main idea. Put beginning or intermediate students with advanced students. Have each pair use the ideas you wrote, or ideas of their own, to write their speech. When they are finished, allow time for students to read their speech to another pair.

Informal Lesson Assessment

	Beginning	Intermediate	Advanced
Task	Ask: *Why did the Pilgrims go to Plymouth?* Give students three choices: religious freedom, money, or better jobs.	Ask: *Why did the Pilgrims go to Plymouth? How did they make decisions there?*	Have students write a paragraph telling why the Pilgrims went to Plymouth and what they did there.
Below Expectations	• the answer is not comprehensible or correct	• no part of the answer is comprehensible or correct	• incorrect ideas • no complete sentences • many errors
Meets Expectations	• answer is partially comprehensible and/or correct	• most of the answer is comprehensible and correct	• appropriate ideas • some incomplete sentences • some errors
Above Expectations	• answer is complete, comprehensible, and correct	• the answer is comprehensible and correct	• appropriate ideas • complete sentences • few errors

Use with Chapter 4, Lesson 4

Build Background

• Before **Introduce**, p. 166
• 10 minutes

Access Prior Knowledge

Have students look at the map of French claims on page 171. Ask: *What other countries claimed land in North America?* Ask: *Who else believed the land was theirs?* Ask students to guess what happened when more than one group claimed or wanted the same area.

Lesson Vocabulary

Have students work in mixed-proficiency groups to create a crossword puzzle using the words **demand, supply, ally,** and **proprietary colony.** Ask them to write definitions for the words on the crossword puzzle. They should skim the lesson to find definitions if they do not know them. Distribute vocabulary cards so that students can compare their definitions with those on the cards. Then have pairs exchange and complete the puzzles.

Additional Vocabulary Review the multiple-meaning words. For *found*, demonstrate the opposites lost and found. Then explain that this word can also mean "establish" or "set up." Explain that when a city is started, we say it is *founded*. Explain the first meaning of *wiped* by demonstrating wiping your desk. Then explain that *wipe* with *out*—*wipe out*—means "to destroy completely."

| found |
| wipe out |

Cognates As students read the lesson, you may wish to point out cognates such as: **control/controlar, governor/gobernador, population/población.**

Build Fluency

Read aloud the following rhyme, and point out words that sound alike. Have students repeat it several times to develop oral language skills. Return to the rhyme throughout the lesson to help develop vocabulary, main idea and details skills, and lesson content.

> Fur was the fashion, the **demand** was high
> In France and the Netherlands fur was in short **supply**.
> Fur brought French traders across the sea
> And made them **allies** of the Huron in their new colony.
> Fur was also what the Dutch wanted most.
> They built New Amsterdam, a Dutch trading post.
> Fur helped settle the French and Dutch claims
> And left America with many French and Dutch names.

Scaffolding the Content

Preview the Lesson

Post the question at the top of page 166 and read it aloud: *Why did the French and the Dutch set up colonies?* Give students a hint, say: *They wanted an important product they could sell for money.* Have students study the pictures and captions on page 171 to see if they can figure out what this product was (animal fur). Then have students work in pairs to list a few things that are made of animal skins and furs today. Confirm that the Dutch and French needed colonies in the Americas for fur trading, and tell students they will learn how these colonies were started.

• During **Teach**, pp. 166–173
• 30 minutes

Modify Instruction

Work with students to outline the chapter. To do so, read the following summary aloud, and stop after each major heading so that students can fill in the matching part(s) of the outline on the blackline master page. Suggest that students write key words, important phrases, and, if possible, also sentences.

I. **New France:** France claimed land in what is now the northeastern United States and Canada. The French set up missions and traded fur. The French only built settlements in Quebec and Montreal.

II. **New Netherland:** The Dutch settled in parts of what are now New York and New Jersey. They built the city of New Amsterdam. At first, the Dutch established a strong fur-trading relationship with the Algonquian. Later, conflicts with the Native Americans broke out. The Algonquian were nearly wiped out, or completely destroyed.

III. **Exploring New France:** Fighting occurred over the fur trade. The Dutch were allies with the Iroquois, and the French were allies with the Huron. The fighting nearly destroyed the Huron population and the French fur trade. The king of France sent explorers to New France. Jacques Marquette and Louis Joliet found the Mississippi River. They did not find the Northwest Passage. The king later sent Sieur de La Salle to explore the Mississippi. He claimed the area for France. He called it Louisiana after King Louis XIV.

IV. **Louisiana:** The king made Louisiana a proprietary colony. That means he gave it to one person, who would own it and rule it. In 1717, Louisiana was given to John Law, a Scottish banker. New France did not grow fast because it did not attract a big enough population.

Extend

Draw a Venn diagram. Label one circle "Dutch." Label the other "French." Label the overlapping area "Both." Ask students for words and phrases from the lesson that tell about the French, the Dutch, or both. Record students' ideas in the correct part of the diagram. When you are finished, ask students to explain what the diagram says about the French and the Dutch during colonization.

• After **Teach**, pp. 166–173
• 10 minutes

Name _____ Date _____

DIRECTIONS Listen to your teacher. Then complete the outline with main ideas and details.

The French and the Dutch

I. New France

_____
_____

II. New Netherland

_____
_____

III. Exploring New France
   A. Wars Over Fur

_____
_____

   B. Explorers
      1. Marquette and Joliet

_____
_____

      2. La Salle

_____
_____

IV. Louisiana
   A. New Orleans

_____
_____

   B. Growth of New France

_____
_____

School-Home Connection Have students take this page home to share with their families. They can use the information in the outline to tell a family member about the French and Dutch settlements and the fur trade.

Apply and Assess

Draw an Advertisement

Begin by reading the assignment aloud and modeling prewriting. Write *New France* and *New Netherland*. Ask students for reasons why people should live in one or both places. Record their answers in the correct column, or, if applicable, in both columns. When you are finished, restate and review the reasons for settling in each location.

- During **Close**, p. 173
- 15 minutes

Remind students that an advertisement should be interesting to look at. Ask for ideas about what should be large or attractive in their advertisement. Ask them what illustrations they should include. Discuss ideas, then record and say them.

Have students work in mixed-proficiency pairs to make their advertisements. They should begin by choosing either New France or New Netherland. Then encourage them to draw ideas (beginning students) and create text and captions (intermediate and advanced students) from the lists you created earlier.

Provide time for partners to show and explain their advertisements to other pairs.

Informal Lesson Assessment

	Beginning	Intermediate	Advanced
Task	Ask: *Why did the French and Dutch come to America?* Give students three choices: gold, fur, and land.	Ask: *Why did the French and Dutch come to America?* Have students explain why in short sentences.	Have students write a short paragraph explaining why the French and Dutch came to America.
Below Expectations	• the student chose the incorrect answer	• the student cannot provide an answer	• incorrect ideas • incorrect paragraph form • many errors
Meets Expectations	• the student chose the correct answer	• the student can name a reason, but cannot provide supporting details	• appropriate ideas • correct paragraph form • some errors
Above Expectations	• the student chose the correct answer and provided a reason why	• the student can name a reason and can provide supporting details	• appropriate ideas • complete sentences • few errors

Use with Chapter 5 — Lesson 1

Build Background

Access Prior Knowledge

Ask students what they know about the Pilgrims. Write their answers on the board. Tell them they will learn about an English colony that was started for religious freedom. Review the goals of the Pilgrims so that students may build on this knowledge as they study the Puritans. Ask: *Where did the Pilgrims come from? What was the name of their colony? What did they want? Why did they need to live in a new place?* Explain that they will read about a new group of people called the Puritans whose goal was similar to the Pilgrims'. Explain that they will learn about the colony and how its location affected life and the economy.

- Before **Introduce**, p. 178
- 20 minutes

Lesson Vocabulary

Using the Vocabulary Cards, lesson illustrations, and gestures, introduce: **dissent, expel, industry, imports, exports, triangular trade route,** and **Middle Passage.** Have students write each word on an index card. Make a statement followed by the question: *What am I?* For example: *I do not support the government. What am I?* Ask students to hold up the card they believe answers the question. Confirm, and elicit the correct answers from volunteers.

Additional Vocabulary Explain the words in the margin and provide examples of their uses. For example, point out that the name *Puritan* is based on the word *pure*. Explain that a *pure* religion means a religion that is not affected by outside ideas. Tell students that the Puritans wanted to practice a pure form of the religion of the Church of England.

disagreement	soil
forest	strict
pure	suffered
rocky	supplies
separate	whale

Cognates As students read the lesson, you may want to point out cognates such as: **industry/industria, route/ruta, separate/separado, suffer/sufrir.**

Build Fluency

Read aloud the following rhyme and point out the words that sound alike. Have students repeat it several times to develop oral language skills. Return to the rhyme throughout the lesson to help develop vocabulary, identifying main ideas and details skills, and lesson content.

> The Puritans of New England
> Were a very strict group indeed.
> They went to church and started schools,
> **Expelling** any who broke their rules.
>
> They raised livestock like cows and sheep.
> They captured whales and cut down trees.
> As **exports** many products were sold like these
> And bought English **imports** like spices and tea.

Success for English Learners

Scaffolding the Content

Preview the Lesson

Refer students to the map on page 180. Ask students to point to the Massachusetts colony, Rhode Island colony, the Atlantic Ocean, and the direction of England and Africa. Explain that this lesson tells about two New England colonies and how they affected these colonists' lives.

- During **Teach**, pp. 178–184
- 30 minutes

Modify Instruction

Review the following summary of the lesson. Read the main ideas in boldface and give students time to find them on the blackline master page. Review the details and guide students in taking notes.

The Puritans started the Massachusetts colony.

Puritans left England to begin a purer Church of England. Their lifestyle was strict. Puritans went to church every Sunday and worked hard. Education was important to them so that they could read the Bible.

New colonies began near the Massachusetts colony.

Puritans expelled, or threw out, colonists who did not follow their rules. They began new colonies near the Massachusetts colony. Roger Williams was expelled because he wanted church and government to be separate. Anne Hutchison was expelled because she questioned the teachings of Puritan ministers. Their colonies joined to form the Rhode Island colony.

Native Americans already lived in locations where colonists settled.

The colonists settled in locations where Native Americans lived. In 1675, King Philip's War began. A Native American named Metacomet led Native Americans in a war with colonists. The British called Metacomet King Philip. Many colonists and Native Americans were killed in the war, including Metacomet.

Geography affected the economy through products colonists sold.

The New England colonists sold cows, sheep, fish, whale oil, and lumber products. Farming was difficult because of rocky soil. They raised sheep and cows. The New England waters had many fish and whales. Whales were used for oil to light lamps. New England forests had many trees that were used to build homes, churches, and ships.

The New England colonies traded with England and Africa.

New England colonies exported, or sent, lumber, fish, whale oil, and furs to England. New England colonies imported, or received, tea, spices, shoes, and paper from England. The New England colonies also imported slaves from Africa.

Extend

Write the main ideas from the lesson on the board. Read aloud numerous details from the lesson. Call on students to identify the main ideas that the details support by pointing to or stating them.

- After **Teach**, pp. 178–184
- 10 minutes

Name _____ Date _____

DIRECTIONS Listen as your teacher reads main ideas. Find them on the graphic organizer below. Then write details that support the main ideas.

The Puritans started the Massachusetts colony.
New colonies began near the Massachusetts colony.
Native Americans already lived in locations where colonists settled.
Geography affected the economy through products colonists sold.
The New England colonies traded with England and Africa.

School-Home Connection Encourage students to take this page home to share with family members. They can use their notes to explain how geography affected the location of the New England colonies.

Unit 2, Chapter 5, Lesson 1

Apply and Assess

Write a Letter

Help students visualize daily life as a Puritan in colonial Massachusetts. Ask them what types of things they would see and hear, what activities they might do, and what difficulties they might have. Note responses on the board in words and phrases.

• During **Close**, p. 184
• 20 minutes

Write a model letter on the board and read it aloud to students. Tell them to follow the structure of your letter as they write their own. Provide beginning students with a letter that includes blanks to fill in using key words. Provide intermediate students with sentence starters, such as *Today I saw . . .* or *Yesterday was a hard day, because . . .* , to complete with original ideas and words. Ask advanced students to compose the letters using original structures and ideas. Have partners read each other's letters aloud.

Informal Lesson Assessment

	Beginning	Intermediate	Advanced
Task	Give students correct and incorrect statements about ways geography affected life and the economy in New England colonies. Have them identify statements as true or false.	Provide statements about ways geography affected life and the economy in New England colonies. Have students identify statements as true or false and correct false statements.	Provide statements about ways geography affected life and the economy in New England colonies. Have students explain why false statements are incorrect.
Below Expectations	• no statement correctly identified	• few or no correct responses • responses are incomprehensible	• no correct response • no comprehensible explanations • many errors
Meets Expectations	• some statements correctly identified	• a few correct responses • responses are mostly comprehensible	• some correct responses • some explanations comprehensible • some errors
Above Expectations	• all statements correctly identified	• all responses are correct • all responses are comprehensible	• all responses are correct • all explanations are comprehensible • few errors

Use with Chapter 5, Lesson 2

Build Background

Access Prior Knowledge

Review reasons new colonies were started. Pair students and ask them to write the answers to these questions: 1) Why did countries want to start colonies in the New World? 2) Which countries had colonies in the New World? 3) Why was it good for colonies to be near water? Consider providing multiple-choice answers for beginning students to circle, and allow intermediate students to answer in phrases. Advanced students should use sentences. Explain that this lesson will tell how the Middle Colonies were started by countries that wanted power, and how the settlers came for reasons like work and religious freedom.

- Before **Introduce**, p. 186
- 20 minutes

Lesson Vocabulary

Post brief definitions to the new vocabulary words using the Vocabulary Cards. Ask students to create word webs of associations between the new words and images students associate with them. For example, make a word web as a class for the term **proprietor,** which may be associated with concepts like *land* and *own.* Ask for one or two additional words from volunteers. Have partners make word webs for the remaining five vocabulary words.

Additional Vocabulary Explain the words in the margin, and provide examples of their uses. For example, tell students that they can understand some words in the lesson by looking at the meaning of each part. One example is *breadbasket.* Draw a loaf of bread on the board and explain that a basket is a woven wood container for carrying things. A breadbasket is a basket for carrying bread. In the same manner, explain *social life* and *port city.*

awakening	minister
background	port city
breadbasket	social life
equal	split
middle	take over

Cognates As students read the lesson, you may want to point out cognates such as: **equal/igual, immigrant/inmigrante, jury/jurado.**

Build Fluency

Read aloud the following rhyme and point out the words that sound alike. Have students repeat it several times to develop oral language skills. Return to the rhyme throughout the lesson to help develop vocabulary, identifying main ideas and details skills, and lesson content.

> Because farmers grew so much corn, rye, and wheat,
> The middle colonies always had plenty to eat.
> Because colonists sold so many goods at ports like New York,
> Blacksmiths and carpenters earned plenty of money for their work.
> Because so many **immigrants** came to these four lands,
> Religious freedom and **diversity** became the rule of the land.

Success for English Learners ■ 79

Scaffolding the Content

Preview the Lesson

Point to the map on page 188. Name the Middle Colonies and ask students to point to them. Next, post true and false sentences about diversity, religion, the economy, and seaports in the Middle Colonies. Have students answer the questions using the summary on page 191. As you check the answers, expand on topics and explain that they are the main ideas in the lesson.

- During **Teach**, pp. 186–191
- 30 minutes

Modify Instruction

Read the following summary of the lesson. Pause after each set of bullet points to allow students to answer the four questions on the blackline master page.

The Start of New York and New Jersey
- King Charles II of England wanted control of New Netherland and sent warships there. Peter Stuyvesant wanted to fight, but settlers did not. England took over.
- The Duke of York split New Netherland into New Jersey and New York.

Religious Freedom and Diversity in the Middle Colonies
- Quakers settled in New Jersey to practice their religion safely. Quakers believed all people are equal. They did not believe in war.
- William Penn was the proprietor of the Pennsylvania colony. He gave people in Pennsylvania freedom of speech, freedom of religion, and the right to trial by jury.
- The Middle Colonies were very diverse. Many immigrants from European countries settled there. There were some free Africans there, but many were enslaved.

Life in the Middle Colonies
- Religion was an important part of life in the Middle Colonies. In the 1720s, the Great Awakening was a movement that renewed people's interest in religion.
- In the country, people met after religious services and invited neighbors to barn raisings to help them build the frame for a new barn. In cities, people went to dances, plays, and concerts. Philadelphia was the biggest city.

The Economy of the Middle Colonies
- Farmers in the Middle Colonies grew wheat, corn, and rye. These crops are used to make bread, so the Middle Colonies were also called the Breadbasket Colonies.
- Farmers sold crops and livestock to merchants. Merchants took them to port cities like Philadelphia and New York. They were shipped to England and to other colonies.
- Colonists also worked in shipping and worked as blacksmiths and carpenters. They learned by being apprentices. Women usually worked in the home.

Extend

Have each student write two details about a Middle Colony and note the colony the detail describes. Ask students to work in small groups. Students should take turns reading a detail and calling on another group member to tell which Middle Colony the detail describes.

- After **Teach**, pp. 186–191
- 10 minutes

Name _____ Date _____

DIRECTIONS Listen as your teacher reads a summary of the lesson. Answer the four questions below.

How were New York and New Jersey started?

Why were the Middle Colonies so diverse?

What was life like in the Middle Colonies?

What kinds of jobs did people have in the Middle Colonies?

School-Home Connection Encourage students to take this page home to share with family members. They can use their notes to tell about the history, economy, and social activities in the Middle Colonies.

Apply and Assess

Write a Letter

Discuss what the day of an artisan would be like. Ask students to imagine working beside an expert all day long. Brainstorm positive and negative aspects of such a job, like living away from home, learning an interesting skill, doing the same types of things each day, and so on. Write phrases and words on the board as you discuss topics.

Write a brief and simple model letter on the board and read it aloud. Tell beginning students that they may copy words and structures from your letter, but they should change a few words to make the ideas original. Have intermediate students use parts of sentences, such as the beginning, but continue with original structures and thoughts. Ask advanced students to use original constructions and ideas, and have them include one or two questions.

- During **Close**, p. 191
- 25 minutes

Informal Lesson Assessment

	Beginning	Intermediate	Advanced
Task	Give students statements about life, history, and the economy in the Middle Colonies. Have them identify which colonies the statements describe, including the options *none* and *all*.	Have students list details about life, history, and the economy in the Middle Colonies. They should list details that describe the group, as well as each colony individually.	Have students write sentences about life, history, and the economy in the Middle Colonies. They should describe the group, as well as each colony individually.
Below Expectations	• no statement correctly identified	• few or no correct responses • responses are incomprehensible	• no correct response • no comprehensible explanations • many errors
Meets Expectations	• some statements correctly identified	• a few correct responses • responses are mostly comprehensible	• some correct responses • some comprehensible explanations • some errors
Above Expectations	• all statements correctly identified	• all responses are correct • all responses are comprehensible	• all responses are correct • all explanations are comprehensible • few errors

Use with Chapter 5 Lesson 3

Build Background

Access Prior Knowledge

Post the names *New England Colonies* and *Middle Colonies*. Ask students to work in mixed groups to list what they know about these colonies. Ask each group to share responses, and write them in the appropriate column on the board. Then, make a third column that identifies main topics. For example, a group may share that New England had *many trees used to build ships*. Record the response under *New England Colonies* and identify the topic of *economy and resources*. Tell students they will learn about a new group of colonies, but the topics covered will be similar to those they have studied before.

- Before **Introduce**, p. 194
- 25 minutes

Lesson Vocabulary

Teach the new vocabulary words using the Vocabulary Cards, examples, and illustrations from the text. Next, have students sort words into two categories: *words that name people* and *words that name things*. Then, have students match the words to the correct definitions.

Additional Vocabulary Explain the words in the margin and provide examples of their uses. For example, point out that the word *rebel* is sometimes used as a noun, but in this lesson, it is used as a verb that means *to work against* or *oppose*. Tell students to notice that the word *shipbuilding* is a compound word that can be understood by looking at the meaning of each part.

assemblies	owe money
dye	prison
forest	proprietors
governor	rebel
indentured servants	shipbuilding
	village

Cognates As students read the lesson, you may want to point out cognates such as: **colony/colonia, governor/gobernador, prison/prisión.**

Build Fluency

Read aloud the following rhyme and point out the words that sound alike. Have students repeat it several times to develop oral language skills. Return to the rhyme throughout the lesson to help develop vocabulary, identifying main ideas and details skills, and lesson content.

> Maryland and Virginia
> Their locations very close,
> Shared a warm, mild climate,
> So tobacco grew well in both.
>
> South Carolina grew indigo,
> But rice was valued there more.
> North Carolina had forests
> That grew products for naval stores.
>
> Crops were sold by planters,
> The richest in the region.
> Crops were grown by people
> Enslaved on Southern plantations.

Scaffolding the Content

Preview the Lesson

Ask students to scan the time line on page 194 and the map on page 196 to find the names of five Southern colonies. Next, have them use the illustrations and captions to identify industries and crops important to one or two colonies. Show the illustration on page 199 and explain that Southern cash crops were grown on plantations.

• During **Teach**, pp. 194–201
• 30 minutes

Modify Instruction

Review the following summary of the lesson. Guide students in taking notes. Have them use their notes to complete the checklist on the blackline master page.

Maryland The Calvert family founded Maryland to make money and to give Catholic people a safe place to practice their religion. Shipbuilding became an important industry. Tobacco was the main cash crop, or crop that was grown to make money. Enslaved Africans farmed it. Maryland had governors and elected assemblies. The Calverts controlled Maryland. Maryland welcomed many religions.

Virginia The climate was mild and tobacco was the main cash crop. Enslaved Africans worked on plantations where it was grown. Virginia had governors and elected assemblies. The king of England controlled Virginia.

North Carolina The Carolina colony was split into North Carolina and South Carolina. In North Carolina, farmers grew tobacco and corn. In Wilmington, there was an important shipping center for forest goods like pine and tar (things used to make boats).

South Carolina Planters brought enslaved Africans who knew how to grow rice. Rice became the most important crop in the colony. Indigo was another major cash crop.

Georgia James Oglethorpe took English debtors to Georgia because King George II of England wanted settlers there. The first settlement there was called Savannah. At first, leaders in Georgia did not allow slavery, but later they decided to allow it. Rice was an important cash crop there due to the wet land.

The Backcountry By the mid-1700s, settlers moved west to unsettled areas, away from the coast, called the backcountry. There were conflicts with Native Americans as more settlers moved into the backcountry.

Africans in the South African families were taken to the colonies to work on plantations. Enslaved people were often beaten. They were not allowed to have an education. They broke tools or acted sick to rebel. Some escaped slavery. In 1738, Fort Moses was formed. It was the first free African settlement in North America.

Economy Southern colonies depended on cash crops grown on plantations. Planters were the richest people in the South. Plantations looked like villages. The planter's house was the main building, and enslaved people lived in cabins. Crops were exported in port cities. Planters paid brokers to sell their crops and to buy products.

Extend

Have students review the answers on the blackline master page. Ask partners to list two or three main ideas about the Southern colonies. Provide key words and topics for the sentences, such as *plantations, cash crops, slavery,* or *the economy*.

• After **Teach**, pp. 194–201
• 10 minutes

Name _____ Date _____

DIRECTIONS Listen and take notes as your teacher summarizes information. Find the information on the graphic organizer below. Then check the correct column or columns.

	The South	Maryland	Virginia	Georgia	North Carolina	South Carolina
1. Indigo was a cash crop.						
2. Tobacco was the main cash crop.						
3. The first settlers were English debtors.						
4. People moved west to the backcountry.						
5. The economy depended on plantations.						
6. This colony was controlled by the king.						
7. This colony was controlled by the Calverts.						
8. These colonies began as one.						
9. Rice was a cash crop.						
10. Enslaved people worked on plantations.						
11. Corn was a cash crop.						
12. Shipbuilding was an industry.						
13. There was a center for shipping forest goods.						
14. Planters paid brokers to buy and sell things.						

School-Home Connection Encourage students to take this page home to share with family members. They can use their notes to tell about the history, economy, and life in the Southern Colonies.

Unit 2, Chapter 5, Lesson 3

Success for English Learners ■ 85

Apply and Assess

Write a Diary Entry

Discuss things Eliza Lucas Pinkney may have done as she experimented with indigo dyes. Review the information about Pinkney on page 200 if necessary. Ask leading questions, such as: *What did Pinkney want in a dye? Did she want a certain color? Did she care if the color washed out?* Then ask students to imagine how Pinkney looked and felt after a day of experimenting with dyes. *What was she wearing? Did she need gloves? Did she work many hours or just a few? Why?* Write phrases and words on the board as you discuss topics.

Write a model diary entry on the board. Read it aloud. Tell students to reference this entry as they write their own.

Help beginning students by underlining phrases in your entry that may be helpful for them to use in their own. Assist them in using the phrases to write brief entries of two or three sentences. Ask intermediate students to choose phrases and structures used in the model, but to complete them with their own words. Have advanced students write diary entries using original language.

• During **Close**, p. 201
• 25 minutes

Informal Lesson Assessment

	Beginning	Intermediate	Advanced
Task	List the Southern Colonies. Give students statements about life, history, and the economy in the Southern Colonies. After each statement, have them circle the colony described.	Have students list details about life, history, and the economy in the Southern Colonies. Allow them to use phrases or short sentences.	Have students write complete sentences about life, history, and the economy in the Southern Colonies.
Below Expectations	• no statement correctly identified	• few or no correct responses • responses are incomprehensible	• no correct response • no comprehensible explanations • many errors
Meets Expectations	• some statements correctly identified	• a few correct responses • responses are mostly comprehensible	• some correct responses • some explanations comprehensible • some errors
Above Expectations	• all statements correctly identified	• all responses are correct • all responses are comprehensible	• all responses are correct • all explanations are comprehensible • few errors

Developing Academic Language

Throughout this chapter, students will be asked to look for cause-and-effect relationships. Students can better comprehend what they read when they understand these relationships and the sentence structures and vocabulary that signal them.

Introduce Cause and Effect

Explain to students that a **cause** is the reason something happens. An **effect** is what happens as a result of something else. State some simple cause-and-effect sentences, such as: *It is dark, so I turn on the light.* Explain that sometimes the effect comes at the end of the sentence, like the one you just shared. However, sometimes the effect comes first in the sentence. For example, *I ate my lunch because I was hungry.* Present the beginnings of sentences that follow these same two patterns, and help students complete them with either a cause or an effect, as appropriate. Then help students identify the causes and effects in each sentence.

- Before **Cause and Effect**, p. 214
- 20 minutes

List some common words and phrases that signal cause-and-effect relationships such as: *because, so that, therefore, so,* and *as a result.* Provide definitions for the words, or have students look them up in a dictionary. Then say a sample sentence using each word or phrase so that students can hear how each is used in a cause-and-effect sentence. Point out that *because* and *so that* introduce causes, and *therefore, so,* and *as a result* introduce effects.

Practice

To help students recognize the structure of cause-and-effect sentences, write the following sentence frames on the board. Line up a few chalkboard erasers and knock them over with your hand. Work together as a class to make up cause and effect sentences to describe knocking over the chalkboard erasers with your hands.

1) The erasers fell over because _____.

2) I pushed over the erasers with my hand. As a result, _____.

3) Because I pushed the erasers with my hand, _____.

Apply

Display the following chart on the board, and have students copy it onto a piece of paper. Give students books and have them look through the illustrations to find cause-and-effect relationships. Begin by helping students find the causes and effects, describe them, and write them down. Gradually provide less help until students can work alone.

Cause	Effect

Success for English Learners

Use with Lesson 1 — Chapter 6

Build Background

Access Prior Knowledge

- Before **Introduce**, p. 222
- 10 minutes

Help students assimilate and apply information from prior lessons. Post and review these facts: *1) British colonies lived under British law and had British rulers. 2) The British had conflicts, or fights, over lands with other countries.* Invite groups of volunteers to act out each fact. Next, take a class vote about the following questions: *Who should fight for the land—the colonists, the British from overseas, or both? If the British pay, should the colonists pay them back?* Explain that this lesson provides details that help answer these questions.

Lesson Vocabulary

Distribute word cards for the vocabulary. Read each word, and say its meaning. Write one of the words, such as **alliance,** on the board and develop a 5 Ws organizer for it. For example, ask: *Who is in an alliance? What is an alliance for? When do people form alliances? Where can you find alliances? Why do people form alliances?* Write the answers, and have students summarize what the organizer shows. Then have mixed-proficiency partners develop similar organizers for **delegate, Parliament, proclamation,** and **budget.**

Additional Vocabulary Explain the meanings and uses of the words in the margin to students.

act of war	ignore
adviser	public
announcement	target
branch	tax
drive out	unite

Cognates As students read the lesson, you may wish to point out cognates such as: **alliance/alianza, connect/conectar, favor/favor, public/público, unite/unir.**

Build Fluency

Read aloud the following rhyme, and point out words that sound alike. Have students repeat it several times to develop oral language skills. Return to the rhyme throughout the lesson to help develop vocabulary, cause-and-effect skills, and lesson content.

> The goals of France and Britain were the same:
> They wanted a big North American claim.
> They fought over The Ohio River Valley, they wanted control.
> Power in North America was their main goal.
> Differences over claims led to war.
> The French and natives fought together as before.
> **Parliament** sent troops from England to help the British fight.
> **Alliances** with natives gave them strength, or might.
> The British won the war and took French lands.
> They soon gave the colonists new demands.
> England said, "No more Moving West!"
> But the pioneering colonists would not rest.

88 ■ Success for English Learners

Scaffolding the Content

Preview the Lesson

Write and say: *French and Indian War.* Next to it, write: French, Native Americans, and British. Circle *French* and *Native Americans* and draw an arrow to the word *British*. Explain that this was not a war between the French and the Native Americans. Then explain that the people we call the American colonists were actually British at that time. This war changed how British colonists and Britain viewed each other.

• During **Teach**, pp. 222–227
• 30 minutes

Modify Instruction

Read the following facts to students and help them take notes. Then refer students to the blackline master page, and read the statements in the boxes entitled "Causes." Pause, and give students time to write in the corresponding "Effects" box. Tell students to listen for words that signal cause and effect, such as *because, caused,* or *so.*

1. Both Britain and France claimed the Ohio Valley. So the two countries decided to force each other to leave the valley.

2. The French sent soldiers to drive, or push, the British out of the Ohio Valley.

3. The French fought from the woods, where they hid behind trees and rocks. The British fought in open fields.

4. The colonies decided not to help France fight against Britain.

5. The Treaty of Paris ended the French and Indian War. The treaty caused the French to lose most lands in North America.

6. Native Americans did not want colonists to settle in lands between the Appalachian Mountains and the Mississippi River. So a chief named Pontiac led a group of tribes in an attack on British forts and colonial settlements.

7. King George III of England wrote the Proclamation of 1763. He did this to stop fighting between colonists and Native Americans. This public announcement said that Native Americans owned the land west of the Appalachian Mountains. The proclamation made colonists angry because they fought for that land in the war. Many colonists ignored the proclamation.

8. The British Parliament wanted the colonists to help pay for the high cost of the war. So it made colonists pay new taxes on imported sugar and molasses. This made colonists angry.

Extend

- Make a two-column chart and label the columns "Reasons" and "Results."
- Ask students to tell you reasons people fought the French and Indian War.
- Then ask them to name some results of the war.
- Repeat accurate ideas and record them.
- When you are finished, have students work in pairs to restate what the chart shows.

• After **Teach**, pp. 222–227
• 10 minutes

Name _____ Date _____

DIRECTIONS Listen as your teacher reads. Read the causes listed on the left and write the effects into the chart.

Causes

- The British wanted to control the Ohio Valley for trade and growth.

- The French wanted the Ohio Valley because it connected land in Canada and Louisiana.

- George Washington led colonists from Virginia to the Ohio Valley. He built Fort Necessity.

- The French attacked the colonists. Native Americans mostly helped the French.

- The colonists needed help to win the war for Britain.

- The British Parliament sent soldiers and supplies from Britain to help the colonists.

- To pay for the war, the British made colonists pay tax on sugar and molasses.

- The king told colonists they could not settle land beyond the Appalachian Mountains.

Effects

School-Home Connection Have students take this page home to share with their families. They can use the information to explain the causes and effects of the French and Indian War.

Success for English Learners — Unit 3, Chapter 6, Lesson 1

Apply and Assess

Write a Newspaper Story

Ask: How would you feel if the government said to you: "Move today"?
Ask: Would you feel even worse if you had just fought for that government in a war? Discuss students' ideas. List them.

• During **Close**, p. 227
• 20 minutes

Review the Proclamation Line by pointing out the Appalachian Mountains on a map. Frame the area to the east where colonists could live, and say: *yes.* Frame or use gestures to encompass the area to the west, and say: *no.*

Review that a newspaper story often tells who, what, when, where, and why. Create a 5 Ws organizer on the board. Work with students to complete it.

Suggest an opening for the story, such as:

> The Proclamation of 1763 has upset many settlers who live _____.
>
> They are upset because _____. They say that _____.

Provide beginning students with a word bank to help them complete the frame. Have intermediate students work with partners to complete the frame. Have advanced students complete the frame and add two or more sentences to it.

Informal Lesson Assessment

	Beginning	Intermediate	Advanced
Task	Provide students with a list of statements about how the French and Indian War changed relations between the British and the colonists. Use correct and incorrect statements. Have students circle correct statements.	Have students use words and phrases to list a few ways the French and Indian War changed relations between the British and the colonists.	Have students write a paragraph telling a few ways the French and Indian War changed relations between the British and the colonists.
Below Expectations	• no response is correct	• no answer is comprehensible or correct	• incorrect ideas • incorrect paragraph form • many errors
Meets Expectations	• some responses are correct	• most answers are comprehensible and correct	• appropriate ideas • correct paragraph form • some errors
Above Expectations	• all responses are correct	• all answers are comprehensible and correct	• appropriate ideas • correct paragraph form • few errors

Use with Chapter 6, Lesson 2

Build Background

Access Prior Knowledge

Hold up an item with a price tag. Ask if you could buy the item if you had the right amount of money. Have students say what they think. If necessary, remind students that some things cost more than what is written on a price tag. That is because people must pay sales tax, too. Explain that taxes help pay the government for things such as roads, schools, and libraries. Sales tax is one way citizens give tax money to the government.

- Before **Introduce**, p. 230
- 30 minutes

Lesson Vocabulary

Remind students that making links between things they know, and things they are trying to learn can help them remember new words and concepts. Post brief definitions of the new vocabulary words, and explain them. When students understand the words, ask them to create word webs of associations between the new words and pictures of things students associate with them. Make a word web as a class for the term **representation**. Help students associate this word with such concepts as *voice*, *rights*, and *leader*. Ask for additional words from volunteers. Have students work in pairs to make word webs for the remaining six vocabulary words. Each student should make a concept web for three words. Ask students to cover the vocabulary words in the center of the web, and see if other students can guess the word based on its associations.

Additional Vocabulary Explain the meanings and uses of the words in the margin to students. Explain that the phrase *open fire* in this lesson means "to shoot." Explain the phrase *speak out against* means "to talk about a disagreement."

Cognates As students read the lesson, you may wish to point out cognates such as: **imperial/imperial, liberty/libertad, protest/protestar, representation/representación.**

cloth	refuse
correspondence	speak out against
liberty	stamp
make fun	tar
massacre	tax collector
open fire	taxation

Build Fluency

Read aloud the following rhyme, and point out words that sound alike. Have students repeat it several times to develop oral language skills. Return to the rhyme throughout the lesson to help develop vocabulary, cause-and-effect skills, and lesson content.

In 1764, it's true,
The colonists did not know what to do.

They felt the king was being unfair,
Deciding to tax them while they weren't there.

The king's demands made the colonists pay,
But the angry group said, "No way!"

The words of the colonists were strong and clear,
"No taxation without **representation**," but did the king hear?

The causes of the conflict were taxes in many forms,
The effects were **boycotts** and angry swarms.

Scaffolding the Content

Preview the Lesson

Read the title of the lesson, and have students look at the pictures on pages 230–236. Ask them to write down any words or phrases that they think of when they look at each picture. Tell students they are going to learn about a time in history when the British Parliament made the colonists pay taxes on many things. The colonists protested, or complained, and trouble started.

- During **Teach**, pp. 230–236
- 30 minutes

Modify Instruction

Read about the following events with students, and guide them as they take notes. Then have students use their notes to sequence the events on the blackline master.

1. Britain spent a lot of money to fight the French and Indian War. The British Parliament decided that the colonists should help pay for that war, too.

2. Parliament ordered the colonists to pay taxes on paper items such as newspapers, letters, and playing cards. This was called the Stamp Act. All the items were stamped after the tax was paid.

3. The colonists became angry. They said it was not fair for the king to tax them without their permission. Many colonists spoke out, or protested, and said they needed to be a part of the decisions made in England.

4. In 1765, the representatives of nine colonies had a formal meeting, or a congress, to speak out against the Stamp Act. Colonists began to boycott, or refuse to buy, products from England.

5. In 1766, Parliament repealed, or stopped, the Stamp Act. However, Parliament decided Britain had full power to make laws for the colonists in America.

6. Colonists wanted to know what was happening in other colonies. They wanted to send information quickly to each other. So they formed the Committees of Correspondence. Members wrote letters about events in their colony.

7. Parliament decided to tax the colonists again. They put a tax on imports, things colonists bought from England, like glass, paint, paper, and tea. These laws were called the Townshend Acts. The colonists stopped buying British products, and the British lost money. So, the British left the tax on British tea but stopped taxes on other products.

8. The British sent many soldiers to the colonies. In Boston, colonists threw rocks and snowballs at British soldiers. The soldiers opened fire on colonists and killed five people. This fight was called the Boston Massacre because colonists were not able to defend themselves from the soldiers' guns.

Extend

Provide an introductory sentence about the causes and effects of taxes that Britain made colonists pay. Have mixed-proficiency pairs of students write a detailed sentence on a strip of paper. Challenge them to put the sentences together to form a paragraph. Revise and edit as a group to make coherent cause-and-effect paragraphs.

- After **Teach**, pp. 230–236
- 20 minutes

Success for English Learners ▪ 93

Name _____ Date _____

DIRECTIONS Listen as your teacher reads. Read the phrase in each box. Write the number of each paragraph in the correct box.

Britain taxes tea.	Parliament passes the Stamp Act.
Colonists and British soldiers fight.	Colonists write letters.
Colonists speak against the Stamp Act, saying they do not want to be taxed without representation.	Parliament repeals, or stops, the Stamp Act.
Colonists boycott products from England.	Britain needs money.

School-Home Connection Encourage students to draw pictures in each box showing what happens. Have them take this page home to share with family members. They can use their drawings and the captions to tell about what happened when Britain created colonial tax laws.

94 ■ Success for English Learners

Unit 3, Chapter 6, Lesson 2

Apply and Assess

Draw a Cartoon

Show students the example of a political cartoon on page 231. Discuss how the cartoon tries to make people believe something or do something. Explain that in colonial times colonists were angry about the British tax laws. Students should draw a cartoon that could have convinced people not to buy British goods.

• During **Close**, p. 236
• 30 minutes

Begin by helping students brainstorm ideas for what to draw. Write the ideas on the board and discuss them. Then give students time to work in mixed-proficiency pairs to decide what they are going to draw.

As students draw their cartoons, talk with them individually about what they are drawing. Suggest ideas for students who are having difficulty getting started.

After students have completed their cartoons, ask volunteers to show and describe their cartoons to the class.

Informal Lesson Assessment

	Beginning	Intermediate	Advanced
Task	Ask: *Why were the colonists angry about the new taxes?* Students may respond with single words, gestures, or by pointing to pictures.	Have students copy this sentence on paper. *New taxes made the colonists feel angry.* Have students continue by writing 3 or 4 sentences to explain why colonists were angry.	Ask students to write a few sentences that tell why the colonists felt angry about the tax laws.
Below Expectations	• no answer is comprehensible and/or correct	• no answer is comprehensible and/or correct	• incorrect ideas • no complete sentences • many errors
Meets Expectations	• some answers are comprehensible and/or correct	• some answers are comprehensible and/or correct	• appropriate ideas • some incomplete sentences • some errors
Above Expectations	• all answers are comprehensible and correct	• all answers are comprehensible and correct	• appropriate ideas • complete sentences • few errors

Use with Chapter 6, Lesson 3

Build Background

Access Prior Knowledge

Present yourself as a serious and determined British general. Ask the class to be colonists. Stand up in front of the class, and give these pronouncements: *We will control the tea trade! We will block Boston Harbor! We will make you feed our soldiers and let them sleep in your houses! We will take your weapons from you!* Each time you call out a pronouncement, have the colonist say: "No, you won't." Discuss with students what your role-play showed.

• Before **Introduce**, p. 238
• 10 minutes

Lesson Vocabulary

Explain the lesson vocabulary by using vocabulary cards and illustrations. Then play a vocabulary game to help students memorize the words. Divide the class in half. Chose one student from each side to come to the board. Show the pair the flash card with the target word so that their teammates do not see. Have the two students sketch pictures so their team members can guess the vocabulary word. To guess, a team member must raise his or her hand first. If the team member is right, the team gets another turn. If not, the other team may guess. The team with the most correct answers wins. If students wish to play when all words have been used, use vocabulary cards from past lessons for further review.

Additional Vocabulary Explain the meanings and uses of the words in the margin to students. Point out that the words *intolerable* and *unacceptable* are synonyms. Both words describe things that people refuse to do because they are impossible or difficult. The words are called synonyms because they mean the same thing. Explain that *assemble* and *gather* are synonyms that mean "to meet."

assemble	gather
coerce	intolerable
competition	militia
deadline	overboard
dock	unacceptable

Cognates As students read the lesson, you may wish to point out cognates such as: **enemy/enemigo, local/local, revolution/revolución, secret/secreto.**

Build Fluency

Read aloud the following rhyme, and point out words that sound alike. Have students repeat it several times to develop oral language skills. Return to the rhyme throughout the lesson to help develop vocabulary, cause-and-effect skills, and lesson content.

> The British said: "We want a **monopoly** on tea!"
> The colonists said: "We'll throw it all into the sea!"
> The British said: "We'll make new laws to punish you!"
> The colonists said: "We've written a **petition.** Don't tell us what to do!"
> The British said: "We'll go to Concord to stop the **Minutemen!**"
> The colonists said: "We'll have a **revolution** then!"

Success for English Learners

Scaffolding the Content

Preview the Lesson

Post the title and headings of sections in the lesson, and explain them briefly by pointing out illustrations in the text: 1) "Disagreements Grow"—Problems between the colonists and British become worse. 2) "The Boston Tea Party"—Colonists throw British tea into the harbor to protest a law. 3) "The Coercive Acts"—British make more laws to punish colonists. 4) "The First Continental Congress"—Colonial leaders meet to decide what to do about the Coercive Acts. 5) "Lexington and Concord"—The British secretly planned to take two colonial leaders and weapons.

- During **Teach**, pp. 238–243
- 30 minutes

Modify Instruction

Read with students about what colonists did when Parliament passed more tax laws. Pause at each cause-and-effect relationship so students can take notes in the corresponding section of the blackline master page.

1 *The Boston Tea Party took place.*

Causes: In 1773, the British Parliament passed the Tea Act. Colonists would have to pay tax on tea, or not drink it at all.

Effects: Colonists were angry. They dressed up as members of the Mohawk tribe and threw tea from British ships into the Boston Harbor.

2 *Colonies formed the First Continental Congress.*

Causes: In 1774, Britain passed laws to punish colonists for the Boston Tea Party. One law closed the port of Boston until colonists paid for the tea they destroyed. Another law forced colonists to give British soldiers food and places to live.

Effects: People in the colonies reacted. They sent representatives to meet in Philadelphia. They voted to form militias, or armies of citizens. They also voted to stop most trade with Britain.

3 *The British decided to capture colonial leaders and weapons.*

Causes: The British learned that the Minutemen had weapons in Concord. The Minutemen was the name for the militia in Massachusetts. General Gage ordered British soldiers to take the weapons. The British secretly planned to march to Lexington.

Effects: Paul Revere learned about the secret plan. He rode to Lexington to warn the Minutemen. The colonists and the British fought. This was the beginning of the American Revolution. A revolution is a complete, sudden change of government.

Extend

Have students work in small groups to copy notes they recorded on the blackline master into sentence strips under the categories "causes" and "effects." Then ask them to express cause and effect by connecting the sentence strips. They should insert words between them such as "because," "so," and other words that indicate which part of the sentence is the reason and which is the result.

- After **Teach**, pp. 238–243
- 10 minutes

Success for English Learners

Name _____ Date _____

DIRECTIONS Listen as your teacher reads. Write causes and effects in the connected boxes.

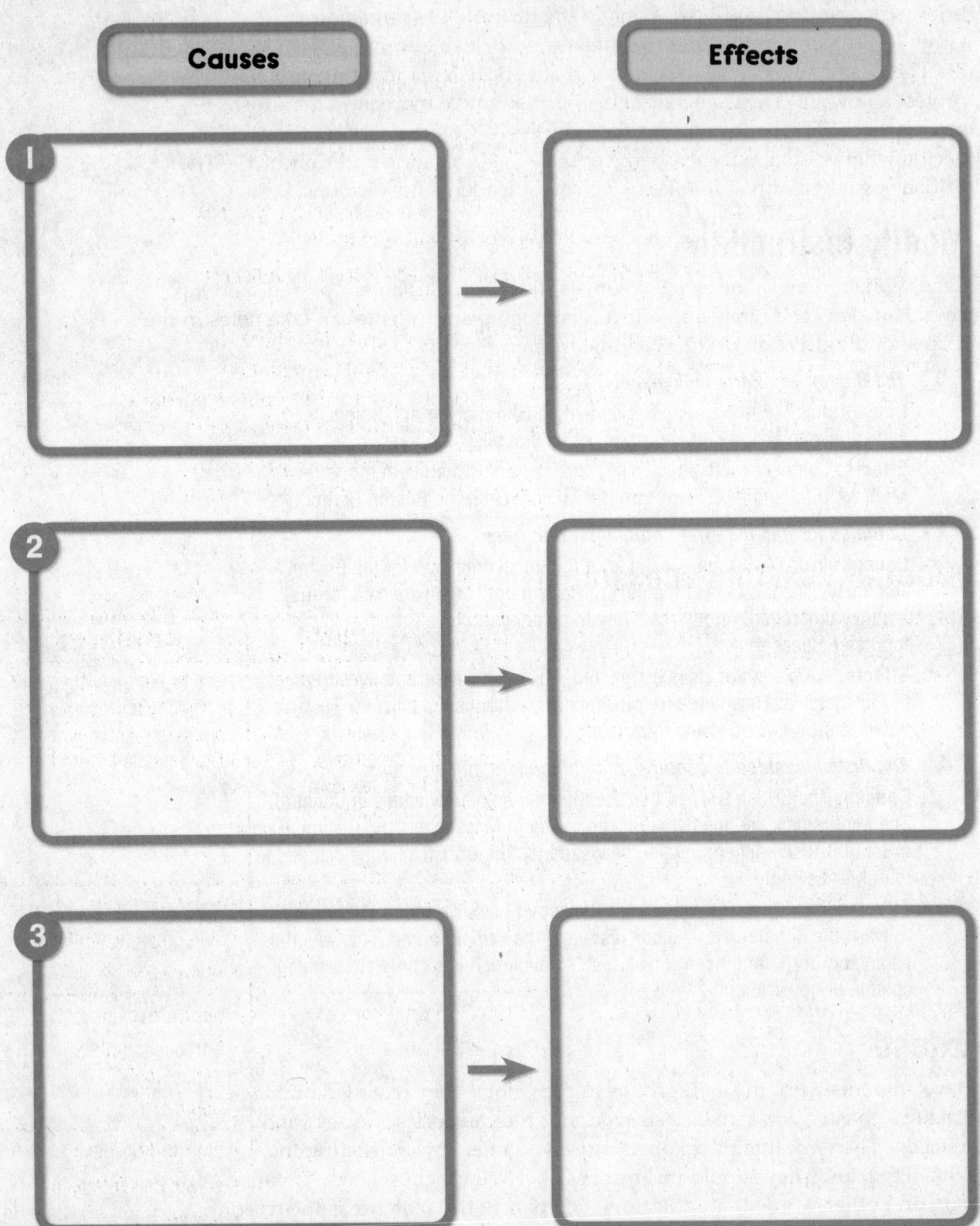

School-Home Connection Have students take this page home to share with their families. They can use the information in the organizers to describe the events that led to the American Revolution.

Apply and Assess

Write a Poem

Begin by writing and saying key information about the battles. Add gestures, such as the sign for secrecy, to help convey information.

• During **Close**, p. 243
• 20 minutes

① The British wanted to make a secret march to Lexington. They wanted to capture Sam Adams and John Hancock there. American colonist Paul Revere rode his horse to warn the Minutemen.

② When the British got to Lexington, the Minutemen were waiting for them. No one knows who fired a gun first, but a battle started.

③ The British marched to Concord. They wanted to take away the colonist's weapons. They did not find the weapons. So the British had to go back to Boston.

④ Many British soldiers died. Some Minutemen died. This fight started the American Revolution.

Have mixed-proficiency groups work together to write poems. Tell them the poems do not have to rhyme. Assure students that their poems can just be sentences or phrases in poem form. Model how to form two or three phrases from Item 1 above: "A secret march the British planned to capture two important men."

Beginning students can illustrate the poems. Provide support to all groups by suggesting first lines, encouraging any progress, and noting what each phrase helps you see or imagine.

Informal Lesson Assessment

	Beginning	**Intermediate**	**Advanced**
Task	Provide students with a few true or false statements about what colonists did when Britain passed more tax laws. Have them label statements "true" or "false."	Have students complete true and false statements about how colonists reacted when Britain passed more tax laws. Have students also correct false statements.	Have students write a few sentences telling how colonists reacted when Britain passed more tax laws.
Below Expectations	• no answers are correct	• no answers are correct	• incorrect ideas • no complete sentences • many errors
Meets Expectations	• some answers are correct	• some answers are correct	• appropriate ideas • some incomplete sentences • some errors
Above Expectations	• all answers are correct	• all answers are correct	• appropriate ideas • complete sentences • few errors

Use with Chapter 6, Lesson 4

Build Background

Access Prior Knowledge

Review what happened at Lexington and Concord: *The British learned that leaders of the Sons of Liberty were in Lexington and that there were weapons in Concord. The British tried to take the weapons and arrest the leaders, but they failed.* Divide the room, and have one side work in small groups to discuss what their next step would be if they were colonial leaders. Have the other side discuss what the next step would be if they were British leaders. For example, would they try to establish peace? Would they gather soldiers and weapons for protection? Have groups share their responses, and post them on the board or overhead. Point out that British and colonial leaders had different opinions about what to do next, but this lesson tells which steps each side decided to take.

- Before **Introduce**, p. 244
- 20 minutes

Lesson Vocabulary

Distribute vocabulary cards for the lesson to each student. Have students work in mixed-proficiency pairs to talk about each definition to be sure that both students understand it. Then turn the questions into a "What am I?" or "Who am I?" game, asking questions such as: "I am a great leader. Who am I?" **(commander in chief)** "These are walls of earth and stone. What am I?" **(earthworks)** "What is an ancient symbol of peace?" **(olive branch)** If several students hold up the wrong card, discuss the definition, providing familiar examples.

Additional Vocabulary Explain the meanings and uses of the words in the margin to students. The word *continental* in this lesson means "the North American continent." It is also a noun used for the paper money used by colonists. *Branch* in a previous lesson meant "part of government," but in this lesson, it means a part of a tree. *Earth* in this lesson refers to dirt, not the planet.

ammunition	olive branch
ancient symbol	part-time
continental	retreat
currency	run out of
earth	step
full-time	

Cognates As students read the lesson, you may wish to point out cognates such as: **ammunition/munición, battle/batalla, petition/petición, symbol/símbolo.**

Build Fluency

Read aloud the following rhyme, and point out words that sound alike. Have students repeat it several times to develop oral language skills. Return to the rhyme throughout the lesson to help develop vocabulary, cause-and-effect skills, and lesson content.

> The Second Continental Congress prepared for war.
> They needed a better army than ever before.
>
> Soon the army met the British on Breed's Hill.
> Many soldiers fought hard, and many were killed.
>
> Congress offered an **olive branch** to King George III.
> Its members hoped to avoid more tragedy.

100 ■ Success for English Learners

Scaffolding the Content

Preview the Lesson

Have students use illustrations, captions, and text from the time line on page 244 to make predictions about the lesson contents. Have them work in small groups to respond to the statements below with *"agree"* or *"disagree."* They should make two columns on their papers, one labeled "before review," which they should complete now, and one labeled "after review," for later.

• During **Teach**, pp. 244–248
• 20 minutes

1) In the Second Continental Congress, colonial leaders decided against a war. 2) In 1775, the colonists and British fought the Battle of Bunker Hill. 3) The British retreated from, or lost, the Battle of Bunker Hill. 4) King George III wanted peace after the Battle of Bunker Hill.

Modify Instruction

Present the lesson as a sequence of events. Have students record each major event, as well as the result of each event, in the appropriate part of the time line on the blackline master page. When you are finished, review the events on the time line. Ask students to explain each major event.

① May 1775: The Second Continental Congress Meets
After the fighting at Lexington and Concord, colonial leaders met in Philadelphia for the Second Continental Congress. Some leaders did not want war. In the end, they decided the colonies should prepare for war. The first step was to form a full-time continental army. Then colonial leaders selected George Washington to be their commander in chief. They had to pay soldiers and buy guns, food, and uniforms, so they also decided to print money. This money was called "continentals."

② June 1775: The Battle of Bunker Hill
Colonial troops on Breed's Hill built earthworks, or walls made of earth and stone. They fired on, or shot, British soldiers who marched up the hill. Colonists had to retreat, or run away, when they ran out of ammunition, or bullets for their guns. The British won the battle. However, the British lost many more soldiers than the colonial troops did. The battle was named after Bunker Hill even though it was fought on Breed's Hill.

③ July 5, 1775: The Olive Branch Petition
Congress wanted the fighting to end. They sent a petition to King George III. It became known as the Olive Branch Petition because it asked for peace. An olive branch is an ancient symbol of peace. However, British leaders were very angry about the Battle of Bunker Hill, so they did not agree to peace.

Extend

Have students work together to check their initial responses to the anticipation guide they completed for "Preview the Lesson". Now that students are familiar with the lesson content, have them work in the same groups as before to record their answers in the "after review" column. As a class, correct any statements that were written incorrectly.

• After **Teach**, pp. 244–248
• 10 minutes

Name _____ Date _____

DIRECTIONS Listen as your teacher reads. Fill in the time line with the information you hear.

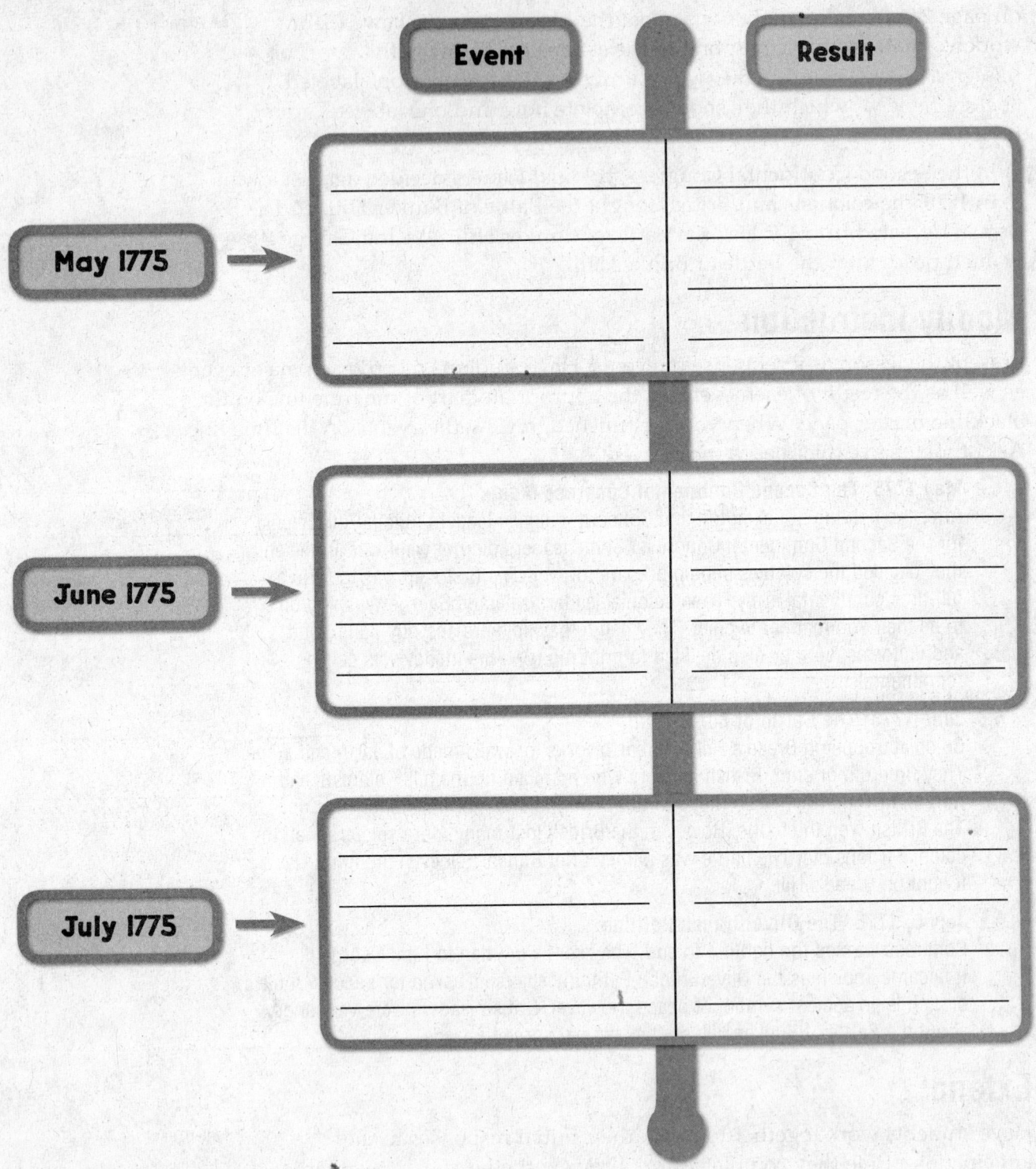

School-Home Connection Have students take this page home to share with their families. They can use the time line to relate some of the first events of the American Revolution.

Apply and Assess

Conduct an Interview

With a student volunteer, demonstrate an interview. Explain that people who do interviews prepare their questions before the interview. Tell students that they are going to write questions for an interview.

- During **Close**, p. 248
- 20 minutes

Write *George Washington* on the board. Ask students what they know about him. Cluster details they suggest, such as: commander in chief, French and Indian War, battles, and Continental Army. Then frame a question that begins with *what*, *why*, or *how* and uses one of the terms in the cluster, such as: *What is the hardest part of leading soldiers in a war?* and *Why do you think you were chosen as commander in chief?* Discuss possible answers.

Have students work in mixed-proficiency pairs to write and answer one or two more questions for their interview. Monitor students as they work, and help them with ideas and the structure of questions as necessary. Provide time for them to practice their interview with each other. Ask volunteer pairs to act out their interview for the class.

Informal Lesson Assessment

	Beginning	Intermediate	Advanced
Task	Ask: *What are three ways that the colonists prepared for war?* Have students respond using sketches and words.	Provide students with sentence starters, and ask them to use them to name three ways the colonists prepared for war.	Have students write three sentences telling how the colonists prepared for war.
Below Expectations	• no answer is comprehensible or correct	• no answer is comprehensible or correct	• inappropriate ideas • no complete sentences • many errors
Meets Expectations	• some answers are comprehensible and/or correct	• some answers are comprehensible and correct	• appropriate ideas • some incomplete sentences • some errors
Above Expectations	• all answers are comprehensible and correct	• all answers are comprehensible and correct	• appropriate ideas • complete sentences • few errors

Use with Chapter 6, Lesson 5

Build Background

Access Prior Knowledge

Write and say: *the Fourth of July.* Write and say: *Independence Day.* Explain that these words talk about the same holiday. Ask students what images and information come to mind when they hear these words. Repeat and record ideas. Explain that Independence Day is like a birthday party for the United States. Write: *July 4, 1776.* Explain that on this day, the Continental Congress decided to accept the final wording of the Declaration of Independence.

- Before **Introduce**, p. 252
- 10 minutes

Lesson Vocabulary

Explain the vocabulary words using the illustration on page 255. Tell students this is a photograph of the Declaration of Independence, which is a statement of freedom. This important document was written by colonists to Britain. Tell students that colonists wanted to make a **resolution,** or a formal group statement, of **independence.** That is why there are many signatures at the bottom of the document. Explain that this is a famous **declaration,** or official statement. Point to the first section of the declaration, and explain that this is called the **preamble,** or the introduction. Point to the body of the declaration, and explain that the colonists wrote their **grievances,** or complaints and problems, in the preamble. Then have students complete the matching exercise below.

Additional Vocabulary Explain the meanings and uses of the words in the margin to students. The word *declare* is a verb that means "to say or announce," and it is the root of the noun "declaration." Mention that *John Hancock* is a person from history. Explain that today his name is used to mean "signature."

Cognates As students read the lesson, you may wish to point out cognates such as: **declare/declarar, independence/independencia, nation/nación,** and **resolution/resolución.**

Articles of Confederation	point of view
break away	rebellion
cut ties	settle differences
declare	signature
John Hancock	succeeding generations
nation	treason

Build Fluency

Read aloud the following rhyme, and point out words that sound alike. Have students repeat it several times to develop oral language skills. Return to the rhyme throughout the lesson to help develop vocabulary, cause-and-effect skills, and lesson content.

"We must have **independence,**" the colonists agreed.
"We want the colonies to be free."
So Jefferson wrote a **declaration** of their goals, or aims,
And many delegates signed their names.
So the beginning of the new nation was the Articles of Confederation.

Scaffolding the Content

Preview the Lesson

Preview the lesson by reading the headings and relating them to the vocabulary students just learned. Start with "Moving Toward Independence." Explain that this describes the colonists' goal of independence from Britain. Move on to "The Declaration of Independence." Point out the picture of this document on page 255. Then move on to "Congress Approves the Declaration" and "Forming a New Government." Point out the illustration on page 258 of the Articles of Confederation.

- During **Teach**, pp. 252–259
- 20 minutes

Modify Instruction

Read the following ideas. Help students take notes in the appropriate categories on the blackline master. Point out the cause-and-effect relationship between the people, their ideas, and the new government.

1. **The People:** Thomas Paine wrote a book called <u>Common Sense.</u> In the book, Paine said that colonists should rule, or govern, themselves. After they read Paine's book, many people wanted to form their own government and country. Richard Henry asked the Second Continental Congress for a resolution, or formal statement, of independence to Britain. Thomas Jefferson wrote most of the declaration, and many people signed it.

2. **The Ideas:** The Preamble is the first part of the Declaration of Independence. It tells why the colonists believed they had the right to form a new nation. The next part tells the colonists' ideas about government, including the right to live, be free, and find happiness. The longest part of the declaration is a list of grievances, or complaints, against the king and Parliament. The last part of the declaration says colonies should be free and independent states. These ideas were dangerous. So the signers knew that the British could kill them to punish them for treason, or acting against the government.

3. **The New Government:** The Second Continental Congress accepted the Declaration of Independence on July 4, 1776. Then, the group formed a new government. The 13 colonies could work together without controlling each other. The national government could start a war and make treaties, or agreements with other countries. However, the government could not control trade or collect taxes. Congress could only ask states for money. States did not have to pay. This government led the states during the Revolutionary War.

Extend

Post and review the steps colonists took to break away from Britain. Have students identify the effects, or results, of each: 1) Thomas Paine wrote <u>Common Sense.</u> 2) Colonists needed to tell Britain about their resolution to form their own government. 3) Colonists needed to plan a government in which 13 states had independence, but worked together as a nation. For beginning students, provide correct and incorrect answers to choose from. Check answers as a class.

- After **Teach**, pp. 252–259
- 10 minutes

Success for English Learners

Name _____ Date _____

DIRECTIONS Listen as your teacher reads. Fill in the circle with the information you hear.

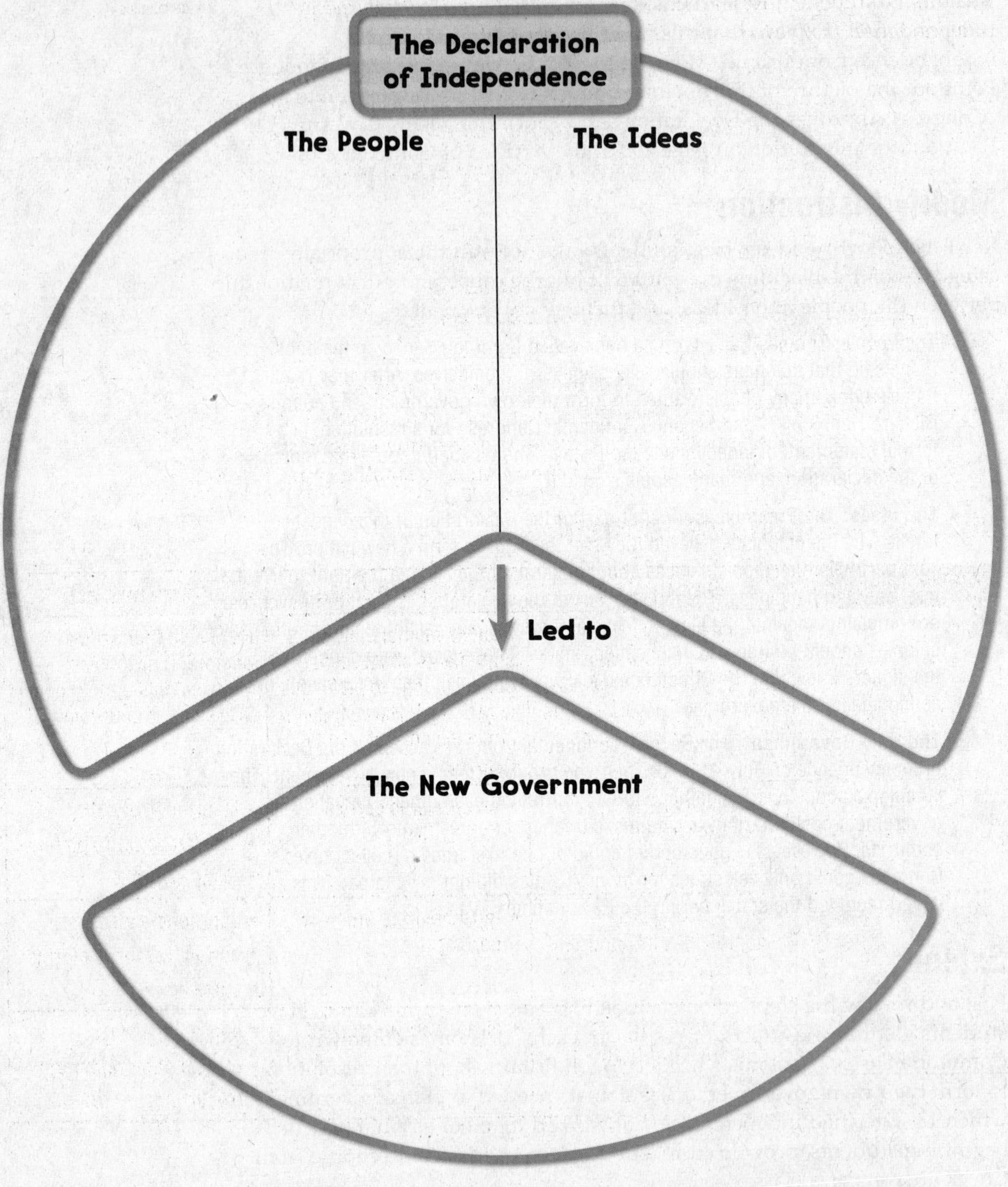

The Declaration of Independence

The People | The Ideas

Led to

The New Government

 School-Home Connection Have students take this page home to share with their families. They can use the organizer to tell about the people, ideas, and government that gave rise to, and resulted from, the Declaration of Independence.

106 ■ Success for English Learners

Unit 3, Chapter 6, Lesson 5

Apply and Assess
Write a Persuasive Letter

Write this opinion statement: *The thirteen colonies should be independent.* Read it, and repeat it. Restate it: *I am for independence for the thirteen colonies. I want the thirteen colonies to be independent.*

- During **Close**, p. 259
- 20 minutes

Ask students to volunteer reasons that support this opinion. Record their ideas. Elicit ideas that review previous content about taxes, being forced to house British soldiers, and about not controlling trade.

Provide students with this frame. Point to each word as you read it:

To the Editor:

I support independence for the thirteen colonies. The most important reason why the colonies should be free is _____. Another reason why they should be free is _____. Also, _____.

Have students write letters to include three reasons that support their opinion. Advanced students may work independently, but monitor the progress of intermediate and beginning students, providing support as needed. Allow time for volunteers to read their letters to small groups.

Informal Lesson Assessment

	Beginning	Intermediate	Advanced
Task	Provide fill-in-the-blank statements about steps colonists took to break ties with Britain. Have students fill in the missing words.	Provide multiple-choice statements about steps colonists took to break ties with Britain. Have students circle the correct response.	Have students write a paragraph describing steps colonists took to break ties with Britain.
Below Expectations	• no answer is comprehensible or correct	• no answer is correct	• incorrect ideas • incorrect paragraph form • many errors
Meets Expectations	• some answers are comprehensible and/or correct	• most answers are correct	• appropriate ideas • correct paragraph form • some errors
Above Expectations	• all answers are comprehensible and correct	• all answers are correct	• appropriate ideas • correct paragraph form • few errors

Success for English Learners

Use with Chapter 7, Lesson 1

Build Background

Access Prior Knowledge

Ask students to imagine that a war takes place in their town. Ask: *How are different people affected in different ways? What bad things can happen to families? To businesses? How can a war divide, or separate people?* List ideas. Then explain that people had many different reactions to the American Revolution.

- Before **Introduce**, p. 268
- 15 minutes

Lesson Vocabulary

Explain the vocabulary words using the Glossary, sketches, and brief definitions. Divide students into pairs to make cards, and play a matching game. Have one student write paraphrased definitions on one side of the cards, leaving the other side blank. Have another student write the vocabulary words on one side of the cards, leaving the other side blank. To play the game, have students place the cards blank side up. The first player turns over two cards. If the definition and the vocabulary word match, the player keeps the cards and has another turn. If they do not match, the cards are turned back over, and the other student gets a turn. The student with the most cards at the end of the game wins.

Additional Vocabulary Explain the meanings and uses of the words in the margin to students. Point out that the root "hard" is a clue to the meaning of *hardship*, which means "difficulty or problem." Explain that *shortage* means "not enough of something." Tell students that the word *blockade* is a group of ships that blocks others from entering a harbor or port.

blockade	hoard
continental	robbed
descent	shortage
divided	side
hardship	wounded

Cognates As students read the lesson, you may wish to point out cognates such as: **continental/continental, independence/independencia, patriot/patriota, rob/robar, veteran/veterano.**

Build Fluency

Read aloud the following rhyme, and point out words that sound alike. Have students repeat it several times to develop oral language skills. Return to the rhyme throughout the lesson to help develop vocabulary, cause-and-effect skills, and lesson content.

Patriots fought for independence. It was their cause.
Loyalists stayed loyal to Great Britain's laws.
The revolution divided them.

Some western settlers were **neutral** and did not fight.
Other western settlers believed the Patriots were right.
The revolution divided them.

Some Native Americans fought with Britain to save their land.
Others fought under Patriot leadership, or command.
The revolution divided them.

Scaffolding the Content

Preview the Lesson

Have students use the illustrations and captions on pages 269, 270, 271, 272, and 273 to identify the following statements as "true" or "false":
1) The British burned homes of some colonists during the war. 2) From 1775 to 1778, more and more imports came into American colonies.
3) Women in colonial times did not participate, or take part in the war.
4) African Americans fought in the Revolutionary War. 5) Some Native Americans fought for the British. Confirm the answers with the class.

- During **Teach**, pp. 268–273
- 25 minutes

Modify Instruction

Read each question and answer below. Have students find the corresponding letter for each question on the blackline master and take notes that answer the question.

A: What personal hardships, or troubles, did colonists suffer because of the war?
British soldiers robbed and destroyed homes and crops.

B: How did the war hurt the economy?
Britain stopped imports from coming into America, so colonists had a shortage, or lack of imports. This caused inflation, or higher prices, so people needed more money to buy products.

C: How did the war change life for women?
Life changed for women after their husbands left home to fight in the war. Some women ran farms and businesses. Some women collected money and clothing for soldiers. Other women fought in the battles.

D: How did the war change life for African Americans?
Many enslaved Africans helped the Patriots because the Patriots promised them freedom. Other enslaved Africans fought for the British, who also promised them freedom.

E: How did the war change the Western settlers' way of thinking?
Western settlers wanted to be neutral. This means they did not want to choose a side. However, many settlers joined the war against Britain because they did not want British people in Western lands.

F: How did the war change the lives of Native Americans?
Many Native Americans stayed neutral at first, but eventually became divided.

Extend

- Name the groups of people affected by the American Revolution.
- For each group, draw a simple cause-and-effect organizer.
- For effects, write the ways in which the group participated in the war.
- For causes, write the reason or reasons why the groups participated as they did.

- After **Teach**, pp. 268–273
- 10 minutes

Name _____   Date _____

DIRECTIONS Listen as your teacher reads. Fill in the sections of the circle with the information you hear.

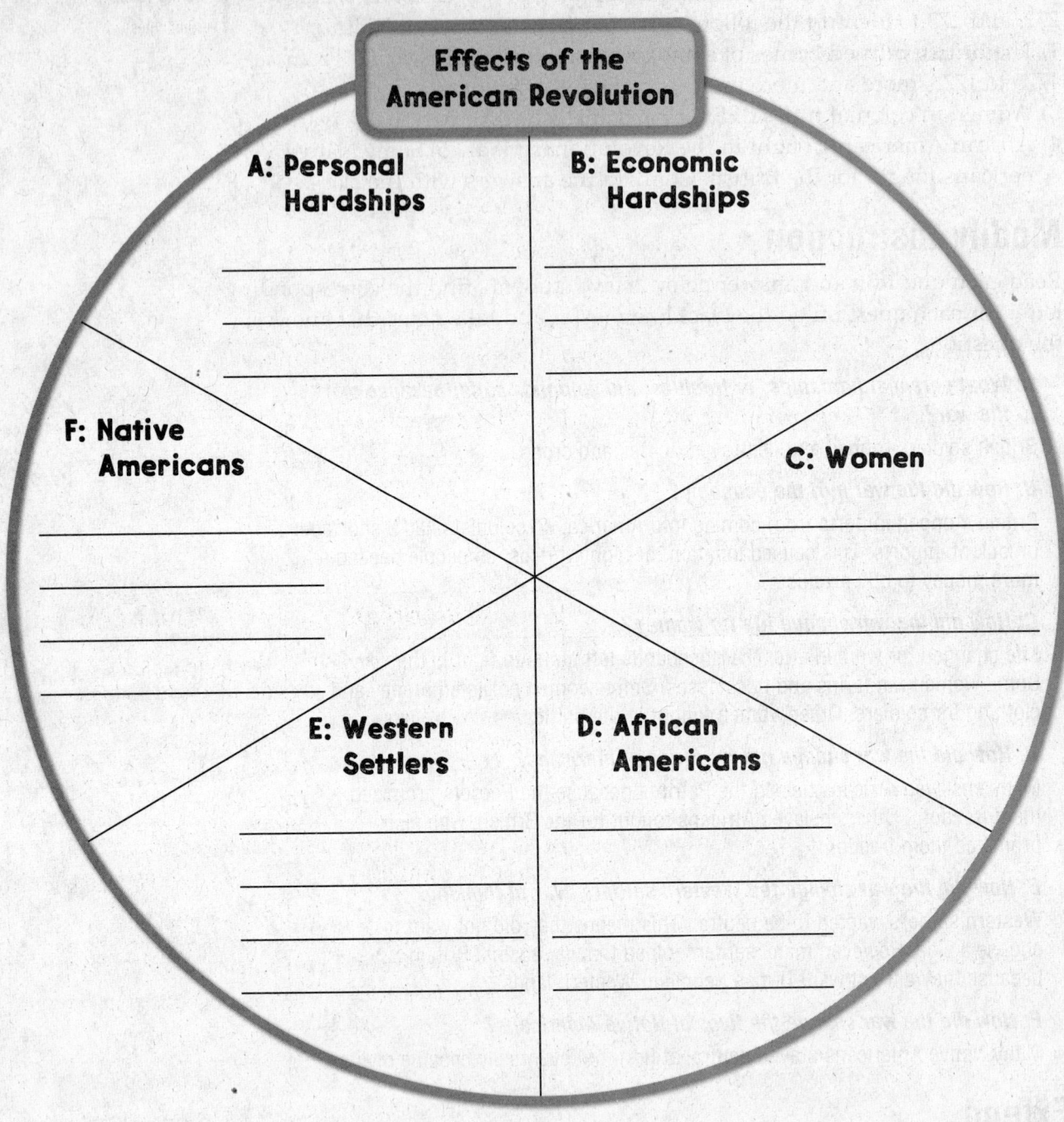

School-Home Connection Have students take this page home to share with their families. They can use the information in the organizer to explain how the Revolutionary War affected people's lives.

Apply and Assess

Write a Conversation

Review and post the words *Patriot* and *Loyalist*. Ask students why a Patriot would support the American Revolution. Repeat and list ideas. Ask students why people would stay loyal to Britain. Repeat and list ideas.

• During **Close**, p. 273
• 20 minutes

Tell students they will write a conversation, or dialogue, between a Loyalist and Patriot. Use an idea from your list of reasons to model this process. For example, you might write:

> Peter, the Patriot, said, "I want the colonies to be free from Britain."
>
> Laura, the Loyalist, answered, "But Britain is our mother country! Our parents were born there!"

Read the dialogue you wrote. Emphasize how each speaker expresses his or her ideas about the American Revolution. Ask students to form small, mixed-proficiency groups to finish the conversation. Have them add one or two more exchanges. Monitor their progress, and provide assistance as needed.

When students are finished, provide an opportunity for them to read their conversations to other groups.

Informal Lesson Assessment

	Beginning	Intermediate	Advanced
Task	Have students name several ways the American Revolution affected people's lives. Allow them to answer using words and sketches.	Have students list several ways the American Revolution affected people's lives using sentences.	Have students write a paragraph identifying several ways the American Revolution affected people's lives.
Below Expectations	• no answer is correct	• no part of the answer is comprehensible or correct	• incorrect ideas • incorrect paragraph form • many errors
Meets Expectations	• some answers are correct	• most of the answers are comprehensible and correct	• mainly correct ideas • correct paragraph form • some errors
Above Expectations	• all answers are correct	• all answers are comprehensible and correct	• correct ideas • correct paragraph form • few errors

Use with Chapter 7 Lesson 2

Build Background

• Before **Introduce**, p. 274
• 15 minutes

Access Prior Knowledge

Ask students what they think is important for soldiers in an army to have in order to win a war. Guide the discussion by asking why soldiers fight. Elicit concepts such as loyalty and bravery, as well as such practical considerations as weapons, food, tents, boots, the attitudes of soldiers, and money. Repeat and write appropriate ideas.

Lesson Vocabulary

Explain the vocabulary words to students by finding them in the lesson, reading them aloud, and using brief explanations to help students understand. Ask students to work in pairs to identify the words: **enlist, mercenary, campaign, turning point,** and **negotiate** using the following hints: 1) a soldier; 2) the first step; 3) a change; 4) discussion; 5) to register; 6) a job; 7) new direction; 8) coming to an agreement; 9) a plan; 10) a strategy.

Additional Vocabulary Explain the meanings and uses of the words in the margin to students. Explain what *axes* and *spears* are by drawing sketches on the board. Help students understand why these weapons were not as the powerful as British guns. Explain that *falling apart* means "dividing into pieces" or "so old that it no longer works well."

axes	falling apart
burned	running low
cannons	spears
everyday	torn
experienced	

Cognates As students read the lesson, you may wish to point out cognates such as: **capture/capturar, enemy/enemigo, negotiate/negociar, point/punto, uniform/uniforme.**

Build Fluency

Read aloud the following rhyme, and point out words that sound alike. Have students repeat it several times to develop oral language skills. Return to the rhyme throughout the lesson to help develop vocabulary, cause-and-effect skills, and lesson content.

> At the beginning of the Revolutionary War
> Many American soldiers had never fought before.
> The British army was experienced and strong,
> But getting supplies took too long.
> The British army had uniforms, guns and meat.
> Would the American army face defeat?
> The British won Long Island in a surprise attack.
> Many American soldiers left and didn't come back.
> A victory in Trenton helped the Americans' mood
> After they marched nine icy miles with little food.
> The Americans won Saratoga after a daring attack,
> And after that, there was no turning back!
> The winter at Valley Forge was cold and long,
> But other countries sent help to keep the Americans strong.

Scaffolding the Content

Preview the Lesson

Divide students into pairs. Assign each pair one of the following years: 1775, 1776, 1777, 1778, 1779, and 1781. Have each pair skim the chapter to find an event that happened for the date they were given. Ask a volunteer from each group to tell the event they found.

- During **Teach**, pp. 274–280
- 25 minutes

Modify Instruction

Explain how armies, events, and other countries influenced the early years of the Revolutionary War. Post important points and have students take notes on the blackline master page.

The Armies

- **The Continental Army** Soldiers from the colonies did not have uniforms. Many men were farmers, not experienced soldiers. Congress gave them little money. There were 15,000 soldiers.
- **The British Army** The British were experienced soldiers. They used guns. They had 50,000 soldiers.

Events

- **The Battle of Long Island (Spring 1776)** Washington's army was in Long Island. The British attacked. The Americans were outnumbered and suffered big losses.
- **The Battle of Trenton (Christmas 1776)** Americans were ready to give up. Washington's army attacked Hessians, or German mercenaries, in Trenton, New Jersey. The Hessians surrendered, or gave up, and the Americans had hope.
- **The Battle of Saratoga (September 1777)** The American general, Benedict Arnold led troops in an attack and captured British cannons and supplies. The British surrendered. This was a turning point. It seemed the Americans might win the war.
- **Winter at Valley Forge (Winter 1777)** Washington and his men camped at Valley Forge in Pennsylvania. Food was running low. Marquis de Lafayette from France came and bought clothes for the Patriots with his own money. Friedrich Wilhelm von Steuben from Germany trained soldiers on better ways to fight and march.

Other Countries

- **France:** The French sent supplies and soldiers.
- **The Netherlands:** This country gave a loan to Congress in 1781.
- **Russia:** The Russians tried to keep the British from blocking trade with the Americans.
- **Spanish:** Bernardo de Gálvez gave guns, food, and money to the Americans.

Extend

Using statements from the activity above, form questions about the armies, the battles, and other countries. Phrase the first few questions so they can be answered with "the Americans" or "the British." For example, *France wanted one side to lose the war. Which side?* Then ask more open-ended questions, such as: *Why was winter at Valley Forge hard for the Americans?* Have students work together in small groups.

- After **Teach**, pp. 274–280
- 10 minutes

Success for English Learners

Name _____ Date _____

DIRECTIONS Listen as your teacher reads. Fill in the time line with the information you hear.

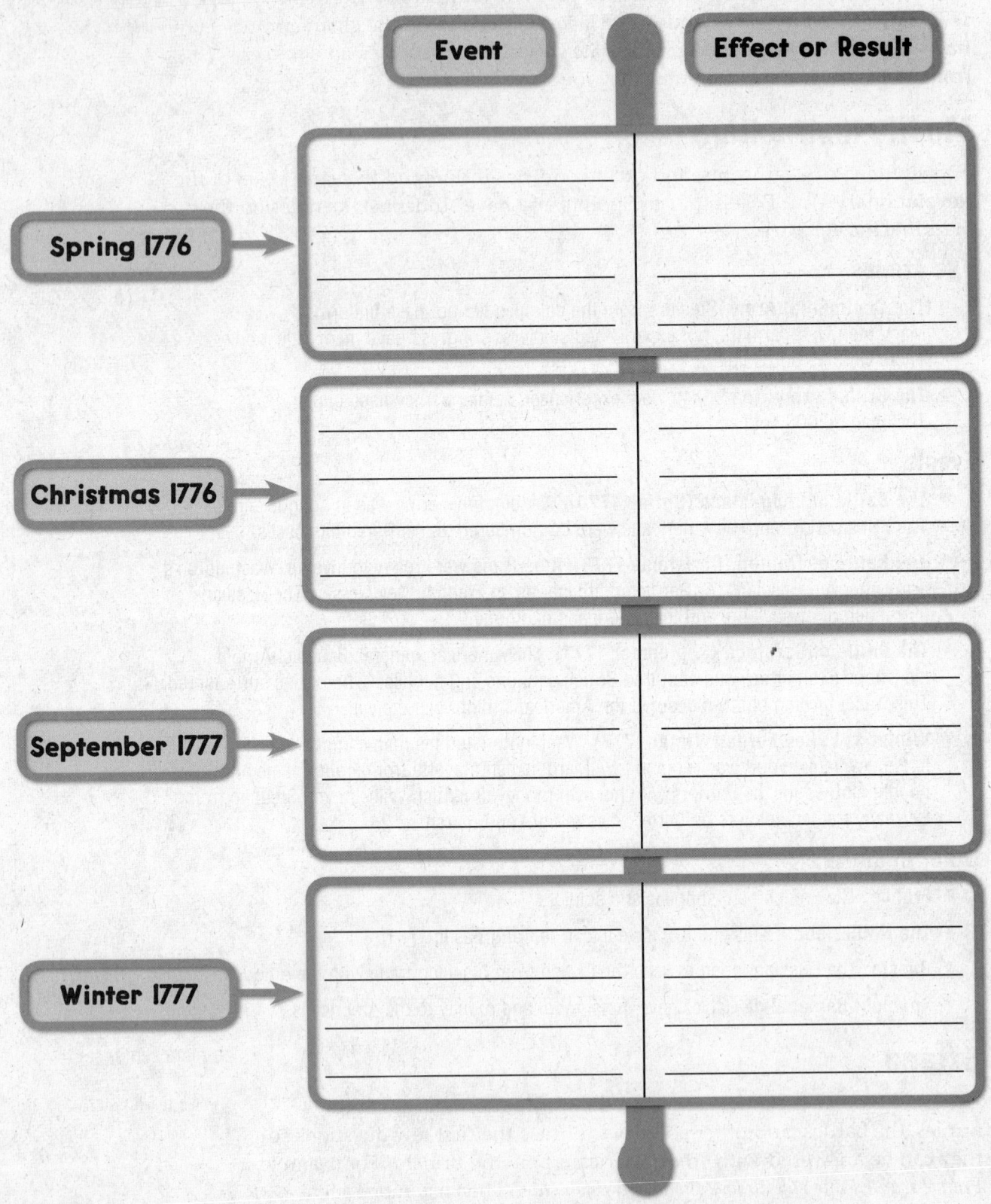

School-Home Connection Have students take this page home to share with their families. They can use the time line to discuss some of the battles and other major events of the American Revolution.

114 ■ Success for English Learners

Unit 3, Chapter 7, Lesson 2

Apply and Assess

Write a Speech

Review how the soldiers felt at Valley Forge where it was very cold, and they had little food, torn clothing, and shoes that were falling apart. Why had the soldiers joined the fighting? What did they want? How did the soldiers keep fighting when they had so few things that they needed? Discuss their responses.

- During **Close**, p. 280
- 20 minutes

Tell students to imagine that they are at Valley Forge. They will write a speech to cheer up the soldiers. Have students volunteer words and images that may make the soldiers feel better, stronger, and more hopeful. Remind students of the Battle of Saratoga, just a few months before, which the Americans won. Note ideas on the board in phrases.

Next, model a speech that uses a few phrases you wrote on the board. Tell beginning students that they may copy the speech, but they have to use different words and phrases. Allow intermediate students to use some sentence structures, but ask them to use mostly their own words. Ask advanced students to use their own words and structures in their speeches. Have students share their speeches with a partner when they are finished.

Informal Lesson Assessment

	Beginning	Intermediate	Advanced
Task	Provide students with a list of early events in the Revolutionary War and a list of their results or effects. Have students match the events with the effects.	Provide students with fill-in-the-blank statements about early events in the Revolutionary War and the results or effects of these events.	Have students write several sentences about early events in the Revolutionary War and the effects or results these events had.
Below Expectations	• no answer is correct	• no answer is comprehensible or correct	• incorrect ideas • no complete sentences • many errors
Meets Expectations	• some answers are correct	• most answers are comprehensible and correct	• correct ideas • some incomplete sentences • some errors
Above Expectations	• all answers are correct	• all answers are comprehensible and correct	• correct ideas • complete sentences • few errors

Success for English Learners

Use with Chapter 7 Lesson 3

Build Background

Access Prior Knowledge

Tell students that they will meet the following people in this lesson: Benedict Arnold, Nathan Hale, John Paul Jones, Nathanael Greene, Molly Pitcher, Tadeusz Kosciuszko, and General Cornwallis. Write the names, say them slowly, and give students a chance to say them. Ask students to skim the lesson and find these names in bold type. Have them use context to understand who these people are and why they are important. Return to this later, and have students confirm or revise the information you recorded.

- Before **Introduce**, p. 284
- 10 minutes

Lesson Vocabulary

Write and say these context sentences:

1) **Civilians** and military helped Americans win the war.

2) Everyone was angry with the **traitor** who gave information to the enemy.

Ask students to use context clues to figure out the meaning of civilian and traitor. Discuss their ideas and reasons. Point out that *traitor* has a word ending, or suffix, that is common to many words that name people. This suffix can be spelled *-or* or *-er*. Ask students if they can think of other words that end in *-or* or *-er* and name people. Elicit such examples as *buyer, seller, banker, author, teacher, translator, sailor,* and *lawyer*. Review meanings for each word. Then post a list of brief statements on the board, and have students note whether they describe a civilian or a traitor.

Additional Vocabulary Explain the meanings and uses of the words in the margin to students.

Cognates As students read the lesson, you may wish to point out cognates such as: **commander/comandante, hero/héroe, nation/nación, traitor/traidor.**

commander	retire
hanged	spy
heart	surround
headquarters	target
rank	volunteer

Build Fluency

Read aloud the following rhyme, and point out words that sound alike. Have students repeat it several times to develop oral language skills. Return to the rhyme throughout the lesson to help develop vocabulary, cause-and-effect skills, and lesson content.

> Help arrived from overseas,
> But the war continued in the colonies.
>
> Heroes like Nathan Hale died to make America free.
> The **traitor** Benedict Arnold helped the enemy.
>
> The British lost at Yorktown on Chesapeake Bay
> and signed the Treaty of Paris on a September Day.
>
> This ended the war and did something great.
> It made a new country, the United States!

Scaffolding the Content

Preview the Lesson

Have students look at the map on page 286 showing major battles of the American Revolution. Ask: *What battles are on this map that we have not yet read about? Where did those "new" battles take place?* Allow students to point out names and locations. Say and write correct responses. Then read the summary on page 289. Explain that this lesson describes how the Americans won the war.

- During **Teach**, pp. 284–289
- 30 minutes

Modify Instruction

Read the following facts about the end of the Revolutionary War. Stop after each number, and ask students to write the number in the correct box on the blackline master. Next, ask students to work in pairs to retell the events in order.

1. Many civilians, or people not in the military, helped Americans win the war. Nathan Hale was a spy who gave his life for America. There were also military heroes like John Paul Jones. He was a navy commander who defeated large British ships.

2. The British army captured many cities in the North, so it moved to the South. The British knew the French were helping the Americans. The British hoped Loyalists in the South would help their army.

3. In 1778, the British attacked American soldiers in Savannah, Georgia, and won. In 1780, the British army took over Charles Town in South Carolina.

4. Benedict Arnold was a Continental Army officer. He was not happy with his rank, or level, in the army. He became a traitor by helping the British in Virginia.

5. General Nathanael Greene commanded the Continental Army in the South. He led Americans to win a major victory at the Battle of Cowpens in South Carolina in 1781. It was a turning point for the war in the South.

6. The British had a victory in North Carolina at Guilford Courthouse in 1781. They still did not win the war, because no single city was the heart, or center, of America.

7. The British General Cornwallis set up a headquarters, or control center, in Yorktown, Virginia, on the Chesapeake Bay. This was a good place for the British to receive supplies. American and French troops surrounded Cornwallis there.

8. French and American troops surrounded Cornwallis for weeks. They attacked him by both land and sea. In 1781, Cornwallis surrendered. Yorktown was the last major battle, but a there were still a few small battles after that.

9. The Treaty of Paris officially ended the war in 1783. This treaty gave America independence. It also forced Britain to remove all soldiers from American land.

10. George Washington retired as commander in chief when the war was over.

Extend

Write and say this cause-and-effect sentence: *There were several causes for the American victory.* Have students name details that support and explain this sentence. Repeat and record ideas below the sentence. Have volunteers restate the ideas.

- After **Teach**, pp. 284–289
- 10 minutes

Success for English Learners ■ 117

Name _____ Date _____

DIRECTIONS Listen as your teacher reads. Read the phrase in each box. Write the number of each paragraph in the correct box.

The British moved to the south.	The British had a victory at Guilford Courthouse.
Cornwallis surrendered at Yorktown.	The French and Americans surrounded Cornwallis at Yorktown.
Washington retired.	The Treaty of Paris ended the war.
Nathan Hale and John Paul Jones became Revolutionary War heroes.	Benedict Arnold became a traitor.
The Battle of Cowpens was fought in the South.	The British took Savannah in Georgia and Charles Town in South Carolina.

School-Home Connection Have students take this page home to share with their families. They can use the page to retell key events that occurred near the end of the American Revolution.

Apply and Assess

Draw a Medal

Explain how soldiers earn medals. Discuss and list ideas such as bravery and courage at a particular battle.

- During **Close**, p. 289
- 20 minutes

Ask volunteers to draw on the board some shapes for medals, such as stars, shields, hearts, and crosses. Ask other volunteers to add designs that might appear within the shapes, or on the edges. As students draw and embellish, discuss the resulting images. Talk about the shapes of real medals, such as the Purple Heart, the Silver Star, and the Distinguished Service Cross.

Students may work individually to create their medals. You might supply cardboard, construction paper, aluminum foil, paste, and other materials.

When students are finished, ask them to show and describe their medal to a partner. Then ask volunteers to show and describe their medal to the class.

Informal Lesson Assessment

	Beginning	Intermediate	Advanced
Task	Provide students with several true and false statements about people, places, and events that led to the American victory in the Revolutionary War. Have students indicate whether each statement is true or false.	Provide students with several true and false statements about people, places, and events that led to the American victory in the Revolutionary War. Have students identify each as true or false, and ask them to correct false statements using words and phrases.	Provide students with several true and false statements about people, places, and events that led to the American victory in the Revolutionary War. Have them identify each as true or false, and ask them to rewrite false statements to make them true.
Below Expectations	• no correct answers	• no answers are comprehensible or correct	• no answers are comprehensible or correct • no complete sentences
Meets Expectations	• some answers are correct	• most of the answers are comprehensible and correct	• most answers are comprehensible and correct • some incomplete sentences
Above Expectations	• all answers are correct	• all answers are comprehensible and correct	• all answers are comprehensible and correct • complete sentences

Success for English Learners

Use with Lesson 4, Chapter 7

Build Background

Access Prior Knowledge

Explain that a consequence of war is an effect of war. It is something that happens as a result. Explain that after the Revolutionary War, the British left North America. Explain that colonists could focus on problems in the new country. Ask students to name problems from prior lessons. Restate and write appropriate ideas. Also, ask students to think about specific groups of people, such as African Americans and Native Americans.

- Before **Introduce**, p. 292
- 10 minutes

Lesson Vocabulary

Put students into mixed-proficiency pairs. Each student in the pair should choose two of the vocabulary words, find them in the lesson, and find their definitions. Explain that the definitions are in the same sentence as the words, or in the next sentence. Add that sometimes the definitions come after the word *or*. When students find the definitions, they should copy them from the lesson, and explain them to their partner. If you want, distribute vocabulary cards so students can compare their definitions with those on the cards.

For additional practice, challenge partners to sort the words into categories that they name and explain. Possibilities include people (**abolitionist**), actions (**abolish**), and things (**territory, ordinance**); words with three (abolish, ordinance), four (territory), or five (abolitionist) syllables; and words related to slavery (abolish, abolitionist) and words related to land (territory, ordinance).

Additional Vocabulary Explain the meanings and uses of the words in the margin to students. Explain that the prefix *anti* means "against," so the term *anti-slavery* means "against slavery."

acre	measure
anti-slavery	section
constitution	sue
jury	township

Cognates As students read the lesson, you may wish to point out cognates such as: **abolish/abolir, model/modelo, region/región, section/sección, territory/territorio.**

Build Fluency

Read aloud the following rhyme, and point out words that sound alike. Have students repeat it several times to develop oral language skills. Return to the rhyme throughout the lesson to help develop vocabulary, cause-and-effect skills, and lesson content.

> After the war, our nation was new.
> People had different points of view.
>
> **Abolitionists** asked: "Didn't we fight to be free? Then let's **abolish** slavery!"
>
> Soldiers said: "We fought in the military, So we should get land in the **territory!**"
>
> Native Americans said: "The land is ours; we will still fight!"
>
> But more and more they lost their rights.

Scaffolding the Content

Preview the Lesson

Point out the illustrations related to slavery and people speaking out against it on pages 292 and 293. Then point out the map on page 295. Read the title; review that territory is land; and explain that after the war, the government wanted people to settle this territory. Then have students scan the time line on pages 296–297, and note that battles over land continued to take place.

• During **Teach**, pp. 292–297
• 30 minutes

Modify Instruction

Discuss how the American Revolution affected, or changed, life in America in many ways. Explain that students will use the blackline master to record some of these ways. Review the categories on the blackline master, and then read aloud the points below. Pause after points, and repeat when necessary to help students record important points.

New Ideas After the war, states had to write their own constitutions, or system of beliefs. The Declaration of Independence said people in America had the right to life and liberty, but new state constitutions did not give women the same rights as men. Most African Americans were still enslaved. Elizabeth Freeman was an enslaved woman who sued, or legally fought the state of Massachusetts, to be free. She won the fight, and Massachusetts abolished, or ended slavery. Other northern states followed.

Western Settlements When the war ended, the United States did not have enough money. Congress needed to pay soldiers. It decided to pay them with land in the West. Many soldiers moved west. Congress also sold land for money, so other settlers moved West.

The Northwest Territory The Northwest Territory was land north of the Ohio River. This territory, or land, belonged to the nation, but was not represented in the government. Congress passed a land ordinance in 1785, or a set of laws that explained how land would be measured and sold. Congress divided the territory into townships, or squares of land. Regions with over 60,000 residents could become states. The ordinance also promised freedom of religion, and it banned slavery.

Battles for Land Before the war, the British helped the Native Americans. Now the Native Americans had trouble stopping settlers from moving onto their land. They united to fight against settlers. In the early 1790s, tribes defeated soldiers in areas where Indiana and Ohio are today. However, by 1795, Michikinikwa and other tribes signed the Treaty of Greenville. They gave up most of their land in the Northwest Territory.

Extend

Create a two-column chart. Label one column "Freedom" and the other column "Land." Ask students to name effects of the war. Restate them, and record them in the correct category. When students finish, ask a volunteer to summarize what the chart shows.

• After **Teach**, pp. 292–297
• 10 minutes

Name _____ Date _____

DIRECTIONS Listen as your teacher reads. Complete the cluster with the information you hear.

New Ideas

Western Settlements

Effects of the War

Battles for Land

The Northwest Territory

 School-Home Connection Have students take this page home to share with their families. They can use the information in the cluster to tell a family member about how the American Revolution affected life in the new United States.

Apply and Assess

Write a News Article

Post this statement: The Jury Frees Elizabeth Freeman. Review facts about Elizabeth Freeman by recording information under columns: *Who, What, When, Where, Why,* and *How.* Discuss the questions as a class, and write notes under each category. Under the *Why* column, note why the jury ruled in favor of Elizabeth Freeman based on the liberties promised in the Declaration of Independence. Also, explain why this decision was historical. Discuss how an enslaved person used American laws to win freedom.

- During **Close**, p. 297
- 20 minutes

Ask students to write a news article about the decision of the jury. Tell students to use the notes on the board. Provide beginning students with sentence starters, and have them complete a one-paragraph article. Ask intermediate students to use original structures, as well as phrases and words from the board to write a two-paragraph article. Have advanced students use original structures, rather than the words posted on the board. Their article should be two to three paragraphs long.

Informal Lesson Assessment

	Beginning	**Intermediate**	**Advanced**
Task	Provide a list of ways the Revolutionary War affected life in the United States. Write some correct statements and some incorrect statements. Have students circle the correct statements.	Have students list a few ways the Revolutionary War affected life in the United States, particularly ideas about liberty and issues concerning land.	Have students write a paragraph explaining three or four ways the American Revolution affected life in the new United States, particulary ideas about liberty and issues concerning land.
Below Expectations	• no answers are correct	• no part of the answer is comprehensible or correct	• inappropriate ideas • incorrect paragraph form • many errors
Meets Expectations	• some answers are correct	• most of the answer is comprehensible and correct	• appropriate ideas • correct paragraph form • some errors
Above Expectations	• all answers are correct	• the answer is comprehensible and correct	• appropriate ideas • correct paragraph form • few errors

Developing Academic Language

Whenever students read in the content areas, they will be asked to draw conclusions. To do so, students must be able to identify main ideas and key details and combine them with their own knowledge. This will enable them to draw conclusions: ideas that are not directly stated in the text, but that flow logically from the text.

Introduce Drawing Conclusions

Write the word *conclusion*. Explain that a conclusion is a statement based on the facts. Sometimes, conclusions are stated on the page. Other times, readers have to use what they already know, in addition to facts on the page, to draw or state a conclusion.

- Before **Draw Conclusions**, p. 310
- 20 minutes

Practice

Write this paragraph, and read it aloud.

In Newtown, the streets are clean. The teachers are happy, and the children do well in school. The town has many clean parks. Most people have small but comfortable houses or apartments.

Have students identify the facts: *clean streets, happy teachers, successful students, clean parks, comfortable houses or apartments.* Have students think about what they already know (*these are all good things to have in a town*). Then work with students to draw a conclusion, and write it on the board:

Newtown is a good place to live.

Apply

Draw the following chart, and have partners copy it onto a piece of paper. Explain that evidence is made up of facts they learn from their reading. Then write and read this paragraph: *Saturdays are busy days for soccer in my town. There are many soccer teams. Sometimes there are not enough fields for teams to play on. Sometimes teams have to go home without playing.* Have students complete the chart. Discuss their work, and write a conclusion as a class: *There are not enough soccer fields in my town.*

Evidence	Knowledge

Conclusion

Use with Chapter 8, Lesson 1

Build Background

Access Prior Knowledge

Review the term *representation*. Then have the class form two groups. Put 75% of the students in one group, and call them Pennsylvania. Put 25% of the students in another group, and call them Connecticut. Say: *Each group gets two votes in Congress. Is that fair?* When students argue, say: *All right, then Pennsylvania, you get 15 votes, and Connecticut, you get five votes.* Ask if that seems fair. Explain that the delegates to the Constitutional Convention had to work out this problem, and think of ways to have fair representation for states.

- Before **Introduce**, p. 316
- 10 minutes

Lesson Vocabulary

Discuss the vocabulary words as a class and have students use the words in sentences. When students understand the meanings of the words, ask them to draw three squares in a horizontal row to represent the vocabulary word **arsenal**. In the first square, have students write a short definition. In the second square, have students write a sentence using the word correctly. In the third square, have students draw a picture or symbol of the object. Provide examples as necessary. Repeat the process for **federal system, republic, compromise,** and **bill**.

Additional Vocabulary Explain to students the meanings and uses of the words in the margin. Explain that in this lesson, *national* means "controlled by the country," and *state* means "controlled by the state." National leaders help control and unite the country, but state leaders have freedom to make decisions that are different from those of other states. Explain that the word *house* in this lesson refers to a group of people coming together to make decisions.

citizenship	outlaw
convention	State House
debate	state militia
debt	storehouse
house	
national army	

Cognates As students read the lesson, you may wish to point out cognates such as: **constitution/constitución, federal system/sistema federal, national/nacional, republic/república.**

Build Fluency

Read aloud the following rhyme, and point out words that sound alike. Have students repeat it several times to develop oral language skills. Return to the rhyme throughout the lesson to help develop vocabulary, the skill of drawing conclusions, and lesson content.

> A convention met to make a new government plan.
> It strengthened the **federal system** for our land.
> Slavery and representation were subjects of debate.
> It took **compromises** to satisfy each state.
> With the new constitution, our **republic** began.
> A government with fair representation was the big plan.

Scaffolding the Content

Preview the Lesson

Read the *What to Know* question on page 316. Explain that the Constitutional Convention was a meeting of delegates from each state. They met to write the Constitution, or the plan of government for the United States. Post and read aloud the main headings in the lesson. Have students predict how the sections will help them answer the question.

- During **Teach**, pp. 316–322
- 30 minutes

Modify Instruction

Have students look at the organizer on the blackline master page. Then have students take notes as you read this information.

Where: Pennsylvania State House, Philadelphia, Pennsylvania

When: May to September, 1787

Who: 55 delegates represented 12 states. They included George Washington, Benjamin Franklin, James Madison, Edmund Randolph, William Paterson, and Gouverneur Morris.

Why:

Shays's Rebellion Some people lost their farms, and some went to prison because they could not pay the money. Poor farmers led by Daniel Shays rebelled, or fought back, by trying to take over an arsenal, or weapons storehouse, in Massachusetts. There was no national army to defend the arsenal. This rebellion made people think the national government could not protect them.

No national leader Each state had a governor, but there was no single national leader. It was difficult to pass laws, because all nine states had to agree.

What:

The relationship between the states and the federal government Some delegates wanted the national government to have more power, but others wanted the states to have more power. The delegates decided to let the states and national government share power.

Law The Constitution became the supreme, or highest, law of the land.

Representation In a republic, people choose representatives to make decisions. At the Constitutional Convention, people had different ideas about how to organize the representatives. They decided that in one house, larger states had more representatives. In the other house, each state had one representative. Either house could present a bill, or an idea for a law.

Slavery The delegates argued about whether to include enslaved African Americans when counting a state's population. The delegates agreed to count three-fifths of the total number of slaves in each state.

Extend

Say this conclusion and write it on the board: *Compromise was very important at the Constitutional Convention.* Have students name details that support this idea. Restate and record appropriate ideas.

- After **Teach**, pp. 316–322
- 15 minutes

Name _____ Date _____

DIRECTIONS Listen to your teacher. Then take notes about the information you hear.

	The Constitutional Convention
Where	
When	
Who	Famous Delegates 1. _____ 2. _____ 3. _____ 4. _____ 5. _____ 6. _____
Why	
What	1. Relationship between the states and the federal government: _____ 2. Law: _____ 3. Representation: _____ 4. Slavery: _____

School-Home Connection Have students take this page home to share with their families. They can use the information in the organizer to tell a family member about the Constitutional Convention.

Unit 4, Chapter 8, Lesson 1

Success for English Learners ■ 127

Apply and Assess

Write a Persuasive Letter

Review issues that required a compromise during the Constitutional Convention. Have students work in small groups to list as many as they can remember. Ask each group to share responses aloud. Note the responses and compromises on the board under headings, and briefly explain the compromise. For example:

Representation
- Some wanted each state to have one vote.
- Some wanted more votes for states with many people.
- Compromise: Congress with two houses, one that counted votes each way listed above.

If necessary, supplement student responses with areas of compromise including slavery, counting population, state and federal power, and the Articles of Confederation. Next, write a model letter on the board explaining why compromise was important during the Constitutional Convention. Use one example of a compromise listed on the board.

Read the letter aloud. Ask students to imagine that they were at the Constitutional Convention. Have them write a letter to a relative that explains why compromise was important at the convention. Ask beginning students to provide one example of compromise. Have them use your model by changing key words and phrases to reflect original ideas. Encourage intermediate students to use their own words, but allow them to use some constructions from your model. Ask advanced students to list three or more examples of issues that required compromise in their own words.

- During **Close**, p. 322
- 30 minutes

Informal Lesson Assessment

	Beginning	Intermediate	Advanced
Task	Provide steps involved in the development of a plan of government that took place at the Constitutional Convention. Have students order them in a time sequence.	Have students list steps involved in the development of a plan of government as they took place at the Constitutional Convention. Allow students to use key words and phrases.	Have students list steps involved in the development of a plan of government at the Constitutional Convention. Ask students to use complete sentences and transitions.
Below Expectations	• no or almost no correct responses	• no correct steps given	• no or very few correct ideas
Meets Expectations	• some correct responses	• one or two correct steps	• some correct ideas
Above Expectations	• correct responses	• three or more correct steps	• correct, complete response

Build Background

Use with Chapter 8, Lesson 2

Access Prior Knowledge

Post the statement: *The Constitution divides power into three parts of government—legislative, executive, and judicial.* Explain that students already know the many people and jobs involved in each branch, or part. Provide these examples: Congress, the President of the United States, lawyers, judges, and police. Ask students if they can tell you which of these people, or groups, do the following: 1) make laws 2) carry out laws 3) make decisions on whether laws were followed.

- Before **Introduce**, p. 328
- 10 minutes

Lesson Vocabulary

Tell students that making connections between ideas they are learning and ideas they have already learned, can help them remember new words and concepts. Provide brief definitions for the new vocabulary words. Then ask students to create word webs between the new words and images they associate with them. Model the activity by having the class help you make a word web for **legislative branch**, which may include concepts like laws, government, and leaders. Ask for one or two additional words from volunteers. Have students work in groups to make word webs for the nine remaining vocabulary words. When they are finished, have them cover the vocabulary words in the center of the web, and see if other students can guess them based on the associations.

Additional Vocabulary Explain the meanings and uses of the words in the margin to students. Tell students that the multiple meaning word *term* in this lesson means "a period of time." Also explain that the expression *to strike down* means "to put an end to something."

Cognates As students read the lesson, you may wish to point out cognates such as: **defend/defender, justice/justicia, office/oficina, supreme/supremo.**

citizen	nominate
common good	principle
consent	reject
court	strike down
electors	term
enforce	version

Build Fluency

Read aloud the following rhyme, and point out words that sound alike. Have students repeat it several times to develop oral language skills. Return to the rhyme throughout the lesson to help develop vocabulary, the skill of drawing conclusions, and lesson content.

> Think of our government like three branches of one tree.
> The **legislative branch** makes the laws that keep us free.
> The **executive branch** makes leadership decisions.
> The **judicial branch** has judges and the court system.
> Think of our government as three branches of one tree.
> Three make one, and one is made out of three.

Success for English Learners

Scaffolding the Content

Preview the Lesson

Ask students to use main headings in the lesson to identify the three branches of government. Ask them to write the names of the three branches on a piece of paper. Beside each branch, ask students to write its function as you review these illustrations and descriptions: the Capitol on page 331—where the legislative branch of the government makes laws; the White House on page 330—where the President of the United States, the head of the executive branch, works to enforce laws; the Supreme Court on pages 331 and 332—where the highest court of the judicial branch decides if laws are fair. Have students quiz each other by naming a function and asking the partner to say the matching branch of government.

• During **Teach**, pp. 328–333
• 30 minutes

Modify Instruction

Present the lesson by using the same headings as in the textbook. Read each summary below. Then pause to ask the main idea question, and have students record the answer and any other important details in the appropriate part of the blackline master.

The Preamble The Preamble is the beginning of the Constitution. It begins with the words "We the People of the United States." The Preamble explains that the purpose of the Constitution is to create a fairer form of government. It also says that the Constitution is based on principles of individual liberty, justice, and peace.

Q: *What does the Preamble say?*

The Legislative Branch The legislative, or lawmaking, branch of the government has the power to make laws to manage conflict, organize an army, declare war, coin and print money, and control commerce. Congress is made up of two houses, the Senate and the House of Representatives. Both houses can propose bills. Congress can also impeach the President, or accuse him or her of a crime.

Q: *What powers does the legislative branch have?*

The Executive Branch The executive branch of the government has the power to enforce laws. The President is the chief executive and also the commander in chief of the military. The President can veto, or reject, bills passed by Congress. Congress can override, or overpower, the President's veto with a two-thirds vote.

Q: *What powers does the executive branch have?*

The Judicial Branch The judicial branch of the government has the power to decide cases that involve the Constitution, treaties, and national laws. The highest court is the Supreme Court. The Supreme Court can strike down laws that go against the Constitution.

Q: *What powers does the judicial branch have?*

Extend

As a class, make a list of about ten powers, or jobs, of the legislative, executive, and judicial branches of the government. Have students work in pairs to identify the branches of government. Next, ask students to think about why it is important to keep the three branches separate from each other. Have pairs share their ideas aloud.

• After **Teach**, pp. 328–333
• 20 minutes

Name _____ Date _____

DIRECTIONS Listen to your teacher. Then answer the questions, and write details in each box.

The Preamble

The Legislative Branch

The Executive Branch

The Judicial Branch

School-Home Connection Have students take this page home to share with their families. They can use the information in the organizer to tell a family member about the Constitution and the three branches of government.

Unit 4, Chapter 8, Lesson 2

Apply and Assess

Write a Set of Rules

Brainstorm classroom rules. Ask volunteers to share ideas, and note a few of them on the board in a column called *classroom rules*. Review important ideas in the Constitution and define them briefly. For example, say: peace *means to have no conflict;* liberty *means freedom;* justice *means fairness.* Have students try to relate classroom rules with ideas from the Constitution. For example, the rule "Do not cheat" relates to fairness.

- During **Close**, p. 333
- 30 minutes

Next, have students form their own list of classroom rules that represent ideas in the Constitution.

- Have beginning students write one or two rules, and show them how to change one or two words from an example to make an original rule. For example, change "Do not cheat" to "Do not yell."
- Have intermediate students make three rules. Allow them to use some words or phrases from the board, but each rule should be new.
- Ask advanced students to make five or more rules without using examples from the board.

Informal Lesson Assessment

	Beginning	Intermediate	Advanced
Task	Provide a list of powers of government branches. Have students classify them as powers of the legislative, executive, or judicial branch of government.	Have students answer this question in short phrases: *What are the powers of the legislative, executive, and judicial branches of government?*	Have students answer this question in complete sentences: *What are the powers of the three branches of government?*
Below Expectations	• no powers are correctly classified	• no part of the answer is comprehensible or correct	• incorrect ideas • no complete sentences
Meets Expectations	• some powers are correctly classified	• most of the answer is comprehensible and correct	• mainly correct or appropriate ideas • some incomplete sentences
Above Expectations	• all powers are correctly classified	• the answer is comprehensible and correct	• appropriate ideas • complete sentences

Use with Chapter 8, Lesson 3

Build Background

- Before **Introduce**, p. 334
- 15 minutes

Access Prior Knowledge

Review information about reasons the Constitution was created, the ideas it includes, and debates delegates had as they wrote it. Write these categories on the board: *Reasons, Ideas,* and *Debates*. Have students work in groups to write facts under each category and share them aloud.

Lesson Vocabulary

Distribute vocabulary cards from this lesson to each student. Have students work in mixed-proficiency pairs to talk about each definition to be sure that both students understand. Then use the definitions for a *What am I?* or *Who am I?* game. Provide clues such as: *If you ever go to jail, you will be glad to have me as your right! What am I?* (**due process of law**) Have students hold up the vocabulary card that they think answers the question. If students hold up the wrong card, discuss the definition, providing examples familiar to students. Continue with **ratify, Federalists, Anti-Federalists, reserved powers, Cabinet,** and **political party**.

Additional Vocabulary Explain to students the meanings and uses of the words in the margin. Explain that in this lesson, the word *bill* means "official list," but in past lessons it meant paper money. Explain that the Bill of Rights is an official list of rights that was added to the Constitution to protect the rights of the people. For example, *freedom of speech* gives people the right to say their personal opinion without being punished by the government.

Cognates As students read the lesson, you may wish to point out cognates such as: **capital/capital, federal/federal, individual/individuo, party/partido, political/político.**

amendment
bill
freedom of press
freedom of speech
head
in favor of
petition
policy
rights
trial

Build Fluency

Read aloud the following rhyme, and point out words that sound alike. Have students repeat it several times to develop oral language skills. Return to the rhyme throughout the lesson to help develop vocabulary, the skill of drawing conclusions, and lesson content.

> "Yes," said the **Federalists**, "let's approve, or **ratify**!"
> "No," said the **Anti-Federalists**, "and let us tell you why.
> The federal government should not be so strong!
> Such a government will not last long!"
>
> Said the Federalists, "a bill will guarantee
> Freedoms for the people and personal liberty."
> And so the Bill of Rights gave freedoms to all
> Including freedom of speech and **due process of law.**

Success for English Learners ■ 133

Scaffolding the Content

Preview the Lesson

Read the events on the time line on page 334. Use the following explanations to highlight two important events: *The Constitution is ratified*—The Constitution is approved; *The Bill of Rights is added to the Constitution*—A new section about the rights of individuals is added to the Constitution. Have students work in pairs to write two questions they have about these events. Answer each group's questions as a class. Explain that this lesson describes how the states made the Constitution the law of the land, and how an important addition to the Constitution protected the rights of the people.

- During **Teach**, pp. 334–339
- 25 minutes

Modify Instruction

Present the lesson as a sequence of events. Have students record each major event, as well as details about it, in the appropriate part of the blackline master.

1787 The Constitution was complete in 1787. For the Constitution to become law, 9 out of the 13 states had to ratify, or approve, it. Many delegates wanted to limit the power of the government, and protect the people's individual rights. Supporters of the Constitution promised to propose a Bill of Rights after the constitution was ratified.

1788 In 1788, the Constitution was ratified. Citizens who liked the Constitution were called Federalists. They wanted a strong federal government. Citizens who disagreed with the Federalists were called Anti-Federalists.

1789 In 1789, George Washington became the first president. He set up a State Department, Treasury Department, and War Department. The heads, or people in charge, of these departments became the members of the first Cabinet to advise the President. Political parties formed when two Cabinet members disagreed about what was best for the United States. Political parties are groups that try to elect a leader who supports their ideas.

1791 In 1791, the Bill of Rights was added to the Constitution. The Bill of Rights is the first ten amendments to the Constitution. The First Amendment protects freedom of religion, speech, and press. The Second Amendment gives people the right to have weapons. The Third Amendment does not allow government to make citizens house soldiers during times of peace. The Fourth Amendment protects citizens from unfair searches. The Fifth through Eighth Amendments are about due process of law. This includes the right to a public trial by a jury. The Tenth Amendment says that the national government can do only what is in the Constitution. All other powers, called the reserved powers, belong to the states or the people.

1797 John Adams became the second president.

1800 The capital was moved to Washington, D.C. The city was planned by surveyor Andrew Ellicott with help from Benjamin Banneker.

Extend

Write this conclusion: *Many important changes took place in the 12 years after the Constitution was ratified, or approved.* Ask students to name the facts that could lead someone to draw this conclusion. Record, and repeat accurate answers. When you are finished, ask volunteers to summarize what you wrote.

- After **Teach**, pp. 334–339
- 10 minutes

Name _____ Date _____

DIRECTIONS Listen to your teacher. Then complete the time line with information you hear.

1787 →

1788 →

1789 →

1791 →

1797 →

1800 →

School-Home Connection Have students take this page home to share with their families. They can use the information in the time line to talk about the government during the early years of the Constitution.

Unit 4, Chapter 8, Lesson 3 — Success for English Learners ■ 135

Apply and Assess

Make a Poster

Write and say *Bill of Rights*. Have students identify some of the rights in the document. Repeat, and list correct answers. Elicit such concepts as freedom of speech, freedom of religion, and freedom of press. As students suggest ideas, categorize them by amendment. For example, the freedoms above are all part of the First Amendment. The freedom from unfair searches is the Fourth Amendment.

Have students work in mixed-proficiency pairs to create a poster that honors the Bill of Rights. Explain that students can do this by listing some of the freedoms it gives. They should also draw, cut out, or print pictures that explain or represent some of those freedoms.

Encourage students to make their posters colorful and interesting. Provide time for students to show and explain their posters to other pairs. Then display the posters, and lead the class in a discussion of the various rights they show.

- During **Close**, p. 339
- 20 minutes

Informal Lesson Assessment

	Beginning	Intermediate	Advanced
Task	Give students several true or false statements on what the Bill of Rights is, and why it was added to the Constitution.	Give students several fill-in-the-blank statements on what the Bill of Rights is, and why it was added to the Constitution.	Ask students short questions about what the Bill of Rights is, and why it was added to the Constitution. Ask them to answer using complete sentences.
Below Expectations	• no answers are correct	• no answers are correct	• no correct answers are written
Meets Expectations	• several answers are correct	• several answers are correct	• several correct answers are written
Above Expectations	• all answers are correct	• all answers are correct	• all answers are correctly written

Use with Chapter 8, Lesson 4

Build Background

Access Prior Knowledge

Create a cluster for the word *democracy* on the board. Ask students for words and phrases they associate with this word. Repeat, and record ideas. Add the word *power* to the cluster. Ask: *Who has the power in a democracy?* Use students' responses to explain that in a democracy, power is shared. Tell students they will learn more about how power is shared in the lesson.

- Before **Introduce**, p. 342
- 10 minutes

Lesson Vocabulary

Explain the meanings of each word using the vocabulary cards, illustrations, and concrete examples when possible. Next, have students paraphrase the definitions and create hints, and use them to create a crossword puzzle. Have students exchange puzzles with a partner. After students complete the crossword puzzles, call out the definitions, and ask students to provide the corresponding vocabulary words.

Additional Vocabulary Explain to students the meanings and uses of the words in the margin. Point out that the multiple-meaning word *exercise* in this lesson means "to use." Also explain that the expressions *keep track of* and *oversee* both mean "to watch over something."

Cognates As students read the lesson, you may wish to point out cognates such as: **basic/básico, declare/declarar, democracy/democracia, popular/popular, union/unión.**

alliance	municipal
draft	oath
empower	override
exercise	oversee
jury	
keep track of	

Build Fluency

Read aloud the following rhyme, and point out words that sound alike. Have students repeat it several times to develop oral language skills. Return to the rhyme throughout the lesson to help develop vocabulary, the skill of drawing conclusions, and lesson content.

> A **democracy** has to be
> A strong authority,
> A protector of liberty.
> The federal government has some powers
> The state governments have other powers
> And some powers are shared.
> Citizens have some powers, too.
> A democracy has to be
> A strong authority,
> A protector of liberty.

Success for English Learners ■ 137

Scaffolding the Content

Preview the Lesson

Explain to students that this lesson shows how the citizens of the United States, the national government, and the state governments all have power. Have students use illustrations, photographs, and captions from the lesson to name one power that each of the three groups has. Have beginning students use key words, and ask intermediate students to use phrases to respond. Ask advanced students to skim topics and introduction sentences in each section to think about how these powers work together.

• During **Teach**, pp. 342–349
• 30 minutes

Modify Instruction

Ask students to listen carefully as you read aloud this chapter summary. Stop after each major heading so students can record details under the matching heading on the blackline master page. Using students' notes, work as a class to draw one or two conclusions for each heading.

Constitution The Constitution describes the powers of the three branches of the federal government. It uses a system of checks and balances, or a way to stop one branch from becoming too powerful. Each branch can check, or block, the power of another branch.

Federal Government The federal, or national, government takes care of things that affect the entire country. This part of the government is in charge of training the military, cleaning the environment, and helping children, ill people, and the elderly.

State Government The Constitution protects the powers of states. State governments can build and manage state highways, state parks, public schools, state colleges and universities, and they can help their citizens. State governments help people who cannot afford food, homes, and medical care. The Constitution also says what states cannot do, such as print money, have an army, or make a treaty with another country.

Local Government In the United States, there are three levels of government: federal, state, and local. Local government is the county or city government. The local government, along with state and federal, can collect taxes. Like other levels of government, local government includes legislative, executive, and judicial branches. The leader of the local government is the mayor.

Citizens In a democracy, people make choices about their government. When citizens vote for leaders, they give them popular sovereignty, or power from the people. At first, not all citizens had the right to vote. Women did not have suffrage, or the right to vote, until 1920. People have a responsibility to act with civic virtue, or in a way that will help the democracy. For example, citizens have to obey, or follow, laws. People who are born in the United States are automatically citizens. Immigrants can become citizens through a process called naturalization.

Extend

Create a Venn Diagram about powers of the national and state governments. In one circle, have students note the powers of the national government that states do not have. In the other circle, have students record the powers of the state government that the national government does not control. In the overlapping portion, have them list powers both national and state governments share.

• After **Teach**, pp. 342–349
• 10 minutes

Name _____ Date _____

DIRECTIONS Listen as your teacher reads. Write important details you hear in the correct row.

	Powers	One or Two Conclusions
Constitution		
Federal Government		
State Government		
Local Government		
Citizens		

School-Home Connection Have students take this page home to share with their families. They can use the information in the organizer to tell a family member about our government.

Unit 4, Chapter 8, Lesson 4   Success for English Learners ■ 139

Apply and Assess

Write a Persuasive Letter

> • During **Close**, p. 349
> • 20 minutes

Help students think of a few issues that they could write about to a local politician. Ask students to work in pairs to list a few things at school or in their neighborhood that need improvement, such as sidewalks or roads in bad condition, dangerous areas, or places that should be cleaned.

Choose one of the issues, write sentences starters, and model how to use them to write a letter about the issue:

I live in/at _____. (area, street, or region)

I am concerned about _____. (the problem)

I would like to ask you to _____. (action you want the politician to take)

Have students write a letter. Have beginning students write a paragraph of three to four sentences and allow them to use sentence starters you modeled. Have intermediate students write a paragraph of five sentences. Ask advanced students to write at least two paragraphs with three to five sentences each.

Informal Lesson Assessment

	Beginning	Intermediate	Advanced
Task	List powers of the national and state governments in the United States. Have students identify each by writing *state*, *national*, or *both* beside each.	Ask students to list a few powers of state and national governments in the United States using key words and phrases.	Ask students to compare and contrast powers of state and national governments in the United States in one or two paragraphs.
Below Expectations	• no answer is comprehensible or correct	• no answer is comprehensible or correct	• incorrect ideas • no complete sentences • many errors
Meets Expectations	• some answers are partially comprehensible and/or correct	• most answers are comprehensible and correct	• appropriate ideas • some incomplete sentences • some errors
Above Expectations	• all answers are comprehensible and correct	• all answers are comprehensible and correct	• appropriate ideas • complete sentences • few errors

Use with Chapter 9 · Lesson 1

Build Background

Access Prior Knowledge

Ask students to imagine that they are going to be some of the first settlers to travel across the American West. Put them in small groups and have each group respond to one of these questions: *What do you think you will find? What people will you meet? What challenges will you have?* Lead a discussion by having each group share their responses aloud.

- Before **Introduce**, p. 354
- 15 minutes

Lesson Vocabulary

Ask students to find the boldfaced vocabulary words in the lesson. Explain the definitions as students study the words in context. Use pictures in the book, sketches on the board, and key words from the definitions to make sure students are comfortable with the vocabulary. Then ask students to draw a picture that represents each word. Help students think of ways to represent the abstract word **consequence**. Put students in pairs to see whether their partner can guess the words from the pictures. Have students change partners and repeat the process.

Additional Vocabulary Explain the meanings and uses of the words in the margin. Define *corps* as an official group of people working together. Mention that *double* is sometimes used as a noun or adjective, but in this lesson it is a verb that means to make two times as large. Point out that the word *report* is often used as a noun, but in this lesson it is a verb that means to announce or tell.

corps	immigrant
cross	overland wagon
double	purchase
expedition	report
hard times	set out

Cognates As students read the lesson, you may want to point out cognates such as: **consequence/consecuencia, explore/explorar, frontier/frontera, immigrant/inmigrante, pioneer/pionero.**

Build Fluency

Read aloud the following rhyme, and point out words that sound alike. Have students repeat it several times to develop oral language skills. Return to the rhyme throughout the lesson to help develop vocabulary, the skill of drawing conclusions, and lesson content.

> On the Gulf of Mexico Jefferson wanted a port for trade.
> 15 million dollars to France is what he paid.
> The country became double the size it was before,
> And Napoleon got money he needed for war.
> Lewis and Clark explored the new land
> And brought back plants and maps drawn by hand.
> Jefferson's questions were all addressed.
> The frontier pushed west and the trip was a success.

Scaffolding the Content

Preview the Lesson

Point out the map on page 357, the heading "Louisiana Purchase," and the time line on pages 358–359. Invite students to name some of what they see on the map and time line. Explain that Lewis and Clark led an expedition, or trip for exploring, across the newly purchased land that the United States bought from France.

- During **Teach**, pp. 354–360
- 30 minutes

Modify Instruction

Present the lesson as a sequence of events. Have students record each major event, as well as details that help describe it, in the appropriate part of the time line on the blackline master page. Review the events on the time line. Ask students to explain each major event.

1. **In the early 1700s and 1800s many immigrants came to the United States.** They were from England, Scotland, Ireland, Germany, and other countries. Some had hard, or difficult, times in their home countries. Others wanted to find land or make money.

2. **In 1801, Thomas Jefferson became the third President of the United States.** He wanted to make the country bigger. One problem the United States had at that time was that there were no ports near the Gulf of Mexico. Farmers had to ship their goods down the Mississippi River to New Orleans. In 1803, the French controlled the port of New Orleans. Jefferson sent representatives to France. Jefferson asked Napoleon Bonaparte, the leader of France, to sell New Orleans and part of Florida to the United States.

3. **In 1803, Napoleon sold Louisiana to the United States in the Louisiana Purchase.** The Louisiana Purchase cost $15 million and doubled the size of the United States.

4. **In 1804, Jefferson set up a trip to learn about the resources in the new land.** Jefferson chose Meriwether Lewis to lead the trip. Lewis chose his friend William Clark to help him. They called their group the Corps of Discovery. York, an enslaved African American, helped them with his hunting and fishing skills. The group left from St. Louis, Missouri, on a boat that traveled up the Missouri River. They spent the winter in a Mandan Indian village in what is now North Dakota. Sacagawea, a Shoshone Native American, helped guide Lewis and Clark through the Shoshone lands.

5. **In 1805, the Lewis and Clark expedition traveled across the Rocky Mountains.** Lewis and Clark's expedition reached the Pacific Ocean.

6. **In 1806, Lewis and Clark returned home.** They brought back seeds, plants, and animals from the new land. They mapped mountains and rivers there. The frontier pushed farther west. Jefferson was proud of their success.

Extend

- Write and say this conclusion: *The Louisiana Purchase changed America in many ways.*
- Have students name ideas, facts, and details that support and explain this sentence. Repeat them and record them below the conclusion.
- Ask students to share their responses.

- After **Teach**, pp. 354–360
- 10 minutes

Name _____ Date _____

DIRECTIONS Listen to your teacher. Complete the time line with information you hear.

1700s and 1800s → Event: _____
Details:

1801 → Event: _____
Details:

1803 → Events: _____
Details:

1804 → Event: _____
Details:

1805 → Event: _____
Details:

1806 → Events: _____
Details:

School-Home Connection Have students take this page home to share with their families. They can use the information in the time line to describe the exploration of the American West.

Unit 4, Chapter 9, Lesson 1

Apply and Assess

Write a Journal Entry

During **Close**, p. 360
30 minutes

Help students imagine what members of the Corps of Discovery saw as they traveled over new lands in the West. On the board, make three columns labeled *Text, Illustrations,* and *Imagination*. Ask students to think of words from the lesson. Next, ask student pairs to look at the illustrations and note geographical features, such as mountains and trees. Finally, have the same pairs imagine other sights they would see when traveling over new lands.

Have students write a journal entry about the sights and geography of the new land they explored. They may use the notes from the board to help them.

- Have beginning students write a few sentences or one paragraph. Write sentence starters to help them generate language in their journal entry.
- Ask intermediate students to write one or two paragraphs. Write suggestions on the board to help guide their thinking, such as: *Tell where you went. Tell what places you saw. Describe how these places looked.*
- Ask advanced students to write an entry of two paragraphs or more. Record major ideas they may want to mention in their journals: where they went, what places they saw, and what the places looked like.

Informal Lesson Assessment

	Beginning	**Intermediate**	**Advanced**
Task	Provide a list of correct and incorrect statements about ways the Louisiana Purchase helped the United States grow. Have students cross out the incorrect statements.	Provide a list of true and false statements about ways the Louisiana Purchase helped the United States grow. Have students identify each as true or false and correct key words and phrases in false statements.	Provide a list of true and false statements about ways the Louisiana Purchase helped the United States grow. Have students identify each as true or false, and rewrite false statements to make them true.
Below Expectations	• no correct response	• no answer is comprehensible or correct	• no answer is comprehensible or correct
Meets Expectations	• some correct responses	• some of the answers are comprehensible and correct	• some of the answers are comprehensible and correct
Above Expectations	• all correct responses	• all of the answers are comprehensible and correct	• all of the answers are comprehensible and correct

Build Background

Use with Chapter 9, Lesson 2

Access Prior Knowledge

Write and say: *War of 1812*. Then write below it: *United States against the British and Indians*. Explain that even after the American Revolution, the British had never left parts of North America, including Canada. The Indians hoped that the British could keep the settlers from going farther west. That is why the British and Indians fought together against the United States. Ask students to note similarities between these details and past conflicts involving Americans, Native Americans, and the British.

• Before **Introduce**, p. 364
• 10 minutes

Lesson Vocabulary

Explain the vocabulary words using the vocabulary cards, illustrations, and examples. Write several hints on the board, such as: *1) a song 2) unfair work 3) pride 4) to seem similar 5) words about a country 6) to work with a group 7) to be forced to work for the enemy 8) to love your country*. In small groups, have students copy each hint onto the front of an index card and write the corresponding vocabulary word on the opposite side. Next, have students practice the words in their groups. One student draws a card and looks only at the back. This player reads the hint aloud, names the word, and spells the word correctly. Another group member reads the front of the card to check the word.

Additional Vocabulary Explain the meanings and uses of the words in the margin. For example, explain that the word *act* has many meanings, but in this lesson it is used to mean law or official action.

act	navy
common man	pride
fire on	removal
First Lady	ruling
give up	tear

Cognates As students read the lesson, you may want to point out cognates such as: **capture/capturar, force/forzar, music/música, nationalism/nacionalismo, symbol/símbolo.**

Build Fluency

Read aloud the following rhyme and point out words that sound alike. Have students repeat it several times to develop oral language skills. Return to the rhyme throughout the lesson to help develop vocabulary, the skill of drawing conclusions, and lesson content.

> One way that the War of 1812 began
> Was with settlers moving to Native American land.
> Tecumseh and the British strengthened boundary lines,
> Then the U.S. fought the British one more time.
> The British fought hard and burned Washington.
> Two years passed before the war was won.
> On the Trail of Tears many Cherokee died
> From bad weather and walking 800 miles.
> The Cherokee tried to learn American ways,
> or **assimilate**,
> But loss and sadness was their fate.

Scaffolding the Content

Preview the Lesson

Work with students to complete these text clues to identify main points in the lesson: 1) *Americans fought against the British and Native Americans in the War of _____.* 2) *Many Cherokee were forced to walk to the Indian Territory on a route called the Trail of _____.* Explain that this lesson will describe what caused the War of 1812, the Trail of Tears, and what happened as a result of these events.

• During **Teach**, pp. 364–369
• 30 minutes

Modify Instruction

Read the following points aloud. Stop after each item so students can locate the corresponding section on the blackline master page. Have students write details that support the conclusions.

1. The British army captured American ships at sea and forced American sailors to work on British ships. This is called *impressment*. Chief Tecumseh united Native Americans to defend their lands from American pioneers.

2. In 1812, President Madison asked Congress to declare war on Britain. Many battles followed. At the Battle of the Thames, Americans defeated the British and Native Americans. Tecumseh died at this battle.

3. The British won battles, too. They marched into Washington and burned the White House and the Capitol. In 1814, the British fired on, or shot at, Americans in Fort McHenry in Baltimore for hours. The Americans did not give up. Francis Scott Key saw the American flag there and wrote a poem called "The Star Spangled Banner." This poem became the national anthem, or official song for the country.

4. The British lost another battle at New Orleans. Neither side knew that a peace treaty, or an agreement that ended the war, had been signed two weeks earlier in Europe.

5. After the war, Americans felt nationalism, or pride for their country. President James Monroe wrote the Monroe Doctrine. It says Europe cannot build colonies in America.

6. In 1828, Andrew Jackson was elected president. He was considered a "common man." In this election, all white men could vote. In past elections, only white men who owned land could vote.

7. In 1830, Jackson signed the Indian Removal Act. It forced the Cherokee and other tribes to go west of the Mississippi River into present-day Oklahoma. The Cherokee had to walk 800 miles to the Indian Territory through bad weather. One of every four Cherokee died during this trip. Today, we call this trip the Trail of Tears.

Extend

Ask students to name words, people, and places related to the War of 1812. Repeat their ideas and list them. Group ideas together to help students form statements. For example, you might group *Tecumseh, Native Americans,* and *British.* Students might form a statement, such as: *Joining with the British did not help Tecumseh and the Native Americans.*

• After **Teach**, pp. 364–369
• 10 minutes

Name _____   Date _____

DIRECTIONS Listen to your teacher. When your teacher pauses, write details that support, or explain, the conclusions in the second column.

	Details	Conclusions
1.		Americans were angry at the British.
2.		Tecumseh believed Native Americans could keep their lands.
3.		President James Madison acted as a brave leader.
4.		The Americans won battles in the War of 1812.
5.		The British won battles in the War of 1812.
6.		News traveled slowly then.
7.		Americans felt a strong nationalism, or pride, for their country.
8.		President Jackson was a symbol of a Democracy for "common people."
9.		The Cherokee suffered and lost all their land in America.

School-Home Connection Have students take this page home to share with their families. They can use the organizer to retell events that happened before and after the War of 1812.

Unit 4, Chapter 9, Lesson 2

Apply and Assess

Write an Article

Help students recall major details to include in their articles about Fort McHenry. Ask them to work in pairs to list facts, including: *who was there, when it happened, where it took place,* and *what happened there.* Discuss responses and post them on the board.

• During **Close**, p. 369
• 20 minutes

Next, ask students to try to imagine what the battle looked like. Ask them to work in the same pairs to list two to three things that witnesses of the battle might have seen. Provide a few examples to help students brainstorm, such as flying bullets and smoke. Have each pair share one or two responses aloud and record these on the board.

Ask students to use the posted information to write an article. Provide beginning students with sentence starters. Remind intermediate students to include the basics of who, what, when, where, and why. Ask advanced students to list the basics of what happened, along with several vivid details to help readers imagine the events in action.

Informal Lesson Assessment

	Beginning	Intermediate	Advanced
Task	Write three events that took place as the United States grew in the early 1800s, and the results that followed, like the War of 1812 and the Indian Removal Act. Have students put the events in the correct sequence.	Provide fill-in-the-blank statements about events that took place as the United States grew in the early 1800s, and results that followed, like the War of 1812 and the Indian Removal Act.	Ask brief questions about events involved in the growth of the United States in the early 1800s, and results that followed, like the War of 1812 and the Indian Removal Act. Have students respond in complete sentences.
Below Expectations	• no correct sequence	• no accurate response	• incorrect ideas • incomplete sentences
Meets Expectations	• partially correct sequence	• some accurate responses	• several correct ideas • some complete sentences
Above Expectations	• correct sequence	• all responses are accurate	• correct ideas • complete sentences

Use with Chapter 9, Lesson 3

Build Background

Access Prior Knowledge

Make a K-W-L chart on the board. Write the words *Travel to the West* above it. Ask students what they already know about how and why people traveled to the American West. Encourage a review of concepts from the previous lessons, as well as any additional knowledge students might have. Then ask students what they still want to learn. Repeat and record their ideas. Return to this chart during the "Extend" activity.

- Before **Introduce**, p. 372
- 25 minutes

Lesson Vocabulary

Explain the vocabulary using the vocabulary cards for the lesson, brief definitions, and sketches when applicable. Ask students to paraphrase each definition. Explain that paraphrasing can involve changing a word, a phrase, or a few words, in each definition. After they paraphrase the definitions, have students quiz a partner by reading the paraphrased definitions and seeing whether the partner can identify the correct word. Ask them to change partners one or two times.

Additional Vocabulary Explain the words in the margin and provide examples of their uses. Point out the illustration of a *covered wagon* on page 375. Explain that the term *given up* is used to describe things that have been given away or thrown away by the owner.

Cognates As students read the lesson, you may want to point out cognates such as: **destiny/destino, dictator/dictador, independence/independencia, ocean/océano.**

covered wagon	missionaries
given up	Mormon
held off	prairie
lone	raised
mission	ranch

Build Fluency

Read aloud the following rhyme and point out the words that sound alike. Have students repeat it several times to develop oral language skills. Return to the rhyme throughout the lesson to help develop vocabulary, the skill of drawing conclusions, and lesson content.

> Texas was once a part of Mexico.
> Settlers wanted independence. Santa Anna said "no!"
> Crockett and other people fought until the end.
> Houston captured the **dictator**, and he gave up his land.
> The country almost reached from ocean to ocean.
> But westward expansion stirred strong emotions.
> **Manifest destiny** had a great cost.
> A war with Mexico began, and many lives were lost.
> The Mexican Cession gave us many new states.
> The country was growing at a very quick rate.
> United States bought California from Mexico.
> During the **gold rush** the population began to grow.

Success for English Learners ▪ 149

Scaffolding the Content

Preview the Lesson

Explain that during the 1830s and 1840s, Texas, California, and surrounding land and trails were important to the growth of our country. Direct students to the map on page 377. Read the names of territories and events. Ask students to read the corresponding dates and point to the regions they refer to on the map. Next, turn to the map on page 374. Explain that settlers used these trails to travel west. Provide hints about the trails and ask students to identify them.

- During **Teach**, pp. 372–379
- 20 minutes

Modify Instruction

Explain the following events to students. Pause after each section and help students find it on the blackline master to record notes. Assist students as they write conclusions under each heading.

Texas Independence

- Antonio Lopez de Santa Anna was the dictator of Mexico. A dictator has total control over a government. Santa Anna sent troops to the Alamo, a fort for Texans, because the Texans wanted to be free from Mexico. American pioneers like Davy Crockett and Jim Bowie held off Santa Anna's army for 13 days. Mexico won the battle. Texans formed an army led by Sam Houston.
- In 1836, the Texan army attacked and captured Santa Anna. Santa Anna gave Texas independence in return for his freedom. Texas became a state in 1845.

Trails West

- The Oregon Trail began in Missouri. Pioneers traveled west on this trail in covered wagons. This was a dangerous trip. People traveled in the spring to avoid winter storms. They walked because the wagons were full of supplies.
- The Mormon Trail was used by Mormons, or members of the Church of Jesus Christ of Latter Day Saints. In 1846, Brigham Young led settlers from Illinois to Utah.

Expanding Borders

- Many people in the United States believed in Manifest Destiny, an idea that the United States was meant to stretch from the Atlantic Ocean to the Pacific Ocean.
- In 1846, the United States declared war on Mexico over the border between Texas and Mexico. In the Treaty of Guadalupe Hidalgo, Mexico sold to the United States present-day California, Nevada, Utah, and parts of New Mexico, Arizona, Colorado, and Wyoming.

The California Gold Rush

- About 90,000 people from other states and countries rushed to California in 1849 to find gold.

Extend

Revisit the K-W-L chart students made during the "Access Prior Knowledge" activity. Ask them to fill out the last column with what they learned about how and why settlers traveled west. Ask them to share the questions they had and answers they found.

- After **Teach**, pp. 372–379
- 10 minutes

Name _____ Date _____

DIRECTIONS Write notes in the chart as your teacher reads. Write a conclusion about why each category was important for the growth of the United States in the 1830s and 1840s.

Growth of the United States in the 1830s and 1840s

Texas Independence

Conclusion:

Trails West

Conclusion:

Expanding Borders

Conclusion:

The California Gold Rush

Conclusion:

School-Home Connection Encourage students to take this page home to share with family members. They can use their notes to explain reasons the United States grew in size and number of states in the 1830s and 1840s.

Apply and Assess

Write a Journal Entry

Remind students that forty-niners came to California for gold from other states and countries. This includes the continents of South America, Europe, and Asia. Ask students to imagine that they are from one of these places. Have them use a classroom map to identify some of the physical features between their imaginary home and the state of California. Tell students they will have to describe these features and other details about their trip in their journal entries.

Model a journal entry by a forty-niner traveling from Ireland. Point to Ireland on a map and a few features between Ireland and California. Then write a journal entry on the board, for example: *I hope today is my last day on the ship from Ireland to the United States. It seems like a very long trip on the Atlantic Ocean. We have plenty of food, but each day, I am nervous that we will not have enough. Everyone is excited to reach land, but I think we still have a long way to go.*

Ask beginning students to write one or two sentences in their entries and to supplement them with sketches. Have intermediate students write three or four sentences. Ask advanced students to write five or more sentences.

- During **Close**, p. 379
- 30 minutes

Informal Lesson Assessment

	Beginning	Intermediate	Advanced
Task	Write the following on the board: *Texas independence, Declaration of Independence, Oregon Trail, Mormon Trail, Louisiana Purchase, California Gold Rush.* Tell students to circle the events that showed growth in the United States during the 1830s and 1840s.	Ask: *How did the United States grow in the 1830s and 1840s?* Students may respond using words, phrases, or a map and verbal descriptions.	Ask: *How did the United States grow in the 1830s and 1840s?* Students should respond using several complete sentences, and they may use maps.
Below Expectations	• no answer is correct	• no answer is comprehensible and/or correct	• incorrect ideas • no complete sentences • many errors
Meets Expectations	• some answers are correct	• some answers are comprehensible and/or correct	• appropriate ideas • some complete sentences • some errors
Above Expectations	• all answers are correct	• all answers are comprehensible and correct	• appropriate ideas • complete sentences • few errors

Use with Chapter 9, Lesson 4

Build Background

Access Prior Knowledge

Ask students to think of three inventions they use that make a job faster, cheaper, and easier. Give the example of a copy machine you use at school. Using it is faster and easier than making copies by hand like people did in the past. It is also cheaper to use the copy machine than it would be to hire a company to print materials. Ask students to share their responses and post them on the board under the columns: *Name of invention, Faster, Easier,* and *Cheaper.*

• Before **Introduce**, p. 380
• 20 minutes

Lesson Vocabulary

Explain the vocabulary words to students using vocabulary cards, paraphrased definitions, examples, and illustrations from the text. Ask for a volunteer to come to the front. Show the volunteer one of the words so that no one else can see. Have another student ask a yes or no question, such as: *Is this a person?* Have the volunteer answer the question and let the student guess at the word. Continue playing until all the words have been used twice. Extend the game by adding words from previous chapters.

Additional Vocabulary Explain the phrases in the margin and provide examples of their uses. Explain that all of the words are related to new inventions and the growth caused by these inventions during the Industrial Revolution. For example, explain that the *steam engine* and *railroad* helped people move goods from one city to another and helped make cities and industries grow.

elevation	railroad
factories	reaper
large-scale	steam engine
mass production	textiles
plow	upstream

Cognates As students read the lesson, you may want to point out cognates such as: **elevation/elevación, invention/invención, obstacle/obstáculo, revolution/revolución.**

Build Fluency

Read aloud the following rhyme and point out the words that sound alike. Have students repeat it several times to develop oral language skills. Return to the rhyme throughout the lesson to help develop vocabulary, the skill of drawing conclusions, and lesson content.

People in textile mills spun cloth,
Canals moved boats using a system of **locks**.
Locomotives and steam engines quickly replaced
Ways people traveled and shipped goods in past days.
The inventions that came with the **Industrial Revolution**
Gave businesses many time-saving solutions.
They changed life in the United States
And made the country's power great.

Scaffolding the Content

Preview the Lesson

Have students use the pictures on pages 380–384 to identify inventions described in the lesson. Have them work in groups to explain one or two inventions to the class. Beginning students in each group can state the name of the invention; intermediate students can tell how the invention made work easier, faster, or cheaper; and advanced students can explain how the invention improved older technology. Explain that students will learn more about new inventions that changed the United States.

• During **Teach**, pp. 380–385
• 30 minutes

Modify Instruction

Explain the following ideas and inventions. Pause after each bullet and help students identify the heading on the blackline master page to record notes.

Inventions

- **National Road** It was difficult to ship things over mountains, so Congress voted to build the National Road in 1818. The road connected Maryland to West Virginia.
- **Canals** Canals were built to connect waterways. The canals moved boats through different elevations using locks, or sections of water held by gates.
- **Steam Engines** The steam engine was invented in Britain. Steamboats could travel upstream and faster than older boats. Steam engines were also used in locomotives, or railroad engines.
- **Cotton Gin** Eli Whitney invented the cotton gin, which removed seeds from cotton. This made it faster and easier to process cotton, so plantations produced more cotton. Plantations then needed more slaves to work in the cotton fields.
- **Interchangeable Parts** Whitney also invented interchangeable parts, or parts that are exactly alike. Interchangeable parts let people use a part of one machine in another machine. This development led to mass production, or producing many goods at one time.
- **Mechanical Reaper** Cyrus McCormick invented a mechanical reaper for harvesting grain. Farmers could cut the same amount of wheat in one day as they could in two weeks with hand tools.

The Industrial Revolution

- Inventions allowed people to use machines to make goods quickly and cheaply. This change was called the Industrial Revolution, which began in Britain.
- In Britain, machines were used to spin thread and weave textiles, or cloth in factories called mills. Britain kept these machines a secret, until a man named Samuel Slater came to the United States. He built the first American textile mill in Rhode Island.

Extend

State a conclusion about inventions in this lesson, such as: *This connected waterways without obstacles, so goods could be transported on water more quickly and easily.* Have students identify the invention. Then give students the opportunity to state a conclusion about inventions in the lesson and inventions that they use.

• After **Teach**, pp. 380–385
• 10 minutes

Name _____ Date _____

DIRECTIONS Use your notes to fill in the chart. In the left column, write the name and purpose of each invention. In the right column, write one conclusion about how each invention changed life in the United States. In the bottom box, write a summary about how the Industrial Revolution affected the United States.

Invention (include name, purpose, inventor)	One Conclusion (about how it changed life in the United States)

Industrial Revolution

School-Home Connection Encourage students to take this page home to share with family members. They can use their notes to explain how inventions changed life in the United States and led to the Industrial Revolution.

Unit 4, Chapter 9, Lesson 4

Apply and Assess

Make an Advertisement

Help students brainstorm information to include in their advertisements. Review the names of inventions, their functions, and why people would want to buy them. Next, discuss advertisements that students have seen in magazines or on television. Ask them to recall phrases from ads, such as: *Everyone loves this product!* Record some phrases on the board.

• During **Close**, p. 385
• 20 minutes

Ask beginning students to include two lines of text in their ad, one with the name of the product and one with a reason to buy it. Ask intermediate students to include three lines of text, including the product, one reason to buy it, and one more line that would interest a reader. Ask advanced students to include four or more lines, including the product, one reason to buy it, and two more lines to grab the reader's attention.

Informal Lesson Assessment

	Beginning	**Intermediate**	**Advanced**
Task	Provide a list of inventions and a list of ways they changed life in the United States during the Industrial Revolution. Have students match the inventions with the changes they caused.	Ask students to list inventions and ways they changed life in the United States during the Industrial Revolution. Ask them to use words and phrases.	Ask students to list inventions and ways they changed life in the United States during the Industrial Revolution. Ask them to use complete sentences.
Below Expectations	• no answer is comprehensible and/or correct	• no answer is comprehensible and/or correct	• incorrect ideas • no complete sentences • many errors
Meets Expectations	• some answers are comprehensible and/or correct	• some answers are comprehensible and/or correct	• appropriate ideas • some incomplete sentences • some errors
Above Expectations	• all answers are comprehensible and correct	• all answers are comprehensible and correct	• appropriate ideas • complete sentences • few errors

Unit 5 Opener

Developing Academic Language

A key skill for understanding social studies is generalizing. When students generalize, they do not rely on former knowledge. Instead, they must understand the facts in a given passage and combine them to make a single, broad statement that expresses the sum total of those facts. Students can learn to generalize by recognizing and using words that signal generalizations and by following a step-by-step process.

Introduce Generalizing

Write the word *generalize.* Explain that to generalize is to form a statement that is true about several details. Note that some words signal generalizing, such as: *most, many, some, all, generally,* and *usually.* Write these words.

- Before **Generalize**, p. 398
- 20 minutes

Note that forming generalizations is also a process. Write and read these steps:

1. Read.
2. Find the facts.
3. Generalize by writing or saying something about the information.

Practice

Write this paragraph, and read it aloud.

> My friend Kim has a dog. My friend Mehmet has a cat. My friend Robyn has a pet rabbit. Even my friend Steve has a pet goldfish.

Have students identify the facts: *My friend Kim has a dog; my friend Mehmet has a cat; my friend Robyn has a rabbit; my friend Steve has a goldfish.* Then have students combine these facts to form a generalization. Repeat it, and record it on the board:

> Many of my friends have pets.

Apply

Draw the following chart, and have partners copy it onto a piece of paper. Write and read this paragraph: *Some houses have porches, but others do not. Some houses have two bathrooms, and some have one. Some houses have a garage, and some do not. Some houses are brick and some are wood. Some houses are small, and some are big.* Have students complete the chart. Discuss, and agree on the best generalization: *All the houses are different.*

Facts

↓

Generalization

Success for English Learners ■ 157

Build Background

Use with Chapter 10, Lesson 1

Access Prior Knowledge

Invite students to recall the differences between Northern and Southern states. Divide students into groups. Post chart paper at stations around the room, and assign a topic to each station: *land, homes, jobs,* and *problems forming a government.* For each topic, have each group write sentences telling how the Northern and Southern states were different (i.e., how each region divided land). Have students move to each station, read what the previous group wrote, and add a sentence. Read aloud responses for each station.

- Before **Introduce**, p. 404
- 35 minutes

Lesson Vocabulary

Use information from prior lessons and concrete examples to explain **sectionalism, industry, free state, slave state, tariff, states' rights,** and **fugitive.** Next, have students record hints for each word, by noting whether it is a person, place, thing, idea, or by listing things the word makes them think of. Finally, have students take turns reading hints and calling on other students to identify the word.

Additional Vocabulary Use context clues to explain the words in the margin. Tell students that the word *Union* is used to mean the United States in this lesson. Add that in this lesson, the word *admitted* means "given permission by Congress to join the Union."

admitted	outlawed
compromise	roughly
federal	turn in
immigrants	Union

Cognates As students read the lesson, you may wish to point out cognates such as: **diverse/diverso, federal/federal, industry/industria, union/unión.**

Build Fluency

Read aloud the following rhyme, and point out words that sound alike. Have students repeat it several times to develop oral language skills. Return to the rhyme throughout the lesson to help develop vocabulary, generalizing skills, and lesson content.

> Northern states had **industries,**
> Southern states plantations.
> Southern states used slavery,
> This caused conflict in the nation.
>
> Northern factory owners liked the **tariff.**
> Rich Southerners did not want to pay.
> This caused more **sectionalism**
> Because each region wanted its way.
>
> Northern and Southern states
> Wanted equal power in the Senate.
> When new states joined the Union
> The balance of power was upset.

Scaffolding the Content

Preview the Lesson

Have students preview the illustrations, captions, and questions at the end of each section. Ask them to try to find three to five topics that caused disagreements between Northern and Southern states. Remind them to look for words they already know as they complete this activity.

• During **Teach**, pp. 404–409
• 30 minutes

Modify Instruction

Highlight the issues that caused conflict between the North and South: *slavery, trade, new states, trade,* and *government*. Write these categories on the board before reading each section, and ask students to listen for those words or phrases so they can complete the corresponding sections of the blackline master.

Different Regions By the middle of the 1800s, the United States had three main regions—the southern, northern, and western regions. They were all very different. The government often made decisions that were good for only one region. This is called *sectionalism*. Northern states had different industries. Immigrants, or people from other countries, came to work in factories there. Farms were small. Southern states made most of their money from plantations. Plantations needed a lot of workers.

Division Over Slavery By 1804, all Northern states made slavery illegal. Enslaved Africans worked on Southern plantations. Plantations and slavery grew. The Mason-Dixon line between Maryland and Pennsylvania divided free states and slave states. Missouri wanted to join the Union as a slave state. This would give slave states more votes in the Senate. In the Missouri Compromise, Congress admitted Missouri as a slave state and Maine as a free state. There would still be a balance of power.

Different Ideas Northern and Southern states disagreed about trade. Northern factory owners needed Americans to buy their products. They wanted a tariff, or tax, on European products. This would make European goods more expensive. Wealthy Southerners bought products from Europe. They did not want the tariff. President Andrew Jackson believed the federal government could set tariffs. Vice President Calhoun believed in states' rights and thought states should decide. Congress passed the tariff in 1832. Sectionalism, or regional loyalty, grew.

More Divisions The United States got more land after the Mexican-American War. The government had to decide whether to create new free states or slave states. California wanted to join the Union as a free state. This would give free states more votes in the Senate. Henry Clay thought of the Compromise of 1850. It made California a free state. It also let people in Utah and New Mexico decide if they wanted slavery, and said that all citizens must return escaped slaves to their owners. The Missouri Compromise had outlawed slavery in Kansas and Nebraska territories. In 1854, Congress let people who lived there decide what to do. People for and against slavery moved to Kansas and fought. Kansas became a free state.

Extend

Ask students to review the blackline master and write a generalization for each category. Have them use compound sentences, such as: *The Northern states believed _____, but the Southern states believed _____.*

• After **Teach**, pp. 404–409
• 10 minutes

Name _____ Date _____

DIRECTIONS Listen as your teacher reads. Take notes about the differences between Northern and Southern states.

	Northern States	Southern States
Slavery		
New States		
Trade		
Government		

School-Home Connection Encourage students to take this page home to share with family members. They can use their notes to explain the conflicts between Northern and Southern states.

Apply and Assess

Make a Chart

Remind students that a chart can show how items in different categories, or groups, are alike. Tell students they will make a chart to show differences between the Northern and Southern states. Tell them that they may use the diagram on the blackline master page for ideas, but they need to add categories, and change the form slightly to make their chart original. Discuss ways to change the chart.

• During **Close**, p. 409
• 30 minutes

Explain that students may use categories listed in the "Access Prior Knowledge" activity and at the beginning of the "Modify" activity in this lesson. Ask beginning students to choose one or two categories, intermediate students to choose two or three, and advanced students to list three or more.

Then ask students to write information in the chart that tells the differences between the Northern and Southern states for each category. Finally, have students present their charts in small groups. They may briefly show the chart and state a few differences they included.

Informal Lesson Assessment

	Beginning	Intermediate	Advanced
Task	Provide sentence strips about beliefs and needs of the states during the 1800s. Have students classify the statements as describing Northern states or describing Southern states.	Provide fill-in-the-blank statements about beliefs and needs of people in Northern and Southern states during the 1800s. Design the statements so that students must use key words from the lesson to complete them.	Ask students to write several sentences comparing beliefs and needs of people in Northern and Southern states during the 1800s.
Below Expectations	• no answer is comprehensible and/or correct	• no answer is comprehensible and/or correct	• incorrect ideas • no complete sentences • many errors
Meets Expectations	• some answers are comprehensible and/or correct	• some answers are comprehensible and/or correct	• appropriate ideas • some incomplete sentences • some errors
Above Expectations	• all answers are comprehensible and correct	• all answers are comprehensible and correct	• appropriate ideas • complete sentences • few errors

Use with Lesson 2, Chapter 10

Build Background

Access Prior Knowledge

Have students discuss what they know about slavery and people who supported and opposed it. Have student pairs list at least two groups of people that supported slavery and two groups that did not. Mention that people's opinion on slavery often depended on their views about government and trade, where they lived, and their religion.

- Before **Introduce**, p. 410
- 30 minutes

Lesson Vocabulary

Explain the two parts of the compound term **Underground Railroad** by reading the fourth paragraph of page 413 where the term is boldfaced. Have students follow along. Explain that *underground* sometimes means secret or illegal, and ask why this might be the case (things that are underground are hidden). Next, ask student pairs to create a concept web of the Underground Railroad. The concept web should contain related words and images. Model how to begin the concept web on the board, and elicit one or two related words from volunteers.

Additional Vocabulary Explain the words in the margin, and provide examples of their uses. Say that *run away* means escape, and a *runaway* is a person who escapes. Explain that a *conductor* usually means the person who drives a train, but in this lesson it is a person who helped move and hide enslaved people along the Underground Railroad.

conductor	resist
equality	runaway
free land	sentiments
journal	sojourner
preach	view

Cognates As students read the lesson, you may wish to point out cognates such as: **convention/convención, problem/problema, resist/resistir, route/ruta.**

Build Fluency

Read aloud the following rhyme, and point out words that sound alike. Have students repeat it several times to develop oral language skills. Return to the rhyme throughout the lesson to help develop vocabulary, generalizing skills, and lesson content.

> Slavery was something many groups resisted.
> "Treat all people equally," women insisted.
>
> Dred Scott tried to win his freedom in court.
> But the legal system did not give him support.
>
> The **Underground Railroad** helped enslaved people flee.
> Abolitionists and former slaves helped set them free.

162 ■ Success for English Learners

Scaffolding the Content

Preview the Lesson

Read the summary on page 414. Then help students identify groups who resisted slavery by scanning the story on page 410, the section headings, and topic sentences. Have students work in groups. Advanced students can scan the story, intermediate students can look for topic sentences, and beginning students can read the section headings to find answers.

• During **Teach**, pp. 410–414
• 20 minutes

Modify Instruction

Read the details about the groups that opposed slavery. Have students take notes that include the names of each group, the names of people associated with the group, and one or two important facts. Have them use their notes to complete the blackline master.

Enslaved Africans
Dred Scott was an enslaved African. When his owner died, he tried to win his freedom in court because he lived on free land at one time. In 1857, the Supreme Court voted not to give him his freedom. This decision upset many people.

White Northerners
William Lloyd Garrison founded the American Antislavery Society. Other white northerners joined the abolitionists and the Underground Railroad.

Women
Women did not have the same rights as men during the 1800s. In 1848, Elizabeth Cady Stanton and Lucretia Mott wrote the *Declaration of Rights and Sentiments*. This document said that all Americans should be treated equally. In 1852, Harriet Beecher Stowe wrote *Uncle Tom's Cabin*. This book told how enslaved workers were mistreated. People in the North stopped ignoring slavery.

Free African Americans
In 1827, Samuel Cornish and John Russworm started the first newspaper owned by African Americans. It was called *Freedom's Journal*. Frederick Douglass escaped slavery and became famous for writing and speaking against slavery. Isabella Van Wagener, who changed her name to Sojourner Truth, escaped slavery and traveled. She preached to people and spoke out against slavery.

Supporters of the Underground Railroad
The Underground Railroad was a set of routes, mostly from Southern to Northern states and Canada, to help enslaved people escape. Workers along these routes were called conductors. They were mostly free African Americans and white abolitionists. Harriet Tubman was an African American who escaped slavery and worked as a conductor along the Underground Railroad.

Extend

Play "Who Am I?" Think of a person who resisted slavery. Call on students to ask a yes or no question, such as: *Was this person a woman?* Allow students to guess after three hints by raising their hands. You may also call on students to see if they can guess.

• After **Teach**, pp. 410–414
• 10 minutes

Name _____ Date _____

DIRECTIONS As your teacher reads, listen for the names of people in each group. Write the name of a person, a group, and one or two facts in the chart.

Person or People	Group	Facts about the Person
1.		
2.		
3.		
4.		
5.		
6.		
7.		
8.		

School-Home Connection Encourage students to take this page home to share with family members. They can use their notes to explain different groups and individuals who resisted slavery in the United States.

Apply and Assess

Make a Poster

Have students work in small groups to make posters about the work of the Underground Railroad. Tell students in advance that they will explain their poster to the class.

• During **Close**, p. 414
• 30 minutes

Have students label each part of the poster, and write a brief explanation about it. Divide the work evenly by giving students different tasks. Beginning students may draw and label, intermediate students may label and write brief descriptions, and advanced students may write brief descriptions and take the lead while explaining the poster to the class.

Informal Lesson Assessment

	Beginning	**Intermediate**	**Advanced**
Task	Write brief statements about individuals and events involved with groups that resisted slavery in the 1800s. Separately, write the names of the groups. Have students identify which group each statement describes.	Ask students to list groups that resisted slavery in the 1800s and identify one event and one person associated with each. Have them use words and phrases.	Ask students to write one or two sentences about several groups that resisted slavery in the 1800s. Sentences should include the names of people and events associated with each group.
Below Expectations	• no answer is comprehensible and/or correct	• no answer is comprehensible or correct	• incorrect ideas • no complete sentences • many errors
Meets Expectations	• some answers are comprehensible and/or correct	• some answers are comprehensible and correct	• correct ideas • some incomplete sentences • some errors
Above Expectations	• all answers are comprehensible and correct	• all answers are comprehensible and correct	• appropriate ideas • complete sentences • few errors

Success for English Learners

Use with Chapter 10, Lesson 3

Build Background

Access Prior Knowledge

Review issues between the Northern and Southern states. Then write the question: *What can happen when two sides of a country want different things?* Ask student pairs to think of three possible results to the conflicts over slavery, trade, government, and new states. Then have them choose the result they believe really happened in the conflict between Northern and Southern states. Tell them to save the list and prediction for the "Extend" activity.

- Before **Introduce**, p. 416
- 30 minutes

Lesson Vocabulary

Explain vocabulary words to students using the vocabulary cards, illustrations, and brief definitions. Next, ask students to complete a fill-in-the-blank exercise to demonstrate their knowledge.

> *Northern and Southern states in this country had conflicts. These conflicts led to a _____. The Southern states wanted to _____, or separate, from the Union. This group was called the _____. States near the division between the North and the South, or _____, did not know which side to choose. The war began when Confederate soldiers fired their _____, or large guns, on the Union soldiers at Fort Sumter.*

debates
election
in Union hands
military force
mounted guns
nominate
raid
run against
spread
torn

Additional Vocabulary Explain the words in the margin, and provide examples of their uses. Tell students that *spread* is a synonym for "grow." Point out that *run against* means to compete with in an election.

Cognates As students read the lesson, you may wish to point out cognates such as: **debate/debate, divide/dividir, election/elección, nation/nación.**

Build Fluency

Read aloud the following rhyme, and point out words that sound alike. Have students repeat it several times to develop oral language skills. Return to the rhyme throughout the lesson to help develop vocabulary, generalizing skills, and lesson content.

> Lincoln did not want slavery to spread to the West.
> Douglas felt that the states should decide what's best.
> Lincoln lost to Douglas when they ran for Senate.
> In 1860 Lincoln won the election for President.
> The Southern states started to **secede**, or leave, the Union.
> After the attack on Sumter war was the only option.

Scaffolding the Content

Preview the Lesson

Have students use illustrations and section headings in the lesson to identify main ideas in the lesson. Provide them with questions that can be answered with key words, such as the following: *1) What debates made Abraham Lincoln famous? 2) Who won the election of 1860? 3) Name a few states that belonged to the Union, the Confederacy, and border states. 4) At what fort did the United States Civil War begin?*

• During **Teach**, pp. 416–421
• 25 minutes

Modify Instruction

Read the following time line. Tell students that it shows events that caused the nation to break apart. After you say each date, have students record corresponding events on the blackline master. Then revisit each year, and ask students to form a generalization about why it was important.

1846 Abraham Lincoln is elected to Congress. Later, he begins the Republican political party to fight the spread, or growth, of slavery.

1858 Lincoln runs against Stephen A. Douglas for Senate. They have debates about slavery. Douglas believes the states should make their own laws about slavery. Lincoln wants to stop slavery from spreading to the West. Lincoln loses the election. Lincoln becomes famous because of the debates.

1859 John Brown leads a raid, or attack, on a government building full of guns. He wants to give the guns to enslaved people to fight for freedom. The raiders, or attackers, are either killed or captured. This divides the country even more because Southerners think Northerners were trying to end slavery.

1860 Abraham Lincoln wins the election for president. He is a Republican. At this time, the Democratic Party has two branches, or parts. Northern Democrats believe states should make their own laws about slavery. Southern Democrats want to protect slavery. When Lincoln wins, many Southern states wanted to secede, or leave the Union.

1861 Alabama, Florida, Georgia, Louisiana, Mississippi, and Texas secedes from the Union. South Carolina had seceded one year earlier. President Lincoln tells the Southern states that he will not use military force against them. However, when Confederate soldiers attack Fort Sumter, he asks Americans to join the Union army to fight against the Confederacy. The civil war begins in the United States.

Extend

Have students refer to the list of possible results from the "Access Prior Knowledge" activity. Ask them to check their lists. Tell students to work in pairs to make a brief time line of important events. Have them place a star by any events on the time line that they predicted.

• After **Teach**, pp. 416–421
• 15 minutes

Success for English Learners ▪ 167

Name _____ Date _____

DIRECTIONS Listen as your teacher reads the time line. Write information about each date, and then write a sentence about why each year was important.

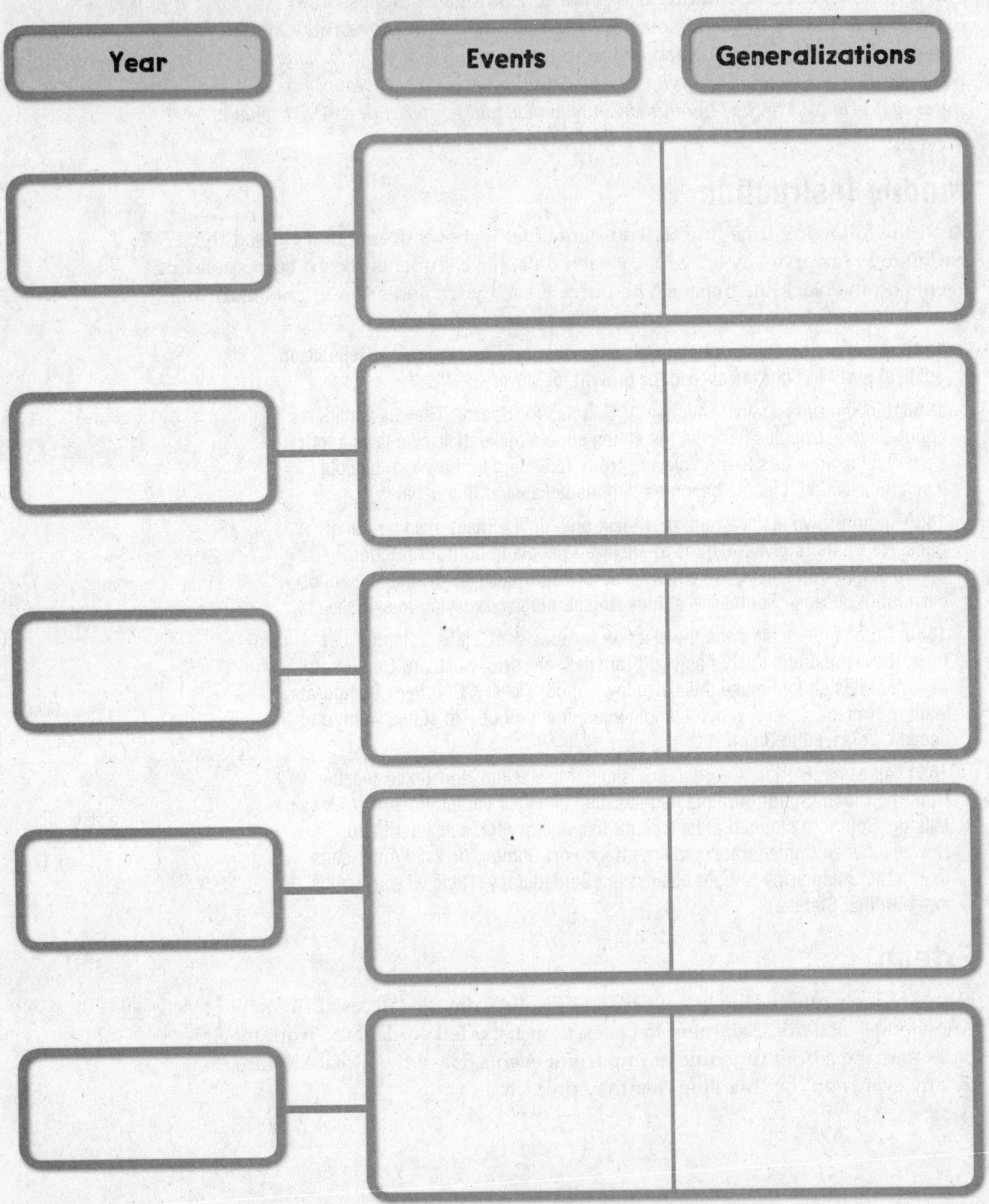

School-Home Connection Encourage students to take this page home to share with family members. They can use their notes to explain events that led to the Civil War in the United States.

Apply and Assess

Write a Newspaper Headline

Remind students that a newspaper headline is the title of an article. Explain that headlines are very short, and they include key words that tell the most important part of the story. Post these examples, and ask students to choose which one they think is better:

> *Lincoln Loses Senate Election to Douglas* or *Douglas Wins Election*
>
> *Brown's Raid in West Virginia Fails* or *Raid in West Virginia*

• During **Close**, p. 421
• 30 minutes

Have students write two to three facts that are important about the election of 1860, including people, issues, and political parties involved. Then ask them to use these points to write headlines in phrases. Give beginning students a few headlines they can use as models. Help intermediate students by recording a word bank on the board. Ask advanced students to produce original headlines without using the word bank.

Informal Lesson Assessment

	Beginning	Intermediate	Advanced
Task	Give students brief multiple-choice questions about events that caused the nation to break apart and led to the Civil War. Have them choose the correct answer.	Ask students what caused the nation to break apart and led to the Civil War. Have them list major events in a time sequence using phrases and single words.	Ask students to write a paragraph about events that caused the nation to break apart and led to the Civil War. The paragraph should include the names of events and their causes.
Below Expectations	• no answer is comprehensible and/or correct	• no answer is comprehensible and/or correct	• incorrect ideas • no complete sentences • many errors
Meets Expectations	• some answers are comprehensible and/or correct	• some answers are comprehensible and/or correct	• appropriate ideas • some incomplete sentences • some errors
Above Expectations	• all answers are comprehensible and correct	• all answers are comprehensible and correct	• appropriate ideas • complete sentences • few errors

Use with Chapter 10, Lesson 4

Build Background

Access Prior Knowledge

Make two columns on the board called "Then" and "Now." Ask volunteers to share facts about Northern and Southern states in the 1800s. Examples include: *Southern states seceded, the country was divided into two parts*, and *slavery existed*. Next have students note facts about the present. For example: *Northern and Southern states are all part of one country*, and *slavery no longer exists*. Explain that the Civil War helped cause some of these changes.

- Before **Introduce**, p. 424
- 30 minutes

Lesson Vocabulary

Use context clues to explain the meanings of the vocabulary words. Ask students to make story strips to demonstrate one vocabulary word. Have student pairs guess the word used on each other's story strip. Let students change partners to see a variety of scenarios. Allow beginning students to draw the story strip and write the word on the back. Have intermediate students write short phrases below each picture to explain events. Ask advanced students to write a sentence that explains events.

Additional Vocabulary Explain the words in the margin, and provide examples of their uses. Explain that *freed* and *trained* are verbs written in the past tense and used as adjectives. In this lesson, *freed* means "those who became free," and *trained* means "those who trained or practiced."

battle lines	regiment
counting on	retreat
freed	scout
invade	spies
prey	trained

Cognates As students read the lesson, you may wish to point out cognates such as: **hospital/hospital, invade/invadir, prejudice/prejuicio, victory/victoria.**

Build Fluency

Read aloud the following rhyme, and point out words that sound alike. Have students repeat it several times to develop oral language skills. Return to the rhyme throughout the lesson to help develop vocabulary, generalization skills, and lesson content.

> President Lincoln wanted to keep the states united. "I want to **emancipate**, or free the slaves," he later decided.
>
> In order to win the war, **strategies** were planned. The North would block Southern ports. The South would defend their land.
>
> African American soldiers faced **prejudice** but fought well.
> Women couldn't fight but ran businesses and hospitals.

Scaffolding the Content

Preview the Lesson

Show students how to get information from questions. Post the question: *Why did the Northern and Southern states fight a Civil War?* Have students work in pairs to discover a fact that the question reveals. (Northern and Southern states fought a Civil War.) Next, have mixed-proficiency groups use the questions at the end of each section to note important facts from the lesson. Require students to produce one to four facts.

• During **Teach**, pp. 424–429
• 25 minutes

Modify Instruction

Read the following events of the Civil War's early years. After you review each event, ask students to record details on the blackline master. Then help students write a generalization about each event.

1. **Event: The Union and Confederate states planned strategies.**
   - The Union wanted to weaken and invade the South. Lincoln planned to blockade Southern ports to stop delivery of weapons and supplies from Europe to the South.
   - The Confederate wanted to defend their lands. Southern leaders thought a long war would make Northerners tired of fighting.

2. **Event: The Union and Confederate states fought battles.**
   - The Battle of Bull Run was the first major battle of the Civil War. Stonewall Jackson led the Confederate soldiers to victory.
   - The Battle of Antietam was fought in Maryland. General Robert E. Lee led the Confederate soldiers. Neither side won. Many soldiers from both sides were killed.

3. **Event: Lincoln wrote the Emancipation Proclamation.**
   - Lincoln wrote the Emancipation Proclamation. It freed enslaved people in Confederate states, but not enslaved people in the border states and areas controlled by the Union.

4. **Event: Women helped in the war.**
   - Only men could join the army in the North and South, but women found ways to help. Dorothea Dix and Clara Barton worked as nurses for the Union. Sally Tompkins ran a hospital for Confederate soldiers. Belle Boyd spied for the Confederacy.

5. **Event: African Americans fought in the war.**
   - About 180,000 African Americans were in the Union army. They were victims of prejudice from people in the North and South. This means some people did not like African Americans because of their color and background.

Extend

Have students revisit the questions at the end of each section. Have them use their notes to form answers.

• After **Teach**, pp. 424–429
• 10 minutes

Success for English Learners ▪ 171

Name _____ Date _____

DIRECTIONS Listen as your teacher reads about events in the Civil War. Write the name and details of each event. Your teacher will help you write a generalization about each event.

Event	Details	Generalization
1.		
2.		
3.		
4.		
5.		

School-Home Connection Encourage students to take this page home to share with family members. They can use their notes to explain early events of the Civil War of the United States.

Apply and Assess

Write a Letter

Help students brainstorm thoughts and questions they may have for an imaginary family member fighting for the Union during the Civil War. Post one or two examples of questions and thoughts, and read them aloud. Examples may include: *Who do you think will win the war?* or *I hope you and the other soldiers have enough food.* Ask students to write two or three questions and thoughts they would want to say to a relative fighting in the war. Call on volunteers to share their ideas and copy them on the board.

- During **Close**, p. 429
- 30 minutes

Next, write a brief letter of your own. Read it to students and tell them to use the structure of the greeting, body, and signature as they write their own letters.

Have students write their letters. Allow beginning students to copy statements from the board, but have them add one or two original thoughts. Tell intermediate students they may use parts of sentences and change or add to them so their letter contains original ideas and questions. Ask advanced students to use only original wording.

Informal Lesson Assessment

	Beginning	Intermediate	Advanced
Task	Provide true and false statements about events that occurred during the early years of the Civil War in the United States. Have students identify the statements as true or false.	Provide true and false statements about events that occurred during the early years of the Civil War in the United States. Have students identify them as true or false, and correct the false statements.	Provide true and false statements about events that occurred in the early years of the Civil War in the United States. Have students identify them as true or false, and rewrite false statements to make them true.
Below Expectations	• no answer is comprehensible and/or correct	• no answer is comprehensible and/or correct	• incorrect ideas • no complete sentences • many errors
Meets Expectations	• some answers are comprehensible and/or correct	• some answers are comprehensible and/or correct	• appropriate ideas • some incomplete sentences • some errors
Above Expectations	• all answers are comprehensible and correct	• all answers are comprehensible and correct	• appropriate ideas • complete sentences • few errors

Use with Chapter 10, Lesson 5

Build Background

Access Prior Knowledge

Ask students to complete a K-W-L chart about the Civil War. Have them work in small groups to list what they know about the war, including the causes, early battles, and other events. Next, have students record what they want to know about the war. They may scan captions and headings in the lesson for ideas. Specify that each student should record one idea in both categories using words, phrases, or sentences.

- Before **Introduce**, p. 432
- 35 minutes

Lesson Vocabulary

Explain the vocabulary words to students using vocabulary cards, key words, and brief definitions. Point out that the word **address** has multiple meanings. Ask students to form a question using each word. Then have them ask the question to a partner. Model the activity with a student volunteer using questions like the following: *Do you know the **address** of the White House in Washington, D.C.? At the beginning of the school year, why does the principal of the school give an **address** to the students?* Ask partners to answer the questions aloud.

Additional Vocabulary Explain the words in the margin and provide examples of their uses. Mention that the phrase *laid siege* means "to surround and attack." Point out that the word *general* has a double meaning, and in this lesson it is used as a title for a leader in the army.

bloodshed	laid siege
cut off	march
effective	tore up
general	wounded
ideals	vain

Cognates As students read the lesson, you may wish to point out cognates such as: **assassinate/asesinar, destroy/destruir, liberty/libertad, victory/victoria.**

Build Fluency

Read aloud the following rhyme, and point out words that sound alike. Have students repeat it several times to develop oral language skills. Return to the rhyme throughout the lesson to help develop vocabulary, generalization skills, and lesson content.

> The South had the great General Lee,
> But General Grant led the Union to victory!
> Gettysburg was the turning point of the war,
> Would the Union stay together from shore to shore?
> Sherman's March to the Sea destroyed so much.
> The South had few supplies and soon gave up.
> At Appomattox Court House, Lee officially surrendered.
> This day in history must always be remembered.

Scaffolding the Content

Preview the Lesson

Read and post the What to Know Question on page 432. Tell students to listen as you read the summary on page 437, and see whether they can identify a few important events that help answer the question. Examples include Union victories at Vicksburg and Gettysburg, damage to the South caused by Sherman's March to the Sea, Lee's surrender to Grant. Tell students that this lesson will explain why these events were important to the Union's victory in the Civil War.

• During **Teach**, pp. 432–437
• 30 minutes

Modify Instruction

Read about the important people and events related to the victory of the Union over the Confederacy. Have students take notes on the blackline master page. Then ask students to work with a partner to form a generalization about the Union's victory.

Ulysses S. Grant General Grant helped the Union win because he was as strong as General Lee, who led Confederate soldiers. Grant led Union soldiers to a victory at Vicksburg. This gave the Union army control of the Mississippi River, which divided the Confederacy into two parts. The Confederacy won a battle at Chancellorsville, Virginia.

The Battle of Gettysburg This battle was a turning point for the Union soldiers. After this battle it seemed like the Union could win the Civil War. Lee's army went back to Virginia. Thousands of Union and Confederate soldiers were killed or wounded.

The Gettysburg Address On November 18, 1863, President Lincoln gave the Gettysburg Address. This address, or short speech, became very famous. It was about freedom, equality, and honoring soldiers who died defending their ideals, or beliefs.

Sherman's March Union General William Tecumseh Sherman was ordered to march from Chattanooga, Tennessee to Atlanta, Georgia. After they left Atlanta, Sherman's men went toward Savannah, Georgia. On their way, now called Sherman's March to the Sea, they burned homes and stores, destroyed crops, and tore up railroad tracks.

Lee's Surrender Grant's army beat Lee's army in the North because Lee ran out of soldiers and supplies. Grant and Lee met at Appomattox Court House where Lee surrendered. The Civil War was over, and the Union had stayed together. More than 600,000 soldiers died during the war. The South was left in ruins. Five days later, Lincoln was assassinated, or murdered, by John Wilkes Booth, a Confederate supporter.

Extend

Have students revisit their K-W-L charts. They should first look at the column where they listed questions and star any that were answered. Next, they should write the answers to these questions in the column that represents what they learned.

• After **Teach**, pp. 432–437
• 15 minutes

Name _____ Date _____

DIRECTIONS Listen as your teacher reads. Write the names of people and events in the first column and important details in the second column. Then work with a partner to write a generalization about the Union victory in the Civil War.

Person or Event	Details
1.	
2.	
3.	
4.	
5.	

Generalization about the Union victory:

School-Home Connection Encourage students to take this page home to share with family members. They can use their notes to explain how the Union won the Civil War.

Apply and Assess

Write a Poem

Remind students that poems do not always need to rhyme or have complete sentences. Brainstorm thoughts about soldiers who fought in the Civil War of the United States. Ask questions, such as: *What was difficult for these soldiers? Why did they fight? How did this war change their lives and ours?* Write ideas on the board. Then write a poem using the details you recorded. Form phrases or sentences. An example poem could read:

• During **Close**, p. 437
• 30 minutes

Fighting bravely
In the cold
In the rain
In the snow
Thank you soldiers
We remember.

Next, ask students to write their own poem to honor soldiers who fought in the Civil War. Beginning students may write two to three lines, intermediate students may write three to four lines, and advanced students should write six or seven lines.

Informal Lesson Assessment

	Beginning	**Intermediate**	**Advanced**
Task	Give students a list of details that describe people and events that led to the Union victory over the Confederacy. Have students identify the names of the people and events described.	Give students a list of people and events that led to the Union victory over the Confederacy. Have students write a few details about the people and events in phrases or short sentences.	Give students a list of people and events that led to the Union victory over the Confederacy. Have students describe the people and events using complete sentences.
Below Expectations	• no answer is comprehensible and/or correct	• no answer is comprehensible and/or correct	• incorrect ideas • no complete sentences • many errors
Meets Expectations	• some answers are comprehensible and/or correct	• some answers are comprehensible and/or correct	• appropriate ideas • some incomplete sentences • some errors
Above Expectations	• all answers are comprehensible and correct	• all answers are comprehensible and correct	• appropriate ideas • complete sentences • few errors

Success for English Learners

Use with Lesson 1, Chapter 11

Build Background

Access Prior Knowledge

Ask students: *Have you ever been punished for something you did? Did it make you change your actions?* Have students work in small mixed-proficiency groups to answer these questions: *Is it a good idea to punish people?* Provide a concrete example, such as: *If a student said something mean to a classmate, which solution would work best? Why?* Discuss answers aloud. Then explain that the President of the United States had to decide whether to punish the Southern states after the Civil War. President Johnson did not want to punish them, but Congress did.

- Before **Introduce**, p. 446
- 25 minutes

Lesson Vocabulary

Explain the words to students using information from prior lessons and concrete examples. Then give students a list that includes each word and two definitions, one that is correct and one that is incorrect. For example:
1) **Reconstruction:** *a. to rebuild the government b. to rebuild the country.* Ask students to circle the correct definition. Then ask them to paraphrase each correct definition and quiz a partner. The first partner should read his or her paraphrased definitions while the other student identifies the correct words. Repeat the process with the other partner.

Additional Vocabulary Explain the words in the margin and provide examples of their uses. For example, remind students this lesson refers to *state* laws and *state* constitutions, or laws and constitutions formed by the state.

Cognates As students read the lesson, you may wish to point out cognates such as: **codes/códigos, constitution/constitución, limit/limitar, society/sociedad.**

carpetbagger	race
charges against	rebuild
corruption	scalawag
former	secret
malice	society
	state

Build Fluency

Read aloud the following rhyme, and point out words that sound alike. Have students repeat it several times to develop oral language skills. Return to the rhyme throughout the lesson to help develop vocabulary, generalizing skills, and lesson content.

> At last there was an end to the bitter war.
> President Johnson wanted peace, as it was before.
> Congress put Southern states
> Under military control.
>
> When Johnson tried to stop
> The **Reconstruction** plan,
> Congress impeached the president.
> But it **acquitted** him, calling him an innocent man.
>
> When President Hayes decided
> That Reconstruction should end,
> The South took control of the government
> And African Americans lost their right to vote again.

■ Success for English Learners

Scaffolding the Content

Preview the Lesson

Read the title of the lesson and have students look at the pictures on pages 446, 447, 448, 449 and 450. Ask them to write down any words or phrases that they think of when they look at each picture. Next, preview the section headings to give students a sense of the lesson's organization. Tell students they are going to learn about how the United States changed after the Civil War.

• During **Teach**, pp. 446–453
• 20 minutes

Modify Instruction

The following sections highlight the types of changes faced by the South during Reconstruction. Read the following points and help students record notes in the appropriate sections of the blackline master. Ask student pairs to form one or two generalizations about changes to life in the South.

New Presidents Lincoln did not want to punish the South for seceding from, or leaving, the Union. Lincoln died 1865. Vice President Andrew Johnson became president. He ended slavery everywhere in 1865 and let most Confederates become full citizens again. Then Ulysses S. Grant became president. He wanted to punish Southern states. Finally Rutherford B. Hayes became president. He ended Reconstruction in 1877.

Political Changes Congress wanted to punish Confederate states. It put them under military rule. Congress made each state write new Constitutions that let African American men vote. President Johnson tried to limit Congress's plan. So Congress impeached, or brought charges against, him. Johnson was acquitted, or found not guilty.

Changes in Law African Americans voted and elected some African American leaders. Secret societies formed. One society was the Ku Klux Klan. These societies used violence to keep African American men from voting. Next, Southerners took back control of their government. They passed laws that stopped African American men from voting. These laws also created segregation, which kept people in separate groups based on their race. By the time Hayes ended Reconstruction, African Americans did not have many rights.

Economic Changes The Civil War hurt the South. Freedmen's Bureau helped many people in the South, especially newly freed families. Many former enslaved people returned to plantations to work, but landowners had little money. They paid workers through sharecropping, or giving a share of crops, rather than money. Taxes in the South were high. The government needed tax money to repair buildings, bridges, and other structures.

Extend

Ask students to create word webs for each of the categories in the "Modify Instruction" section. They may use words or images from the summaries but should also use some of their own words.

• After **Teach**, pp.446–453
• 15 minutes

Name _____ Date _____

DIRECTIONS Write notes below each topic as your teacher reads about changes that happened in the South during Reconstruction. Then, think about generalizations you can make about each type of change. Work with a partner to write one or two of them.

Changes In Southern Life During Reconstruction

New Presidents	Political Changes

Changes in Law	Economic Changes

School-Home Connection Encourage students to take this page home to share with family members. They can use their notes to explain changes in Southern life during Reconstruction.

Apply and Assess
Write a Conversation

Ask students to work in small groups. Each group should pretend to be Northerners or Southerners and write brief statements that they could have said during Reconstruction. Ask students to share one or two statements. Note them on the board in columns labeled *Northerners* and *Southerners*.

• During **Close**, p. 453
• 30 minutes

Next, write a sample conversation on the board, such as:

> **Northerner:** I am glad that Southern states are being punished. They did not follow the laws of the Union. Now they are trying to stop African Americans from voting!
>
> **Southerner:** We wanted to be separate so we could make our own laws. We do not want to live the way Northern states do. Leave us alone!

Next, have groups think about the actions and opinions of Northern and Southern states during Reconstruction. Tell them they will write a conversation between a Northerner and Southerner. Have beginning students write at least one line for each side. Intermediate students should write a few lines, and advanced students should write several lines for each side.

Informal Lesson Assessment

	Beginning	Intermediate	Advanced
Task	Ask: *How did the South change during Reconstruction?* Students may respond with single words, gestures, or by pointing to pictures.	Have students copy this sentence frame on paper and fill in the blank. *After Reconstruction, ____ changed in the South.*	Ask students to write two or three sentences about changes to Southern life during Reconstruction. Ask them to use a generalization in the introduction or conclusion.
Below Expectations	• neither answer is comprehensible and/or correct	• neither part of the answer is comprehensible and/or correct	• incorrect ideas • no complete sentences • many errors
Meets Expectations	• one answer is comprehensible and/or correct	• one part of the answer is comprehensible and/or correct	• appropriate ideas • some incomplete sentences • some errors
Above Expectations	• student gives three or more correct answers	• all answers are comprehensible and correct	• all answers are comprehensible and correct

Success for English Learners

Build Background

Use with Lesson 2, Chapter 11

Access Prior Knowledge

Remind students that the frontier was unsettled land in the West. Explain that some of the reasons people moved to the frontier are similar to the reasons people move to a new country. Ask: *Why do people move to new countries?* Have volunteers provide answers, and note them on the board. If necessary, supplement with responses such as: *new opportunities, to make money,* or *to escape from problems.* Explain that frontier life was difficult, but people chose to move West to find money, land, and a new way of life.

- Before **Introduce**, p. 454
- 20 minutes

Lesson Vocabulary

Post brief definitions for the vocabulary words, and explain them. Ask the class to create word webs of associations between the new words and images students associate with them. Model making a word web with the word **prospector,** which may be associated with the words *gold, money,* and *risk.* Ask volunteers for one or two additional words. Have student pairs make word webs for the remaining vocabulary words, so that each student makes a web for one or two words. Ask students to cover the vocabulary words in the center of the web to see if other students can guess them based on the associations.

Additional Vocabulary Explain the words in the margin and provide examples of their uses. As you explain each word, point out their relation to the West during the 1800s. For example, *sod* is dirt. People used it to build homes when they got free land from the government.

buffalo	drought
cattle	finds
cow towns	mining
cowhand	rancher
drew	sod

Cognates As students read the lesson, you may wish to point out cognates such as: **buffalo/búfalo, insects/insectos, mining/minería.**

Build Fluency

Read aloud the following rhyme, and point out words that sound alike. Have students repeat it several times to develop oral language skills. Return to the rhyme throughout the lesson to help develop vocabulary, generalizing skills, and lesson content.

> People went West to work in the mines.
> They dreamed of the gold they hoped to find.
> People came West to sell cattle's meat.
> Then they sent it by railroad to the East.
> The Homestead Act sent many people West
> For a lot of free land, hard work, and no rest!

Scaffolding the Content

Preview the Lesson

Use the illustrations in the text to preview major themes in the lesson. Have students identify topics of the illustrations on pages 452–456 in words, phrases, or sentences depending on their language proficiency. Confirm the topics and provide a few details about why they were important as people moved West. For example, the photograph on page 455 shows a mining town. Explain that settlers built these towns quickly because many people moved West to find gold, silver, or other metals.

- During **Teach**, pp. 454–457
- 20 minutes

Modify Instruction

Review the following questions and answers, and tell students to record notes on the blackline master. Put students in pairs to form a generalization using their notes.

Q: Why did mining bring people West in the late 1800s?

Many prospectors, people in search of metal and minerals, went to Nevada in 1859. They set up mining camps. Towns grew around the camps. Settlers built the towns quickly. Business owners sold products that miners needed. The economy and population boomed, or grew quickly. When the metal was gone, there were busts, or quick losses in population or money.

Q: Why did cattle trails bring people West in the late 1800s?

The East got very busy after the Civil War. Many ranchers, or people who raised animals like cows, lived in the West. They wanted to sell meat to people in the East. Transporting the animals East was difficult, so they made trails and sent animals by trains. People built "cow towns" along the railroad. African American and Mexican cowhands taught American cattle drivers about moving cattle.

Q: Why did the Homestead Act bring people West in the late 1800s?

In 1862, Congress passed the Homestead Act. This law gave land on the Great Plains to people who lived there for five or more years. Many Americans and 100,000 immigrants from Europe rushed to claim some of this land. These people were called homesteaders. Homesteaders had difficult lives. They built houses from sod, or dirt.

Q: What happened to Native Americans as settlers went West?

As settlers developed the West, Native Americans lost buffalo and land. Some tribes signed treaties with the United States. The treaties forced the tribes, including the Sioux, Nez Perce, and Apache, onto reservations, or land for use only by Native Americans.

Extend

Play a game with students. Divide the room into two sides. Give brief true and false statements and call on a side to answer the question. If that side answers correctly, they get another turn. If not, the other side gets to try.

- After **Teach**, pp. 454–457
- 10 minutes

Success for English Learners ■ 183

Name _____ Date _____

DIRECTIONS Take notes under each topic as your teacher reads. Then work with a partner to write one or two generalizations about why people moved West during the late 1800s.

Q: Why did mining bring people West?

Q: Why did cattle trails bring people West?

Q: What happened to Native Americans as settlers went West?

Q: Why did the Homestead Act bring people West?

Generalize why people moved West.

 School-Home Connection Encourage students to take this page home to share with their families. They can use their notes to explain why people moved West during the 1800s.

Apply and Assess

Prepare a Question List

Remind students that homesteading was a dream for many people from America and Europe. These people wanted land but did not have enough money to buy it. Tell students to imagine that they are homesteaders preparing for the trip West. Explain that they need to plan well to make sure they get land and know how to live on the frontier.

• During **Close**, p. 457
• 30 minutes

Explain that the frontier will have few or no stores, so students will need to bring things to farm, build a home, cook, and bathe. Even if there are stores, they are very far from most homes.

Have students think of questions that will help prepare them for the move and for getting their land. For example: *How do I tell the government I am there when I arrive? Will I have neighbors?* Give beginning students sentence starters that require one or two words, such as: *Will I have _____?* Provide intermediate students with question starters that require a few words, such as: *"When I get to the land, how will I _____?"* Ask advanced students to try to form questions without assistance.

Informal Lesson Assessment

	Beginning	**Intermediate**	**Advanced**
Task	Have students list things that brought people West during the late 1800s. They may answer using sketches, words, or phrases.	Have students list things that brought people West during the late 1800s. They may answer using phrases and short sentences.	Ask students to write a few sentences about things that brought people West during the late 1800s. They should answer in complete sentences.
Below Expectations	• no answer is correct or comprehensible	• no answer is comprehensible and/or correct	• incorrect ideas • no complete sentences • many errors
Meets Expectations	• some answers are correct and comprehensible	• some answers are comprehensible and/or correct	• appropriate ideas • some incomplete sentences • some errors
Above Expectations	• all answers are correct and comprehensible	• all answers are comprehensible and correct	• appropriate ideas • complete sentences • few errors

Use with Chapter 11 Lesson 3

Build Background

Access Prior Knowledge

Post and read this statement: *Inventions change our lives.* Ask students to work in small groups to write the name of one invention they learned about in a previous lesson. Ask them to tell how the invention changed the way of life during that time. Explain that long ago in the United States people could not talk on the phone, travel across the country, or fight for their rights at work. Ask students how being able to do these things would change people's lives.

- Before **Introduce**, p. 462
- 20 minutes

Lesson Vocabulary

Explain vocabulary words to students using the vocabulary cards, illustrations, and brief definitions. Then instruct students to work in groups of three to make vocabulary squares for the vocabulary words. Model the activity using the word **skyscraper.** On the board, draw three squares in a horizontal row. In the first square, write a short definition: *a tall building.* In the second square, write a sentence using the word correctly: *In big cities, I see many skyscrapers.* In the third square, draw a picture of a skyscraper. Leave the sample on the board, so students can refer to it as they work. Help students think of ways to illustrate more abstract concepts, such as **strike.** Tell students to make squares for two words, and then have groups show their squares to the class.

Additional Vocabulary Explain the words in the margin, and provide examples of their uses. Explain that words with the root "electric" are related to electricity. So, *electrical* means "to work by way of electricity." Also mention that *working conditions* refers to what life is like for people at work.

communicate	raw materials
iron ore	station
kerosene	steel
electrical lightbulb	tracks
power station	working conditions

Cognates As students read the lesson, you may wish to point out cognates such as: **condition/condición, electrical/eléctrico, petroleum/petróleo, unión/unión.**

Build Fluency

Read aloud the following rhyme, and point out words that sound alike. Have students repeat it several times to develop oral language skills. Return to the rhyme throughout the lesson to help develop vocabulary, generalizing skills, and lesson content.

> A **transcontinental railroad** from shore to shore
> Helped people travel, ship, and sell more!
> Carnegie saw how the British made steel
> And in Pennsylvania he built the first mill.
> Life was easier because of many inventions,
> For example, the telephone changed communication.
> **Labor unions** improved life in many ways.
> They caused safer conditions and shorter workdays.

186 ■ Success for English Learners

Scaffolding the Content

Preview the Lesson

Ask students to scan section illustrations, captions, and section review questions for developments or inventions. Have them record what they find and share one or two responses with the class. Record responses on the board. Provide a brief explanation of how the development or invention changed life in the United States. For example: *Unions made workplaces better.* Tell students they will learn how new industries and invention changed life at the end of the 1800s.

• During **Teach**, pp. 462–467
• 20 minutes

Modify Instruction

Read the following points, and help students record notes about each development on the blackline master. Then ask students to form a generalization about the developments.

The Transcontinental Railroad
- In 1869, workers from China and Ireland finished a railroad that crossed the entire country. People could now travel across the country by train. People could also sell goods all over the country. Cities grew near the railroad.

Industries and Inventions
- People began selling many goods by train, so they needed bigger and stronger trains and railroads. In 1872, while traveling in Britain, Andrew Carnegie saw a way to make steel. He built a steel mill in Pennsylvania. People used steel for many things, like skyscrapers, or tall buildings. The steel industry spread to Cleveland, Ohio and Chicago, Illinois. Many people moved to these cities for jobs.
- In 1863, John D. Rockefeller set up an oil refinery. This is a factory that makes oil into products people need. He bought many refineries and joined them into one business called Standard Oil Company. It was so successful that other oil companies could not compete.
- In 1874, Thomas Alva Edison opened a laboratory to make inventions. He worked with a team of inventors. Their best-known invention was an electric lightbulb. In 1882, Edison set up the first central electrical power station. Lewis Lattimer was a famous African American engineer on the team who directed the station.
- In 1876, Alexander Graham Bell designed a new telephone. The next year he began the first telephone company in the country.

Workers Struggle
- Owners of railroads, mills, and factories became rich. Sometimes they paid workers little money and made them work long hours in dangerous places. Workers joined labor unions. The unions organized strikes and forced employers to make changes.

Extend

List hints about one development from the lesson until a student names it correctly. Use sketches, gestures, and simple language. Then allow volunteers to provide the class with hints about another invention or industry from the lesson.

• After **Teach**, pp. 462–467
• 10 minutes

Name _____ Date _____

DIRECTIONS Take notes about each topic as your teacher reads. Then write a generalization about the industries and inventions of the late 1800s.

Industry or Invention	Details
1.	
2.	
3.	
4.	
5.	
6.	

How They Changed Life in the United States

School-Home Connection Encourage students to take this page home to share with their families. They can refer to it to explain how industries and inventions changed life in the United States during the late 1800s.

188 ■ Success for English Learners

Unit 5, Chapter 11, Lesson 3

Apply and Assess

Create a Chart

Refer students to the chart they completed about industries and inventions on the blackline master page. Explain that they will make a similar type of chart. The new chart will have different column names as well as pictures.

- During **Close**, p. 467
- 35 minutes

Provide the following steps for students to make the chart:

1. Decide the number of rows and columns to use.
2. Decide where the pictures will go.
3. Draw the chart.
4. Write information in the boxes.
5. Draw pictures.

Tell beginning students to make a chart about at least two industries or inventions. Intermediate students should include at least four industries or inventions. Advanced students should have six industries or inventions on their charts. When students finish, have them show and explain their charts in small groups.

Informal Lesson Assessment

	Beginning	Intermediate	Advanced
Task	Provide a piece of paper with a list of industries and inventions on one side and their influence on life in the United States in the 1800s on the other side. Have students match them by drawing lines.	Provide a list of ways life in the United States changed during the late 1800s. Ask students to provide the name of the industry or invention that caused the change.	Provide a list of industries and inventions. Have students write sentences describing how the developments changed life in the United States during the late 1800s.
Below Expectations	• no answer is correct	• no answer is comprehensible and/or correct	• incorrect or incomprehensible ideas • incomplete sentences • many errors
Meets Expectations	• some answers are correct	• some answers are comprehensible and/or correct	• appropriate ideas • some incomplete sentences • some errors
Above Expectations	• all answers are correct	• all answers are comprehensible and correct	• appropriate ideas • complete sentences • few errors

Use with Lesson 4, Chapter 11

Build Background

- Before **Introduce**, p. 468
- 15 minutes

Access Prior Knowledge

Write the word *immigration* on the board. Then write the following categories: *countries, reasons,* and *problems*. Ask students to work in pairs to list facts they learned in previous lessons about immigrants who came to the United States. After five minutes, ask students to pass their paper to the pair beside them. Have student pairs review responses on the papers, add to them, and then share the answers aloud. As students share responses, note them on the board.

Lesson Vocabulary

Explain the vocabulary words to students using brief definitions, gestures, sketches, and context clues. Ask students to make story strips with three to four pictures to represent one vocabulary word. Pair students and have them guess their partner's word. Have them change partners a few times to see a variety of story strips. Allow beginning students to draw the story strip and write the word on the back. Have intermediate students write short phrases below each picture to explain events. Ask advanced students to include a complete sentence with each picture.

Additional Vocabulary Explain the words in the margin and provide examples of their uses. Tell students that *migration* is a word that describes a person's moving from place to place in their own country. Work with students to help them understand the difference between immigration and *migration*.

challenging	newcomer
customs	poverty
faced	processing center
foreign-born	
health care	support
migration	

Cognates As students read the lesson, you may wish to point out cognates such as: **escape/escapar, examine/examinar, immigration/inmigración, opportunity/oportunidad, tradition/tradición.**

Build Fluency

Read aloud the following rhyme, and point out words that sound alike. Have students repeat it several times to develop oral language skills. Return to the rhyme throughout the lesson to help develop vocabulary, generalizing skills, and lesson content.

> In the 1800s, immigrants came to the United States.
> They had hard lives. They wanted to escape.
> They worked very hard, but many were poor.
> They lived in dirty **tenements,** and could not afford more.
> Some worried immigrants would take their jobs
> To keep some immigrants out, Congress passed a law.
> **Reformers** helped immigrants by giving them tools
> Like food, health care, clean water, and schools.

Scaffolding the Content

Preview the Lesson

Write the subheadings from the lesson on the board. Invite children to scan the pictures and captions for each section. Ask them to take turns predicting what information they will find. Write each prediction on the board. An example might read: 1) *New Immigrants: a) This section tells reasons immigrants came to the United States and what countries they came from. b) This tells where many immigrants worked and describes schools.*

- During **Teach**, pp. 468–472
- 20 minutes

Modify Instruction

Read the following information about immigration and the lives of immigrants. Tell students to use their notes to complete the blackline master page.

Many Immigrants Arrive

- Between 1860 and 1910, about 23 million immigrants came to the United States. Many came to escape violence and poverty, to find freedom, and to have a better life. The Ellis Island Immigration Station in New York opened in 1892.
- Many immigrants lived in crowded, poorly built apartment buildings called tenements. Immigrants sometimes got sick because tenements often did not have clean water. Garbage filled the streets. Immigrants had difficulty finding jobs. Sometimes children worked all day to help their families.

Reactions to Immigration

- Many Americans did not want new immigrants in the country. Some thought they were not educated. Other Americans were afraid immigrants would take their jobs.
- In 1882, Congress passed the Chinese Exclusion Act. This law said Chinese immigrants could not come to the United States for ten years.
- Reformers, or people who wanted to change society, tried to solve some of the immigrants' problems. They started settlement houses that gave immigrants food, medicine, and schools.

Migration and Immigration

- Between 1910 and 1930, African Americans moved to cities in the North. Some African Americans found jobs in factories.
- After the Civil War, most immigrants came from countries in Europe. Now, most immigrants come from countries in Asia and Latin America. Almost one-fourth of today's immigrants come from countries in Asia.
- Immigrants practice customs and traditions unique to their cultures.

Extend

After reading the Modify Instruction section, ask the class what they think was the biggest challenge for immigrants in America in the late 1800s and early 1900s. Have students give reasons that support their thoughts. For example: *I think it is difficult not to know English. It is hard to find a job in a place where you do not speak the language.*

- After **Teach**, pp. 468–472
- 10 minutes

Success for English Learners

Name _____ Date _____

DIRECTIONS Take notes as your teacher reads. Write about challenges United States immigrants faced during the late 1800s and early 1900s. Work with a partner to write one or two generalizations about life for immigrants.

Challenge #1

Challenge #2

Challenge #3

Challenge #4

Challenge #5

Generalizations:

 School-Home Connection Encourage students to take this page home to share with family members. They can refer to it to explain immigration and to provide details about the way of life for immigrants in the United States during the late 1800s and early 1900s.

Apply and Assess

Write a Diary Entry

Help students brainstorm before they write. Put students in pairs to imagine a few emotions, goals, and expectations a child coming to the United States might have. Suggest that students recall their own immigration experiences, as appropriate. Ask students to share some of their responses, and record them on the board.

• During **Close**, p. 472
• 25 minutes

Next to the responses, post a model diary entry. Include the date and one hope you have for life in the new land. Read the entry aloud to students. Tell them they should use the same form when they write their own diary entries.

Allow beginning students to copy most of the sample entry but replace a few important words to express original thoughts. Have intermediate students use words from the board and phrases from the sample entry. Ask advanced students to use original language in their entries.

Informal Lesson Assessment

	Beginning	Intermediate	Advanced
Task	Have students describe challenges immigrants in the United States had during the late 1800s and early 1900s. Allow them to use single words and sketches in their responses.	Have students describe challenges immigrants in the United States had during the late 1800s and early 1900s. Ask them to use phrases and short sentences in their responses.	Have students describe challenges immigrants in the United States had during the late 1800s and early 1900s. Ask them to use complete sentences.
Below Expectations	• no answer is comprehensible and/or correct	• no answer is comprehensible and/or correct	• incorrect ideas • no complete sentences • many errors
Meets Expectations	• some answers are comprehensible and/or correct	• some answers are comprehensible and/or correct	• appropriate ideas • some incomplete sentences • some errors
Above Expectations	• all answers are comprehensible and correct	• all answers are comprehensible and correct	• appropriate ideas • complete sentences • few errors

Unit 6 Opener

Developing Academic Language

Summarizing is a key skill that begins with careful reading. To summarize, students have to be able to understand key facts and important details. Then they have to state those ideas in a way that accurately reflects what they read.

Introduce Summarizing Skills

Post the word *summarize*. Explain that to *summarize* is to tell the important ideas briefly and in different words. Write and say these three steps:

- Before **Summarize**, p. 486
- 20 minutes

1. Read.
2. Identify main ideas and important details.
3. Summarize by writing or saying the main ideas and important details in your own words.

Practice

Write this paragraph, and read it aloud.

> **The huge store was full of sporting goods. It sold equipment, like skates, golf clubs, hockey sticks, and helmets. It also sold all kinds of sports clothing, such as ski jackets, swimsuits, and baseball pants.**

Have students identify the important details in each sentence, and circle them. Then work with students to summarize important information.

> **The huge store sold sporting goods. It sold balls, equipment, and sports clothing.**

Apply

Draw the following chart, and have partners copy it onto a piece of paper. Explain that paragraphs can have different numbers of important facts, and note that students can add more key facts to the chart if needed. Then read this paragraph: *The house was huge! It had fifteen rooms, including a game room and a family room. It had six bedrooms. It also had a giant backyard big enough for a game of baseball.* Work with students to write the main idea and important details in the chart. Then discuss what their organizers show, and compose a summary together.

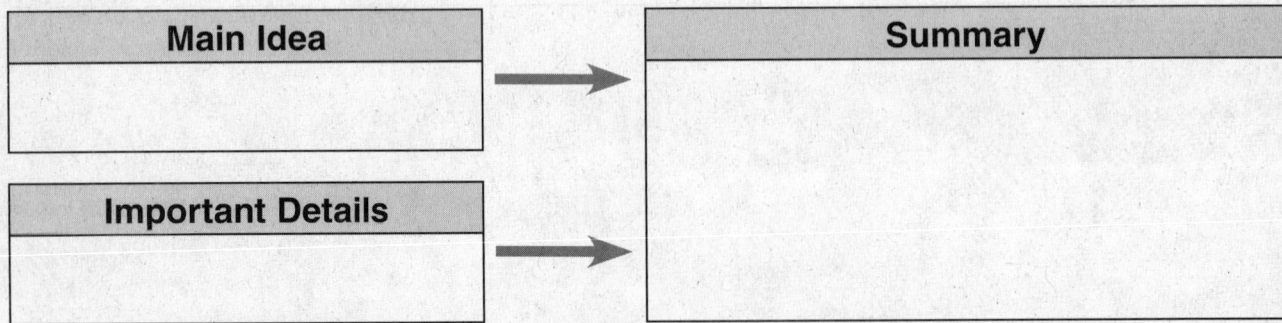

Build Background

Use with Chapter 12, Lesson 1

Access Prior Knowledge

Quiz students about the size of the United States and its territories. Ask students to say "true" or "false" in response to the following sentences: 1) *The United States is made up of 50 states.* 2) *Puerto Rico is a territory of the United States.* 3) *Two states do not touch other states.* 4) *The United States has territory in Asia.* Review the correct answers. Tell students that they will be learning about the expansion of the United States during the 1900s.

- Before **Introduce**, p. 494
- 25 minutes

Lesson Vocabulary

Help students find the vocabulary words in the Glossary and discuss the definitions as a class. Then ask students to draw three squares in horizontal rows to represent each word. In the first square, they will write a short definition. In the second square, they will write a sentence using the word. In the third square, they will draw a picture or symbol of the object. Ask students to share their vocabulary squares in small groups.

Additional Vocabulary Explain the words in the margin and provide examples of their uses in the lesson. For example, tell students that *territory* is often used as a synonym for land, but in this lesson, it means land that belongs to a country. Mention that territories can have their own governments and work like independent countries.

abroad	imprisoned
annexed	segregation
armistice	standard
assassinated	sugar
canal	territory
expand	

Cognates As students read the lesson, you may want to point out cognates such as: **assassinated/asesinado, canal/canal, prison/prisión, territory/territorio.**

Build Fluency

Read aloud the following rhyme and point out the words that sound alike. Have students repeat it several times to develop oral language skills. Return to the rhyme throughout the lesson to help develop vocabulary, summarizing skills, and lesson content.

> Two cents an acre was Alaska's price.
> It was a small price for land so nice.
> When the queen was imprisoned in 1898,
> Hawaii was annexed by the states.
>
> Trouble in Spanish colonies,
> In Cuba, and the Philippines
> Led to the Spanish-American War
> After the Maine exploded on Cuban shores.
>
> The end of the war
> Caused the states to expand.
> Spain gave the United States
> Control of new lands.

Success for English Learners ▪ 195

Scaffolding the Content

Preview the Lesson

Ask students to work in pairs to preview information. Have beginning students scan headings to note two states that were added to the country and when. Ask intermediate students to use the summary to find the name of a war and what the United States gained from it. Have advanced students skim pages 496 and 498 to tell the names of two Presidents and a few decisions each made. Confirm answers. Explain that students will learn how the United States grew during the late 1800s and 1900s.

• During **Teach**, pp. 494–499
• 30 minutes

Modify Instruction

Review the following events that led to expansion of the United States. Use a map to show students unknown locations as necessary. Guide students in taking notes. Then have them complete the blackline master page.

The United States Expands
In 1867, the United States bought Alaska from Russia for $7.2 million, or 2 cents an acre. In 1893, Hawaii was an independent country. Americans farmed sugar there. The queen of Hawaii changed laws that affected American farmers. Americans imprisoned her. In 1898, the United States annexed Hawaii, or made Hawaii a United States territory.

The Spanish-American War
In the 1890s, the United States declared war on Spain. People in Cuba were fighting Spain for independence. President William McKinley sent the battleship *Maine* to Cuba to protect Americans there. The *Maine* exploded and Americans blamed Spain. The United States and Spain fought. Then the Spanish-American War ended. Spain gave the United States control of Spanish Cuba, Puerto Rico, the Philippines, and Guam.

Changes at Home and Abroad
In 1900, William McKinley was elected President and Theodore Roosevelt was elected Vice President. Soon after, McKinley was assassinated, or killed. Roosevelt became President. In 1904, Roosevelt began the building of the Panama Canal to connect the Atlantic and Pacific Oceans. The Panama Canal was completed 10 years later. President Roosevelt was supported by progressives who felt the government and citizens could make life better. In 1909, W.E.B. DuBois and other leaders formed the National Association for the Advancement of Colored People (NAACP). This group worked to change laws that prevented African Americans from having rights. The group also worked to end segregation. In 1959, Alaska became the 49th state of the United States. That same year, Hawaii became the 50th state.

Extend

Ask pairs to review their notes from the lesson and summarize events in two or three sentences. Confirm their responses. Next, post several questions on the board, such as: *Who became President in 1900?* Use questions that can be answered with one or two words if possible. Ask students to practice asking and answering the questions with a partner.

• After **Teach**, pp. 494–499
• 10 minutes

Name _____ Date _____

DIRECTIONS Listen to your teacher. Take notes as your teacher discusses events that took place during the dates below. Review the lesson to find events for each date.

How Did the United States Expand?

- 1867
- 1893
- 1898
- 1900
- 1904
- 1909
- 1959

School-Home Connection Encourage students to share this page with family members. They can tell about Alaska and Hawaii, territories gained in the Spanish-American War, and accomplishments of President Theodore Roosevelt.

Unit 6, Chapter 12, Lesson 1 Success for English Learners ▪ 197

Apply and Assess

Make a Time Line

Ask students to make time lines modeled after the one on page 494. Read aloud the short descriptions following the dates, and explain how to use key words telling *who* and *what* to turn details from their notes into similar descriptions. Have students do the following:

- During **Close**, p. 499
- 30 minutes

① Paraphrase their notes into short descriptions to use with their own time lines.

② Construct their time lines horizontally like the one on page 494. Place their descriptions by the appropriate dates.

③ Illustrate each date with a sketch or picture.

When students are finished, ask them to share their time line with a partner, reading the dates and the events aloud.

Informal Lesson Assessment

	Beginning	Intermediate	Advanced
Task	Provide a list of events. Have students match each event with the territory or state that was added to the United States as a result.	Provide students with a list of territories and states. Ask them to list events that caused the territory or state to become part of the United States.	Provide a list of places. Ask students to write a sentence about each, describing how the place became part of the United States.
Below Expectations	• no statement correctly identified	• few or no correct responses • responses are incomprehensible	• no correct response • no comprehensible explanations • many errors
Meets Expectations	• some statements correctly identified	• a few correct responses • responses are mostly comprehensible	• some correct responses • some comprehensible explanations • some errors
Above Expectations	• all statements correctly identified	• all responses are correct • all responses are comprehensible	• all responses are correct • all explanations are comprehensible • few errors

Use with Chapter 12, Lesson 2

Build Background

Access Prior Knowledge

Discuss the concept of war. Post the names of wars students have studied, such as the Revolutionary War, the War of 1812, the French and Indian War, and the Spanish-American War. Ask students to list factors common to these wars. On the board, record an example, such as: *fighting between countries or sides*. Discuss responses aloud and note them on the board. Explain that in this lesson, students will learn about World War I.

- Before **Introduce**, p. 500
- 25 minutes

Lesson Vocabulary

Read aloud the vocabulary words in the context of lesson sentences and have students follow along. Provide further detail using gestures, sketches, and examples as needed. Help students practice the words. Say a key word that can be associated with one or more vocabulary words, like **war**. Call on a student to say the vocabulary word(s) that involve this concept. Call on a second student, and ask if he or she agrees with the answer. Confirm the correct answer. When students seem to understand the words, have them practice spelling in pairs, one calling out a word and the other spelling it aloud or in writing.

Additional Vocabulary Explain the words in the margin, and provide examples of their uses.

Cognates As students read the lesson, you may want to point out cognates such as: **alliance/alianza, military/militares, million/millón.**

alliance	rebel
Archduke	stay out of
enlist	supplying
increased	surrendered
million	warfare

Build Fluency

Read aloud the following rhyme and point out the words that sound alike. Have students repeat it several times to develop oral language skills. Return to the rhyme throughout the lesson to help develop vocabulary, summarizing skills, and lesson content.

> The events of World War I began
> When a rebel killed Archduke Ferdinand.
> Long before that, European countries had become allies.
> This means they had formed strong ties.
> Americans joined the Allies late in the **war**.
> Soldiers fought in ways they had never fought before.
> Women took jobs and the children grew crops.
> The war ended in 1914, and the fighting stopped.

Scaffolding the Content

Preview the Lesson

Help students focus on section headings to preview lesson topics. Post the headings: *Causes of World War I, Fighting the War, The War at Home,* and *The Effects of the War.* Ask students to work in mixed-proficiency pairs to identify topics in each section of the lesson. Provide beginning students with topics they can match with the headings. Ask intermediate students to use bold-faced words and subheadings to identify topics in the sections. Have advanced students use topic and conclusion sentences.

- During **Teach**, pp. 500–505
- 30 minutes

Modify Instruction

Review the following summaries with students. Use a map to point out the countries and locations mentioned. Guide students in recording the topic and taking notes. Then have them complete the checklist on the blackline master page.

Causes of World War I
In 1914, the Allied Powers, or the Allies, included Britain, France, Russia, Italy, and Serbia. The Central Powers included Germany, Austria-Hungary, the Ottoman Empire, and Bulgaria. A Serbian rebel killed Archduke Francis Ferdinand of Austria-Hungary. Austria-Hungary declared war on Serbia and the Allies backed Serbia. The Central Powers backed Austria-Hungary. President Woodrow Wilson and many Americans wanted the United States to stay out of the war. In 1917, Germany threatened to attack all ships in the Atlantic, and so the United States joined the Allies.

Fighting the War
The United States had a small army. Congress made men ages 21 to 30 sign up for a military draft. The government chose men to fight in the war. Soldiers used trench warfare. This meant they dug trenches for protection. Each side tried to reach "no man's land," a place between the trenches. Soldiers used new machine guns, tanks, poison gas, and airplanes. Millions of soldiers died. About 26,000 of these soldiers were Americans.

The War at Home
Many workers left their jobs to fight in the war. People fighting the war needed many products. In order to get enough workers, businesses increased pay and hired more women and African Americans. About 500,000 African Americans moved north to work in factories. Families grew vegetables to send to soldiers.

The Effects of the War
The American troops helped the Allies. In 1918, Germany surrendered. Allied leaders met in Paris to discuss peace. The Treaty of Versailles, the peace plan, formed the League of Nations to help nations solve problems peacefully. The United States did not join the League of Nations. Women won suffrage, the right to vote, in 1920.

Extend

Prepare index cards with short-answer questions about what the United States did before, during, and after World War I. Record answers on the back. Have students work in small groups, taking turns drawing cards and answering questions. Then have them exchange their questions with other groups until each group has practiced all questions.

- After **Teach**, pp. 500–505
- 10 minutes

Name _____ Date _____

DIRECTIONS Listen as your teacher discusses the topics below. Take notes on three to five details. Then work with a partner to summarize them.

The United States and World War I

Topic	Details	Summarize
Causes of World War I		
Fighting the War		
The War at Home		
The Effects of the War		

School-Home Connection Encourage students to take this page home to share with family members. They can use their notes to tell about the United States' involvement in World War I and ways life changed during and after the war.

Apply and Assess

Write a Letter

Help students to imagine that they have a relative who is a soldier in World War I. Brainstorm topics they would want to talk about with this relative. Note responses on the board in words and phrases.

- During **Close**, p. 505
- 30 minutes

Write a short model letter on the board and read it aloud. Use key words from the board to form questions and statements. Ask students to follow the structure of your letter as they write their own.

- Have beginning students write brief letters of two to three sentences. Help them construct statements and questions.
- Provide intermediate students with sentence starters, such as: *I want to tell you about . . .* or *What types of things do you . . . ?* Have them complete the sentences and use them in the letter.
- Ask advanced students to write a letter using their own words.

Have students read their letters aloud in pairs. Then have them exchange the letters and read their partner's letter aloud.

Informal Lesson Assessment

	Beginning	Intermediate	Advanced
Task	Ask students to list things the United States did before, during, and after World War I. Allow them to use key words and sketches.	Ask students to list things the United States did before, during, and after World War I. Have them answer using phrases and brief sentences.	Have students write one or two paragraphs about things the United States did before, during, and after World War I.
Below Expectations	• no response is comprehensible or correct	• few or no correct responses • responses are incomprehensible	• no correct response • no comprehensible explanations • many errors
Meets Expectations	• some responses are comprehensible and correct	• a few correct responses • responses are mostly comprehensible	• some correct responses • some comprehensible explanations • some errors
Above Expectations	• all responses are comprehensible and correct	• all responses are correct • all responses are comprehensible	• all responses are correct • all explanations are comprehensible • few errors

Use with Chapter 12, Lesson 3

Build Background

Access Prior Knowledge

Explain that the Great Depression was a time when many Americans were poor and life was difficult. Tap students' prior knowledge about poverty from images on television, movies, or from real life. Have them work in small groups to list the problems faced by families in poverty, such as *no money* or *no job*. Note responses on the board.

- Before **Introduce**, p. 506
- 25 minutes

Lesson Vocabulary

Help students find vocabulary words in the Glossary. Explain them further by using sketches and examples when possible. Next, pass out index cards on which you have already written one of the words. Repeat the words as often as necessary to ensure that you have enough cards for everyone. Ask students to sketch a picture representing the word written on the other side. Circle the room as students work to be sure their images match the words. Have students visit other students in the class, look at their pictures, and guess the words represented.

Additional Vocabulary Explain the words in the margin and provide examples of their meanings. For example, point out that *crash* has multiple meanings, but in this lesson it means "to collapse or fall." Tell students that *stocks* are ownership in a company that people can buy and sell. The *stock market crash* was a time when stock prices fell and no one wanted to buy stocks anymore.

automobile	musician
consumer	panicked
crash	savings
dust	stocks
jazz	unemployed
loan	

Cognates As students read the lesson, you may want to point out cognates such as: **assembly/asamblea, consumer/consumidor, musician/músico.**

Build Fluency

Read aloud the following rhyme and point out the words that sound alike. Have students repeat it several times to develop oral language skills. Return to the rhyme throughout the lesson to help develop vocabulary, summarizing skills, and lesson content.

> **Consumer goods** like refrigerators and washing machines
> Made it much easier to cook and clean.
> The 1920s brought movies, music, radio, and art.
> Then the **stock market** crash tore the world apart.
> Banks lost money and had to close.
> People lost savings, work, and homes.
> Then Franklin Delano Roosevelt thought of a plan.
> His New Deal would bring jobs to every American.
> In some ways the programs didn't succeed,
> But they did give hope to people in need.

Scaffolding the Content

Preview the Lesson

Preview the following illustrations and captions: consumer goods, p. 507; impoverished people, p. 509; and Franklin Delano Roosevelt, p. 512. Point to the heading *The New Deal* and explain that this program made life easier for some Americans. Have students complete these sentence frames: 1) *Consumer goods made life easier in the _____s.* 2) *After 1929, many people lost their _____.* 3) *President _____ tried to help Americans.* Tell students that in this lesson they will learn why so many Americans lived in poverty during the Depression and how President Roosevelt tried to help people.

• During **Teach**, pp. 506–512
• 30 minutes

Modify Instruction

Review the summaries below. Define unknown vocabulary words and concepts as necessary. Guide students in taking notes in the appropriate boxes on the blackline master page. Then help them summarize each topic.

The Good Times
After World War I, factories made new products like vacuum cleaners, refrigerators, and radios. These products were called consumer goods. Henry Ford used a moving assembly line to manufacture automobiles cheaper and faster than ever before.

New Art Forms
Jazz came from African American music in the South. Louis Armstrong and Duke Ellington were jazz musicians. They performed in Harlem, a part of New York City. People enjoyed listening to the radio and watching movies.

The End of the Good Times
The stock market is a place where people can buy shares of a business. In 1929, many people sold stock, so prices became very low. People panicked and sold all of their stock, so then the stock market crashed. This crash caused the economy to collapse.

The Hard Times
Big companies had less money, so factories closed. Workers lost their jobs. Many people went to banks to get their savings. Banks loaned money they did not have. Banks closed, and people lost their savings. People lost their homes. Many people went hungry and stood in lines for free food. The Midwest had a drought and dust storms. This area was called the Dust Bowl.

The New Deal
Franklin Delano Roosevelt became President in 1932. He began the New Deal, a program to help the economy. The program gave people hope but did not work completely. One program was Social Security. It paid people after they retired, or stopped working. Another program was the Tennessee Valley Authority, or TVA. This was a system of dams to make electricity. The Civilian Conservation Corps, or CCC, gave jobs to young people.

Extend

Create a paragraph with cloze sentences for each section of the lesson. For example, the first sentence under "The Good Times" could read: *After World War I, factories made _____ _____ like vacuum cleaners, radios, and cars.* Give advanced students more sentences to complete.

• After **Teach**, pp. 506–512
• 10 minutes

Name _____ Date _____

DIRECTIONS Take notes as your teacher discusses each topic below. Then summarize the details on the bottom half of each box.

The Good Times

Summary:

New Art Forms

Summary:

The End of the Good Times

Summary:

The Hard Times

Summary:

The New Deal

Summary:

School-Home Connection Encourage students to take this page home to share with family members. They can use their notes to tell about life in the United States after World War I, the stock market crash and the Great Depression, and accomplishments of President Franklin Roosevelt.

Apply and Assess

Write a Letter

Ask students how people traveled before cars. Ask students questions that highlight ways that cars improved life, for example: *How did cars help people who had relatives far away? How did cars help people who needed to carry many things?* Record responses on the board in phrases and sentences.

• During **Close**, p. 512
• 30 minutes

Write a model letter on the board and read it aloud. Use key words from the board to form questions and statements. Ask students to follow the structure of your letter as they write their own.

- Have beginning students write brief letters of two to three sentences and help them incorporate phrases or sentences from the board.
- Ask intermediate students to include three to five sentences using phrases from the board.
- Ask advanced students to include two brief paragraphs in their letter, and ask them to paraphrase information from the board.

Informal Lesson Assessment

	Beginning	Intermediate	Advanced
Task	Provide multiple-choice statements about ways the stock market crash changed American life. Ask students to choose the correct answer.	Provide cloze sentences about ways the stock market crash changed American life. Have students fill in the blanks using key words.	Ask brief questions about ways the stock market crash changed American life. Have students answer using sentences.
Below Expectations	• no statement correctly identified	• few or no correct responses • responses are incomprehensible	• no correct response • no comprehensible explanations • many errors
Meets Expectations	• some statements correctly identified	• a few correct responses • responses are mostly comprehensible	• some correct responses • some comprehensible explanations • some errors
Above Expectations	• all statements correctly identified	• all responses are correct • all responses are comprehensible	• all responses are correct • all explanations are comprehensible • few errors

Use with Lesson 4, Chapter 12

Build Background

Access Prior Knowledge

Review United States events before, during, and after World War I and the Depression. Write questions on the board: *1) What is the military draft? 2) What countries were part of the Allies? 3) How did the war create jobs? 4) What happens to people during a Depression?* Assign each group a question and have students share responses. Highlight points that relate to events during World War II. For example, during the Depression, Americans were poor and needed hope; explain that Germans also needed hope during a depression, and this led to World War II.

- Before **Introduce**, p. 514
- 25 minutes

Lesson Vocabulary

Briefly explain the meanings of **dictator, rationing,** and **internment camps**. Use examples, simple language, and sketches. Then ask students to use the words in sentences. Provide cloze sentences for beginning students. Provide sentence starters for intermediate students. Ask advanced students to produce original sentences. Then quiz students by writing sentences on the board that use the words both correctly and incorrectly. Have students select incorrect sentences, and work together to correct them as necessary.

Additional Vocabulary Explain the words in the margin and provide examples of their uses. Point out that *coupon* is frequently used to mean *paper that gives a reduced price at stores.* In this lesson, it means *paper that limited products people could buy in stores.*

bomb	limiting
civilian	powerful
coupon	supplies
draft	surrender
in ruins	tanks

Cognates As students read the lesson, you may want to point out cognates such as: **bomb/bomba, dictator/dictador, tank/tanque.**

Build Fluency

Read aloud the following rhyme and point out the words that sound alike. Have students repeat it several times to develop oral language skills. Return to the rhyme throughout the lesson to help develop vocabulary, summarizing skills, and lesson content.

> Adolf Hitler started a war
> To make his country as strong as it was before.
> He attacked Poland, then Britain and France
> Joined the war to stop his advance.
> Japan and Italy also began
> The race to take over foreign lands.
> At first the United States stayed out of the war—
> just like before.
> But after the bombing of Pearl Harbor, they joined the war.
> In North Africa, then in France
> The Americans improved the Allies' chance.
> Then, on VE-Day in 1944,
> Germans surrendered and ended the war—
> just like before.

Scaffolding the Content

Preview the Lesson

Read aloud the time line on page 514. Ask: *1) What is the name of the War we will study? 2) When did the war begin and end? 3) When did the United States join the war?* Record the answers on the board. Next, write the names of these countries on the board: *Germany, Italy, Japan, United States, Britain, France,* and *Soviet Union*. Point to each country on the map on page 520. Read aloud the third paragraph on page 517. Have students say *Axis* or *Allies* after you name each country.

- During **Teach**, pp. 514–521
- 30 minutes

Modify Instruction

Review the following summary. Guide students in taking notes in the appropriate boxes on the blackline master page. Then help them summarize each topic.

Before the War
After World War I, Germany's economy was in ruins. Adolf Hitler led the Nazi party. He became dictator in 1933. Hitler promised to solve Germany's problems. He wanted to make Germany powerful again.

A Global Conflict
In the 1930s, Japan, Italy, and Germany began taking over countries. In 1939, Germany invaded Poland. Britain and France declared war on Germany. This began World War II. By 1941, Germany controlled most of Europe. In 1940, President Franklin Delano Roosevelt was elected a third time. He wanted to prepare the country in case of an attack. A military draft began. On December 7, 1941, Japanese planes bombed military ships in Pearl Harbor, Hawaii.

Americans and the War
The United States declared war on Japan and joined the Allies. The Allies included Britain, France, and the Soviet Union. Germany, Italy, and Japan were the Axis Powers. The government began limiting goods people could buy. People had special coupons to buy butter, sugar, meat, and gasoline. In 1942, President Roosevelt ordered the army to put Japanese Americans into internment, or prison, camps.

The War in Europe and Africa
The Allies needed to defeat the Germans and the Italians in North Africa in order to gain control of the Mediterranean Sea. American General Dwight D. Eisenhower invaded Morocco and Algeria, and in 1943, the Allies won North Africa. The Allies wanted to defeat German troops in France. They invaded on June 6, 1944. This day was called D-Day. On May 8, Germany surrendered. This day is Victory in Europe Day, or V-E Day. The war in Europe was over. Harry S. Truman became President when Roosevelt died in 1945. The United States dropped atom bombs on Japanese cities Hiroshima and Nagasaki. Japan surrendered.

Extend

Post three different summaries of the above events. Make two of them unacceptable and one acceptable. Ask students to identify the accurate summary by comparing it to the information in their notes. Have students circle inaccuracies they find in the incorrect summaries.

- After **Teach**, pp. 514–521
- 10 minutes

Name _____ Date _____

DIRECTIONS Take notes as your teacher discusses each topic below. Then number the boxes below from 1 to 12.

America dropped atom bombs on the Japanese cities Hiroshima and Nagasaki.	The government began rationing goods.
The Allies defeated German troops in France on D-Day.	Japanese planes dropped bombs on military ships in Pearl Harbor, Hawaii.
The United States joined the Allies.	A military draft began.
Adolf Hitler became dictator of Germany.	General Dwight D. Eisenhower led American troops invading Morocco.
Roosevelt ordered American military to put Japanese Americans in internment camps.	The war in Europe ended when Germany's surrender was accepted.
In 1939, Germany invaded Poland.	Germany, Japan, and Italy began taking over countries.

School-Home Connection Encourage students to take this page home to share with family members. They can use their notes to tell about the countries involved in World War II, events that caused fighting, and how the war ended.

Unit 6, Chapter 12, Lesson 4   Success for English Learners ■ 209

Apply and Assess

Make a Time Line

Review the time line on page 514. Tell students to use it as an example as they make their own. Post these dates on the board: 1939, 1940, 1941, 1942, 1943, 1944, and 1945. Outline this process for students to follow in making their time lines:

- During **Close**, p. 521
- 30 minutes

❶ Scan notes for the dates.

❷ Identify the important event that happened on each date.

❸ Copy this information onto the time line.

For beginning students, consider providing events on strips of paper to arrange and paste to a time line. Give intermediate students a word bank to use that includes key words they may use in writing their events. Ask advanced students to paraphrase events from their notes independently.

Informal Lesson Assessment

	Beginning	**Intermediate**	**Advanced**
Task	List events that happened during World War II. Have students circle actions by the United States that supported the Allied victory.	Have students list actions the United States took during World War II that supported the Allied victory. They may use words or phrases.	Have students write a paragraph that includes a few actions the United States took that supported the Allied victory.
Below Expectations	• no event correctly identified	• few or no correct responses • responses are incomprehensible	• no correct response • no comprehensible explanations • many errors
Meets Expectations	• some events correctly identified	• a few correct responses • responses are mostly comprehensible	• some correct responses • some comprehensible explanations • some errors
Above Expectations	• all events correctly identified	• all responses are correct • all responses are comprehensible	• all responses are correct • all explanations are comprehensible • few errors

Use with Chapter 12 — Lesson 5

Build Background

Access Prior Knowledge

Make a K-W-L chart on the board. Write the words *Europe after World War II* above it. Ask students what they already know about Europe after the war. Encourage a review of concepts from the previous lesson, as well as anything students might already know about the Holocaust and concentration camps. Then ask students what they still want to learn. Repeat and record their ideas. Return to this chart after you teach the lesson.

- Before **Introduce**, p. 524
- 25 minutes

Lesson Vocabulary

Explain the vocabulary words using vocabulary cards and by connecting them to countries and people. Then have students number their papers from 1 to 5. Call out paraphrased definitions and have students record the words next to the correct number. Examples include: *1. event in which many Jews were killed 2. to take the lives of one group 3. industries and property are owned by government 4. place where Nazis held civilians 5. countries that were against communism.*

Additional Vocabulary Explain the words in the margin and provide examples of their uses. For example, help students understand the number of war victims by writing out 20 million and 30 million in digits. Remind students of words they learned in previous lessons, such as *industry*, and *property*, and explain them in the context of Communism.

airlift	murdered
blockade	Nazi
blocked	property
industry	trial
million	

Cognates As students read the lesson, you may want to point out cognates such as: **communism/comunismo, million/millón, United Nations/ Naciones Unidas.**

Build Fluency

Read aloud the following rhyme and point out the words that sound alike. Have students repeat it several times to develop oral language skills. Return to the rhyme throughout the lesson to help develop vocabulary, summarizing skills, and lesson content.

> At Hitler's **concentration camps** during World War II,
> Europe lost 6 million Jews.
> Hitler carried out his hateful **genocide,**
> And innocent men, women, and children died.
>
> Another change took hold of Europe too—
> Belief in **communism** grew.
> As the Soviet Union pushed the Nazis back,
> It planted new governments in their tracks.
> Soviets blockaded the city of Berlin.
> They didn't want the Allies to get in.
> So the Allies airlifted supplies to the town,
> And the Soviets finally backed down.

Success for English Learners

Scaffolding the Content

Preview the Lesson

Read the story on page 524 and point out Anne Frank's picture. Explain that the Nazis sent many families to concentration camps. Show the photograph on page 525. Explain that Allies freed people from these camps after the war, and they also took control of Western Berlin. Explain that students will learn the effects of World War II on Germany, other countries, and people in Europe.

- During **Teach**, pp. 524–527
- 30 minutes

Modify Instruction

Review the following changes brought on by World War II. Guide students in answering the questions in the appropriate sections of the blackline master page.

The Holocaust
- Hitler and the Nazis murdered men, women, and children in concentration camps.
- Nazis murdered more than 6 million Jews. This event is called the Holocaust.
- In 1945, Allies began to bring Nazi leaders to trial to punish them for these crimes. The most important trials were in Nuremberg, Germany.

The United Nations
- In World War II, about 20 million soldiers died. About 30 million civilians, or people who were not soldiers, died.
- In April 1945, representatives from 50 countries met in San Francisco to form the United Nations. They wanted to keep world peace and prevent more world wars. Today the UN is located in New York.

The Soviet Union
- The Soviet Union fought on the side of the Allies during World War II.
- The Soviet Union was Communist. This meant the government owned industries and property.
- As the Soviet Union pushed Nazis back into Germany, it set up communist governments in the countries it marched through. As a result, Eastern Europe was controlled by the Soviet Union.

The Berlin Airlift
- The United States, Britain, and France controlled West Germany. The Soviet Union controlled East Germany, so East Germany had a Communist government.
- Part of Germany's capital city, Berlin, was in the East, and part was in the West.
- In 1948, the Soviets blockaded Berlin so Allies could not travel from Berlin to West Germany. The Allies started the Berlin Airlift to get supplies into West Berlin. In 1949, the Soviets ended the blockade.

Extend

Have students revisit the information under each category on the blackline master. Ask them to follow two steps in writing summaries: *1) Circle two important facts in each category; 2) Write one sentence that contains both facts.* Model by summarizing the category *The Holocaust*.

- After **Teach**, pp. 524–527
- 10 minutes

Name _____ Date _____

DIRECTIONS Listen to your teacher talks about changes that happened because of World War II. Take notes as your teacher discusses each topic below.

| What happened during the Holocaust? | Why was the United Nations formed? |
| Why did Communism expand after World War II? | Why did the Allies airlift supplies to Berlin? |

School-Home Connection Encourage students to take this page home to share with family members. They can use their notes to tell ways World War II affected Europe.

Apply and Assess

Write an Essay

On the board, write the questions: *Why is it important to have a place to discuss problems? How does this help keep peace?* Discuss the questions aloud. Record ideas on the board.

• During **Close**, p. 527
• 30 minutes

Explain that an essay is a form of writing that explains a point of view. If possible, read aloud a brief example for students.

- Provide beginning students with an essay that contains cloze sentences. Explain the point of view expressed in the essay and ask them to fill the blanks in using appropriate key words.
- Support intermediate students by providing topic sentences for paragraphs of an essay. Have them provide information and ideas that support each topic sentence.
- Have advanced students write an essay of a few paragraphs to explain their point of view on the questions recorded on the board.

Informal Lesson Assessment

	Beginning	**Intermediate**	**Advanced**
Task	Write phrases on the board that indicate changes in Europe after World War II and details about them: Holocaust, Making Peace, Communism. Have students classify details under the changes they describe.	Provide students with a list of changes that came about in Europe after World War II. Have students describe them by writing phrases or sentences.	Have students describe changes that took place in Europe after World War II. Ask them to use complete sentences.
Below Expectations	• no detail correctly classified	• few or no correct responses • responses are incomprehensible	• no correct response • no comprehensible explanations • many errors
Meets Expectations	• some details correctly classified	• a few correct responses • responses are mostly comprehensible	• some correct responses • some comprehensible explanations • some errors
Above Expectations	• all details correctly classified	• all responses are correct • all responses are comprehensible	• all responses are correct • all explanations are comprehensible • few errors

Build Background

Use with Chapter 13, Lesson 1

Access Prior Knowledge

Help students recall previous lessons about post-war situations to predict changes that happened in the United States after World War II. Ask students to work in small groups to respond with *yes* or *no* to the following questions: 1) After World War II, did the United States economy become stronger because people wanted to buy many products? 2) Did the United States refuse to help the country of South Korea after World War II? 3) Did the United States and Russia compete to show who was more advanced? Then have students explain their answers. Tell students they will check their responses after reading.

- Before **Introduce**, p. 532
- 25 minutes

Lesson Vocabulary

Divide the class in half. Choose one student from each side to come to the blackboard. Show him or her a vocabulary card so that no one else can see it. Allow the student to sketch pictures or provide clues so that team members can guess the word. To guess, a team member must raise his or her hand. If the team member is right, the team gets a point and another turn. If not, the other team gets a turn.

Additional Vocabulary Explain the words in the margin and provide examples of their uses in the text. For example, explain that *boom* is a loud noise. However, in this case, it means a sudden and large increase. Say: *The baby boom was a sudden and large increase of babies born.* Have students practice each word by using them in sentences.

appliances	exploration
baby boom	orbit
charges	proof
communist	shortage
competed	space

Cognates As students read the lesson, you may want to point out cognates such as: **baby/bebé, communist/comunista, satellite/satélite.**

Build Fluency

Read aloud the following rhyme and point out the words that sound alike. Have students repeat it several times to develop oral language skills. Return to the rhyme throughout the lesson to help develop vocabulary, generalizing skills, and lesson content.

> South Korea attacked from the North.
> The UN sent troops to South Korea for support.
> Finally a **cease-fire** ended the fighting.
> A border was set, and Korea was divided.
>
> People had to use rations during the second World War,
> So afterward they bought more than ever before.
> People bought homes, and more children were born.
> Outside of big cities, **suburbs** were formed.
>
> The Soviet Union and United States raced
> To have more weapons and to explore space.
> In 1957, Soviets made strides
> With Sputnik, the world's first space **satellite**.

Success for English Learners • 215

Scaffolding the Content

Preview the Lesson

Have students refer to headings, illustrations, and captions in the lesson to complete the following cloze exercise: *The decade of the 19_____s was successful in many ways. The United States helped South Korea in the _____ War. There was a growing _____ because Americans bought many products. Many people enjoyed watching _____. The United States and the Soviet Union fought a _____ War, or a war of ideas.* Briefly discuss each point. Tell students they will learn how the United States changed after World War II.

• During **Teach**, pp. 532–537
• 30 minutes

Modify Instruction

Read the summaries below. Use a world map to provide locations of countries students may not be familiar with. Guide students in taking notes. Then have students summarize their notes by answering the questions on the blackline master page.

The Korean War
North Korea invaded South Korea in 1950. The United States went to the United Nations (UN) to ask them to help South Korea. The UN voted to send soldiers to Korea. Communist nations of the Soviet Union and China helped communist North Korea. In the end, a border was made, and a cease fire was called.

A Growing Economy
People lived with rationing, or a limited amount of products, during World War II. When the war ended, people began to buy many products, like cars, and appliances, like refrigerators. They also began to buy homes. Suburbs, or communities outside of cities, formed. Americans had more children.

A New Way of Living
Television was the most popular pastime, or fun thing to do, during the 1950s. In 1952, President Dwight D. Eisenhower was the first President to use television commercials in a presidential campaign. The trial of Senator Joseph McCarthy was also televised. He accused Americans of spying for the Soviet Union. People saw that McCarthy had no proof of these charges.

The Cold War
The United States and the Soviet Union had a Cold War, or a war of ideas. They had an arms race, and each country tried to buy more weapons than the other. They also had a space race, or a competition to explore space. As a result, in 1957, the Soviet Union launched Sputnik, the world's first space satellite.

Extend

Ask partners to revisit the questions they answered during the "Preview" activity. Have them work in the same groups to review their answers and to revise them by recording new responses to the same question. Discuss each point. Next, make additional statements about the material. Call on individuals to answer *true* or *false* and explain their answers.

• After **Teach**, pp. 532–537
• 10 minutes

Name _____ Date _____

DIRECTIONS Listen to your teacher. Take notes as your teacher discusses events that took place during the 1950s. Answer each question by summarizing your notes.

What happened during the Korean War?

Why did the United States economy grow in the 1950s?

Why was television important during the 1950s?

How did the United States and the Soviet Union compete against each other during the Cold War?

School-Home Connection Encourage students to take this page home to share with family members. They can use their notes to tell about the United States during the 1950s.

Apply and Assess

Write a Letter

Ask students to imagine that they have never watched a television show. Ask questions to help students formulate ideas and express their thoughts, for example: *What would surprise you? Is television more exciting than the radio? Why or why not? How is television different from reading a book or playing outside?*

• During **Close**, p. 537
• 30 minutes

Write responses on the board. Then write a model letter. Read it aloud to students and ask them to follow the form as they write their own letter.

- For beginning students, provide a few sentences with fill-in-the-blanks that can be completed with original ideas.
- For intermediate students, provide several sentence starters.
- Ask advanced students to write original letters using ideas from the board for help.

Informal Lesson Assessment

	Beginning	**Intermediate**	**Advanced**
Task	Provide a list of United States traits, including some from earlier decades and several that began during the 1950s. Ask students to circle the traits that show changes made during the 1950s.	Provide students with fill-in-the-blank statements to be completed with key words describing changes made in the United States during the 1950s. Have students supply the key words.	Ask brief questions about changes made in the United States during the 1950s. Ask students to respond in one or two sentences per question.
Below Expectations	• no trait correctly identified	• few or no correct responses • responses are incomprehensible	• no correct response • no comprehensible explanations • many errors
Meets Expectations	• some traits correctly identified	• a few correct responses • responses are mostly comprehensible	• some correct responses • some comprehensible explanations • some errors
Above Expectations	• all traits correctly identified	• all responses are correct • all responses are comprehensible	• all responses are correct • all explanations are comprehensible • few errors

Use with Chapter 13, Lesson 2

Build Background

Access Prior Knowledge

Hold up the photographs on pages 541 and 542. Ask students to describe what they see, and list ideas on the board. For the picture of the astronauts, ask: *Why is this picture in the lesson? Why do you think it is important?* For the pictures of the soldier and Vietnam protesters, ask: *Why do you think these people are so angry? What is the relationship between these two pictures?* Tell students that they are going to learn about important events that happened when President Kennedy and President Johnson led the United States.

- Before **Introduce**, p. 538
- 25 minutes

Lesson Vocabulary

Explain the vocabulary words using the vocabulary cards and concrete examples. Ask students to write each word on the front of an index card. On the back, have them write two hints about each word. For example, hints for **developing country** might be: *a place* and *making progress*. In small groups, have them combine their cards. Ask one student to draw a card, read the hints, and call on another student to guess the word.

Additional Vocabulary Explain the words in the margin and provide examples of their uses from the text. For example, explain that *insurance* is a product people buy to prevent losing money. Point out that there are many types of insurance, and the kind mentioned in this lesson is health insurance.

astronaut	insurance
blockade	moon
conquered	society

Cognates As students read the lesson, you may want to point out cognates such as: **astronaut/astronauta, crisis/crisis, society/sociedad**.

Build Fluency

Read aloud the following rhyme and point out the words that sound alike. Have students repeat it several times to develop oral language skills. Return to the rhyme throughout the lesson to help develop vocabulary, generalizing skills, and lesson content.

> The young president, John F. Kennedy,
> Faced a **crisis** with an enemy.
> The Soviets put missiles near our shores,
> And Kennedy had to act quickly to prevent war.
> In the Peace Corps, teachers and engineers
> Helped people in countries far and near.
>
> Johnson supported programs too—
> He encouraged people to reach the moon.
> President Johnson's Great Society made
> Programs like Head Start and Medicaid.
> When North Vietnam invaded the South,
> The United States sent troops, but then pulled out.
> When the Vietnam War was fought,
> Some people supported the war, but many did not.

Scaffolding the Content

Preview the Lesson

Post these topics on the board: *President Kennedy, Peace Corps, Cuban Missile Crisis, Space Exploration,* and *the Vietnam War*. Ask students to work in pairs to record the lesson page number with a photograph related to each topic and to tell a fact about each. Allow students to use photo captions, text, and the lesson summary. Record facts on the board. Tell students that in this lesson they will learn about events that happened in the United States during the 1960s.

- During **Teach**, pp. 538–543
- 30 minutes

Modify Instruction

Review the following points. Guide students in taking notes on the blackline master page. Then have pairs work together to summarize events of the 1960s.

John F. Kennedy
- **Peace Corps** This is a program that sends Americans to developing countries all over the world. Americans in the Peace Corps help people by working as teachers, health educators, and engineers.
- **Space Exploration** In 1961, President Kennedy asked Congress to give money for space exploration. The Soviet Union and the United States put men in space. Kennedy wanted to send an astronaut to the moon before the Soviet Union did.
- **Cuban Missile Crisis** In 1962, the Soviet Union put missiles in Cuba. Cuba is very close to the United States. President Kennedy ordered a blockade of Cuba so Soviet ships could not bring more missiles. Then Nikita Khrushchev, the Soviet leader, took the missiles out of Cuba. A nuclear war was prevented.

Lyndon B. Johnson
- **Programs** Johnson had a plan called the Great Society to make life better for Americans. Many programs in this plan still exist. Head Start provides education to young children before they go to school. Medicaid gives free health care to Americans who are poor. Medicare gives health insurance to older Americans.
- **Man on the Moon** In 1962, John Glenn was the first American to orbit, or circle, Earth. On July 20, 1969, Neil Armstrong and Buzz Aldrin, Jr. were the first people to walk on the moon.
- **The Vietnam War** In 1964, President Johnson sent American soldiers to South Vietnam to help defend the country from attacks by communist North Vietnamese. The war divided the United States. In 1973, President Nixon ordered a cease fire. American troops came home. Two years later, North Vietnam conquered the South.

Extend

Post categories *John F. Kennedy* and *Lyndon B. Johnson* on the board. Using their notes, have students copy events from the 1960s onto index cards. Collect the cards. Read a card and give it to a student. Have the student place the card under a category. Ask the class if the card was placed correctly. Confirm the correct category, and repeat the process.

- After **Teach**, pp. 538–543
- 10 minutes

Name _____ Date _____

DIRECTIONS Listen to your teacher. Take notes as your teacher discusses events that took place during the 1960s. Then summarize the events in two or three sentences.

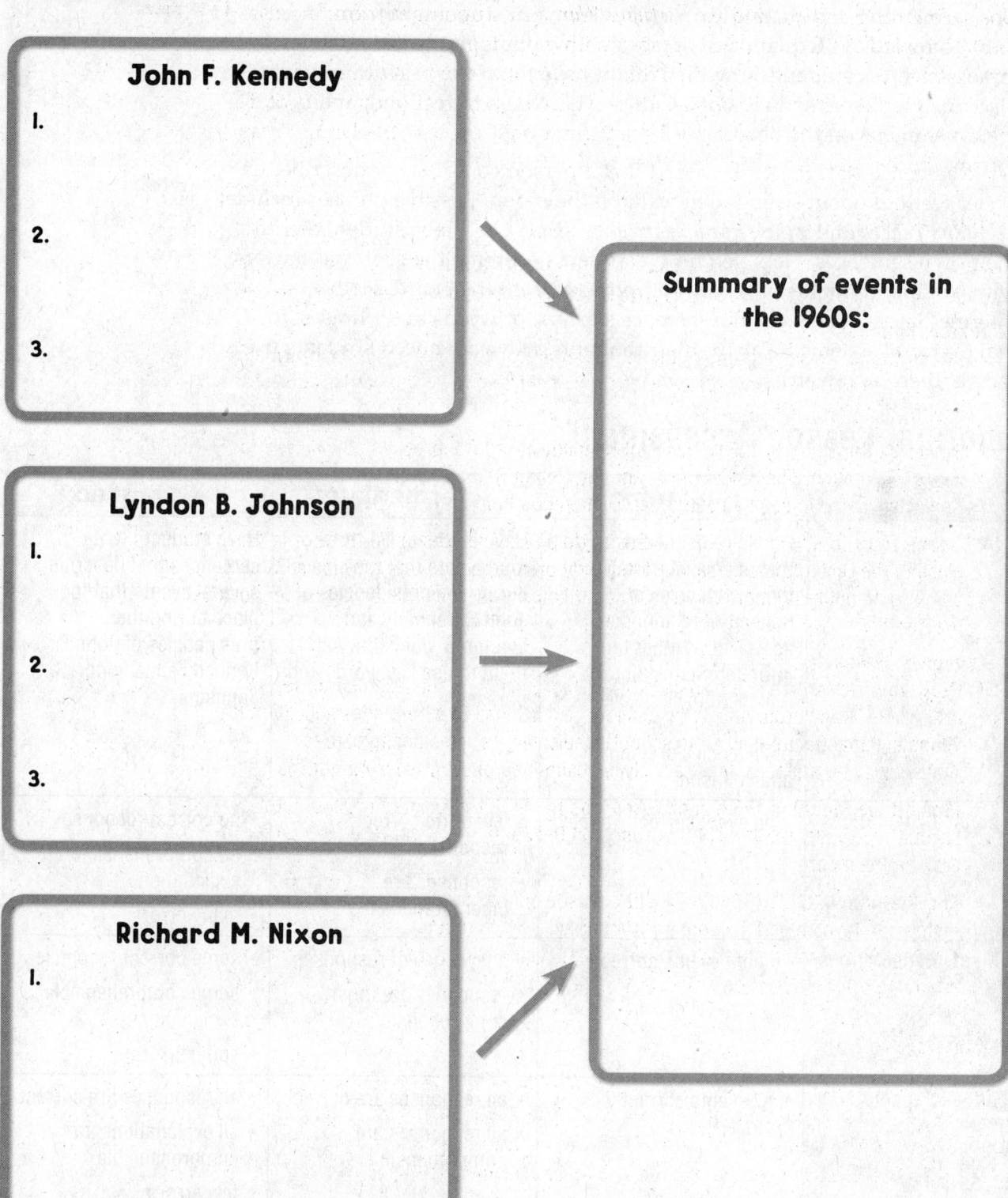

School-Home Connection Encourage students to take this page home to share with family members. They can use their notes to tell about events and accomplishments of the 1960s.

Unit 6, Chapter 13, Lesson 2 Success for English Learners ▪ 221

Apply and Assess

Write a Journal Entry

Help students understand the importance of the walk on the moon by Neil Armstrong and Buzz Aldrin, Jr. Review your discussion from "Access Prior Knowledge." Explain that at one time walking on the moon seemed impossible. Ask students how they might have felt if they saw this event take place for the first time in history. Call on volunteers to respond, and note their comments on the board.

• During **Close**, p. 543
• 30 minutes

Write sentence starters on the board that a person could use to describe his or her feelings about seeing men walk on the moon. Possible phrases include: *I couldn't believe* and *When I saw them take a step, I . . .* Have students write their own sentences. Help beginning students combine the sentence starters with original thoughts or words and phrases from the board. Help intermediate students use the sentence starters, or words and phrases, to make several statements about their thoughts. Have advanced students use mostly their own words.

Informal Lesson Assessment

	Beginning	Intermediate	Advanced
Task	Provide a list of events that happened during the presidencies of Kennedy and Johnson as well as at other times in United States history. Ask them to circle events that happened during the presidencies of Kennedy and Johnson.	Have students list three or four events that took place during the presidencies of John F. Kennedy and Lyndon B. Johnson. Ask them to use key words and phrases.	Have students write sentences that describe several events that took place during the presidencies of John F. Kennedy and Lyndon B. Johnson.
Below Expectations	• no event correctly circled	• few or no correct responses • responses are incomprehensible	• no correct response • no comprehensible explanations • many errors
Meets Expectations	• some events correctly circled	• a few correct responses • responses are mostly comprehensible	• some correct responses • some comprehensible explanations • some errors
Above Expectations	• all events correctly circled	• all responses are correct • all responses are comprehensible	• all responses are correct • all explanations are comprehensible • few errors

Use with Chapter 13, Lesson 3

Build Background

Access Prior Knowledge

Have students complete an "Equal Rights" K-W-L chart. Tell students to work in groups to record information they know about equal rights. Ask questions to help generate ideas, such as: *What does it mean to have equal rights? Who are some famous people who fought for equal rights?* Next, have students list questions about the Civil Rights Movement, including *What was the goal of the Civil Rights Movement?* They will complete the charts during the "Extend" activity.

- Before **Introduce**, p. 546
- 25 minutes

Lesson Vocabulary

Have students create word webs to connect new vocabulary words and associated images. Make a class web for **integration,** which may be associated with equal, fair, and together. Have students make webs for **civil rights** and **nonviolence** and share them with a partner.

Additional Vocabulary Explain the words in the margin and provide examples of their uses from the text. For example, the word *case* has multiple meanings. However, in this lesson, it refers to a court case, or when two sides present a problem and let a jury or judge decide the correct answer.

assassinated	national origin
boycott	refused
case	segregated
gender	separate
hire	treat

Cognates As students read the lesson, you may want to point out cognates such as: **origin/origen, violence/violencia.**

Build Fluency

Read aloud the following rhyme and point out the words that sound alike. Have students repeat it several times to develop oral language skills. Return to the rhyme throughout the lesson to help develop vocabulary, summarizing skills, and lesson content.

The Civil Rights Movement had a goal—
Civil rights for every single soul.
Many schools were segregated.
This meant blacks and whites were separated.
The family of Linda Brown
Went to court to turn this around.
Rosa Parks set an example for all of us
By refusing to give up her seat on the bus.
The preacher Martin Luther King, Jr.
Made a speech about his dream—
People not judged by the color of the skin
But by the person who they are within.

Success for English Learners ■ 223

Scaffolding the Content

Preview the Lesson

Take students on a picture walk through the lesson. Ask: *What are these people doing? Why?* Read the summary on page 550 aloud. Write the following question on the board: *The Civil Rights Movement helped a) African Americans only b) women only c) many minorities.* Model how to answer the question by breaking apart the summary. Invite students to support their answers by using information in the pictures. Explain that they will learn about the goals of the Civil Rights Movement.

• During **Teach**, pp. 546–550
• 30 minutes

Modify Instruction

Review the following points. Help students take notes on the blackline master page. Then have partners summarize events of the Civil Rights Movement.

Segregation in Schools In the early 1950s, the family of Linda Brown fought segregation in schools. A lawyer named Thurgood Marshall argued this case to the Supreme Court. In 1954, the Supreme Court outlawed segregation in public schools. Schools had to be integrated.

Segregation on City Buses Until the 1950s, in many cities African Americans had to sit at the back of the bus. On December 1, 1955, a young African American woman named Rosa Parks refused to move. She was arrested for breaking state law. Thousands of African Americans boycotted, or stopped using, city buses. The city buses lost a lot of business. Soon it became illegal to have segregated seating on city buses.

Civil Rights Act of 1964 Many restaurants, playgrounds, and stores segregated African Americans and whites. Martin Luther King, Jr. was an African American leader who led people through peaceful speeches and marches. He believed people could cause change without using violence. Congress passed the Civil Rights Act of 1964. This law gives all Americans the right to use public places and services. It also says employers cannot refuse to hire people because of their race, religion, country of birth, or gender. This law was a victory for the Civil Rights Movement. The goal of the movement was to change the United States Constitution to make sure that all minorities have full civil rights.

Violence The Civil Rights movement became violent in many parts of the country. There were riots because of integration in schools. An African American leader named Malcolm X supported separation between races. Someone assassinated, or killed, him in 1964. Martin Luther King, Jr. was assassinated in 1968.

Rights for All Minorities Cesar Chavez formed the United Farm Workers (UFW). He wanted migrant farm workers to have better wages. In addition, new laws said employers must treat men and women equally.

Extend

Ask students to complete the "Equal Rights" K-W-L chart. First, have them review the questions they asked about equal rights and record any answers they found in the lesson. Next, have them record other details they learned, such as the goals of the Civil Rights Movement. Then have students share the details aloud.

• After **Teach**, pp. 546–550
• 10 minutes

Name _____ Date _____

DIRECTIONS Listen to your teacher. Take notes as your teacher discusses different aspects of the Civil Rights Movement. Then summarize each section.

Notes	Summary
Segregation in Schools	
Segregation on City Buses	
Civil Rights Act of 1964	
Violence	
Rights for All Minorities	

School-Home Connection Encourage students to take this page home to share with family members. They can use their notes to tell about the Civil Rights Movement.

Unit 6, Chapter 13, Lesson 3

Apply and Assess

Deliver a Speech

On the board, record vocabulary words from Martin Luther King Jr.'s "I Have a Dream" speech. Explain their meanings. Then read the speech aloud. Pause after major parts and explain the content to students. Ask questions to assess comprehension as you go.

- During **Close**, p. 550
- 30 minutes

Next, have pairs practice reading parts. Have beginning students take turns reading the speech sentence by sentence. Have one student read a sentence and have the partner repeat it. Have intermediate students take turns reading the speech by paragraph. Ask advanced students to read the speech individually. Circle the room and point to parts for students to read aloud. Listen to their pronunciation and ask questions to assess comprehension.

Informal Lesson Assessment

	Beginning	Intermediate	Advanced
Task	Ask students to choose the main goal of the Civil Rights Movement from a list of several statements.	Have students identify the main goal of the Civil Rights Movement in writing. They may use words and phrases.	Have students describe the main goal of the Civil Rights Movement in one or more sentences.
Below Expectations	• an unrelated idea was chosen	• response is incorrect or incomprehensible	• response is incorrect or incomprehensible
Meets Expectations	• a related idea was chosen	• response is correct but parts are incomprehensible	• response is correct but parts are incomprehensible
Above Expectations	• the goal was correctly chosen	• the entire response is correct and comprehensible	• the entire response is correct and comprehensible

Use with Chapter 13, Lesson 4

Build Background

Access Prior Knowledge

Write *Jimmy Carter, Ronald Reagan, Richard Nixon,* and *Mikhail Gorbachev* on the board. Ask questions, such as: *Which of these people were American Presidents? Which was a leader of Russia? Why were they important?* Then ask: *Do leaders ever break the law? Do people always support their leaders?* Discuss students' answers. Point out that these people were world leaders during the 1970s and 1980s. In this lesson, students will learn about these leaders' accomplishments as well as their mistakes.

- Before **Introduce**, p. 556
- 25 minutes

Lesson Vocabulary

Explain vocabulary words using vocabulary cards and by reading them in the context of lesson sentences. Ask students to create a picture cue or symbol for each word. For example, model making a visual for the word **inflation** by drawing a dollar sign and an arrow pointing up to symbolize the higher prices that occur during inflation.

Additional Vocabulary Explain the words in the margin, and provide examples of their uses from the text. For example, explain the phrasal verb *cover up* means to hide, and it often refers to hiding illegal activity.

Cognates As students read the lesson, you may want to point out cognates such as: **reform/reforma, scandal/escándalo**.

against the law	cut taxes
Berlin Wall	declined
bills	hostage
cover up	reform
	resign

Build Fluency

Read aloud the following rhyme and point out the words that sound alike. Have students repeat it several times to develop oral language skills. Return to the rhyme throughout the lesson to help develop vocabulary, summarizing skills, and lesson content.

During the 1970s, Nixon eased the Cold War,
Then did something no president had done before—
He committed a crime and caused a **scandal**.
His resignation was a lot for Americans to handle.
Carter helped Egypt and Israel make peace; this was a first!
Then his luck got worse and worse.
America suffered gas lines and **inflation**
And Carter earned the anger of the nation.
Students took American hostages in Iran.
The hostages were freed as the Reagan presidency began.
The 1980s brought the biggest changes yet.
Reagan cut taxes, and this created a huge budget **deficit**.
The Berlin wall that divided East and West
Came down in '89 and finally put the Cold War to rest.

Scaffolding the Content

Preview the Lesson

Use lesson pictures and headings to help students preview important people and events they will read about. Ask questions, such as: *Who were the presidents of the United States during the 1970s and 1980s? What was one problem people faced during this time?* Tell students they will learn about important events that happened during the 1970s and 1980s.

- During **Teach**, pp. 556–561
- 30 minutes

Modify Instruction

Read the summaries below. Guide each student in taking notes. Then have students summarize their notes by answering questions on the blackline master page. Review by covering questions and recalling as many details as possible.

President Richard Nixon
President Nixon met with Soviet leader Leonid Breznev. They agreed on a plan for arms control, or limiting weapons of each nation. In 1972, Nixon was reelected. During his campaign, people working for him broke into an office of the Democratic Party in the Watergate building. He tried to cover it up. This caused a scandal, and he resigned.

President Jimmy Carter
Jimmy Carter was elected President in 1976. Arab leaders limited oil shipped to the United States. This caused high gas prices and inflation. In 1979, a group of students in Iran took Americans hostage. Americans wanted Carter to stop the crisis, and they blamed him for problems in the economy.

President Ronald Reagan
Reagan was elected in 1980. He cut taxes. The economy got stronger, and inflation declined. The government did not have enough tax money to pay bills, so it borrowed money. This created a budget deficit, or shortage. Reagan spent money to build a stronger military to win the Cold War. The Soviet Union made more weapons, too.

Soviet Leader Mikhail Gorbachev
Gorbachev became the leader of the Soviet Union in 1985. He and Ronald Reagan agreed to limit missiles. Gorbachev reformed the Soviet Union and gave the people more freedoms. In November 1989, the Berlin Wall was removed, and the next year Germany reunited. In 1991, Gorbachev outlawed the Communist party. Because of that, there was little reason to reunite the fifteen Soviet republics. These fifteen Soviet republics declared independence.

Extend

Review the important events that occurred under Richard Nixon, Jimmy Carter, Ronald Reagan, and Mikhail Gorbachev. Write a summary of important events under each leader. Have students match the summaries to the leader by drawing lines. Then read events and have students identify the leader under whom each event happened.

- After **Teach**, pp. 556–561
- 10 minutes

Name _____ Date _____

DIRECTIONS Listen to your teacher read the lesson summary. Record details that answer the questions as your teacher explains them. Then cover the question and recall as many related details as possible.

What did President Richard Nixon do during the 1970s?

Whom did Americans blame for the troubles in the 1970s?

What did President Ronald Reagan do during the 1980s?

What did Soviet leader Mikhail Gorbachev do during the 1980s?

School-Home Connection Encourage students to take this page home to share with family members. They can use their notes to tell about important events of the 1970s and 1980s.

Unit 6, Chapter 13, Lesson 4

Success for English Learners

Apply and Assess

Write a Diary Entry

*During **Close**, p. 561
*30 minutes

Help students imagine the feelings between people of the Soviet Union and the United States during the Cold War. For example, ask: *What was it like living during the Cold War? Were you scared of nuclear weapons?* Record responses on the board.

Next, help students imagine how people's emotions changed when the Cold War ended. On the board, record words like: *excited, curious, surprise,* and *shock.* Explain why people felt this range of emotions at the end of the Cold War.

Write a model diary entry on the board. Read it aloud and tell students to follow the form. Underline phrases that beginning students can copy and complete using original words. Tell intermediate students to consider using parts of sentences, like the beginning, and add their own thoughts to the end. Ask advanced students to use original words and thoughts.

Informal Lesson Assessment

	Beginning	Intermediate	Advanced
Task	List important events and people of the 1970s and 1980s. Ask students to specify whether each occurred during the 1970s or 1980s.	Have students use phrases to list important people and events of the 1970s and 1980s. Then have them list differences during those decades in the United States.	Ask students to write a paragraph describing differences in the United States during the 1970s and 1980s.
Below Expectations	• no event correctly classified	• few or no correct responses • responses are incomprehensible	• no correct response • no comprehensible explanations • many errors
Meets Expectations	• some events correctly classified	• a few correct responses • responses are mostly comprehensible	• some correct responses • some comprehensible explanations • some errors
Above Expectations	• all events correctly classified	• all responses are correct • all responses are comprehensible	• all responses are correct • all explanations are comprehensible • few errors

Use with Chapter 13 · Lesson 5

Build Background

Access Prior Knowledge

Read aloud the list of *People* and *Places* on page 562 and write them on the board in columns. Have students work in small groups to brainstorm information they know about them. As the class is working, call up groups to record a detail or two in the appropriate columns on the board. Once all groups have been called, review the information on the board together. Revise any inaccurate details and circle any that will surface in this lesson.

• Before **Introduce**, p. 562
• 25 minutes

Lesson Vocabulary

Explain the vocabulary words using brief definitions and sketches or symbols. Read and show the definitions on the vocabulary cards and ask questions to assess students' comprehension, for example: *Which word describes the economy?* Have students work in mixed-proficiency pairs to create a crossword puzzle using the words from the lesson. Ask them to write definitions, or hints for the words, and exchange puzzles with another pair to complete.

Additional Vocabulary Explain the words in the margin and provide examples of their uses from the text. For example, explain that *budget* means a plan for spending money, and budgets are used by families, schools, governments, and businesses to spend money wisely. Explain that when a country spends too much money, it can cause problems in the economy.

budget	popular
embassy	spending
fame	under oath
gulf	unemployment
lying	welfare

Cognates As students read the lesson, you may want to point out cognates such as: **embassy/embajada, gulf/golfo, popular/popular, terrorism/terrorismo.**

Build Fluency

Read aloud the following rhyme and point out the words that sound alike. Have students repeat it several times to develop oral language skills. Return to the rhyme throughout the lesson to help develop vocabulary, summarizing skills, and lesson content.

> The 1990s brought new challenges and lessons.
> President Bush dealt with unemployment and a **recession.**
> Then Iraq attacked Kuwait, so he led America to war.
> In 1991, he formed Operation Desert Storm.
> Under Bill Clinton, the economy grew.
> There were millions of jobs, and a balanced budget too!
> But **terrorism** was a problem that wouldn't go away.
> Terrorists attacked us at home and far away.

Success for English Learners ■ 231

Scaffolding the Content

Preview the Lesson

Preview lesson pictures, captions, headings, and topic sentences. Ask questions that can be answered using these features. For example, point to the picture on page 564 and say: *The United States fought a war in the 1990s. Find the name of that war in the heading on this page.* Have students write or say their answers. Next, read the summary on page 563 aloud and point to photographs in the lesson that relate to key topics. Explain that students will learn how the United States changed during the 1990s.

- During **Teach**, pp. 562–567
- 30 minutes

Modify Instruction

Read each category aloud. Show students the locations of countries on a world map, as necessary. Have students find the corresponding heading on the blackline master page. Guide students in taking notes on each topic. Then help them summarize information under each one.

President George H.W. Bush
In 1988 George H.W. Bush was elected President. Before that he was Vice President under Ronald Reagan. After the Cold War, the economy had a recession, or time of slow activity. Millions of Americans lost their jobs. Many people worried about the economy.

The Persian Gulf War
In 1990 Saddam Hussein led Iraq in an invasion of Kuwait, a producer of oil in the Middle East. President Bush built a coalition, or a group with the same goal, of 33 nations. The United States led an attack called Operation Desert Storm, or the Gulf War. The Allies won. General Colin L. Powell became a national hero during the Gulf War.

President Bill Clinton
Bill Clinton was elected President in 1992. During his presidency, businesses created millions of new jobs, unemployment dropped to a very low level, and the President and Congress balanced the national budget. President Clinton and Congress made a law that people could receive welfare for only two years. President Clinton was also involved in controversy. He was impeached, or accused of crimes, including lying under oath. He was not convicted.

Terrorism
In 1993, foreign terrorists set off a bomb at the World Trade Center in New York City. The bomb killed six people and wounded about 1,000. In 1995, an American citizen who was angry with the government set off a bomb at a government building in Oklahoma. Outside of the United States, bombs exploded at two American embassies in Africa. Terrorists also bombed the USS *Cole*, a United States Navy ship docked near the country Yemen.

Extend

Have students use a Venn diagram to compare the presidencies of Bill Clinton and George H. W. Bush. Tell them to include actions and problems of each president, as well as events that occurred under each.

- After **Teach**, pp. 562–567
- 10 minutes

Name _____ Date _____

DIRECTIONS Listen to your teacher read each category. Take notes about each category. Then summarize information on each topic.

Notes	Summary (one or two sentences)
President George H. W. Bush	
The Persian Gulf War	
President Bill Clinton	
Terrorism	

School-Home Connection Encourage students to take this page home to share with family members. They can use their notes to talk about how the United States changed during the 1990s.

Apply and Assess

Write an Editorial

Explain that an editorial is an article in a newspaper that states an opinion. Write this question on the board and ask student to state their opinions: *Why is it important for the President and Congress to work together?* If necessary, review information about Clinton's working with Congress to balance the budget, as well as the roles of the President, Congress, and Senate. Record important points on the board.

• During **Close**, p. 567
• 30 minutes

Have students form groups to write editorials. Have beginning students illustrate the editorial with labels identifying names and objects shown. Ask intermediate students to outline the points that will be made and to ensure that all group members understand the points. Ask advanced students to write the editorial independently.

Informal Lesson Assessment

	Beginning	Intermediate	Advanced
Task	Have students list changes that happened during the 1990s. Allow them to use pictures and key words to express their knowledge.	Have students list changes that happened during the 1990s. Ask them to use phrases and short sentences to express their knowledge.	Ask students to write several sentences describing changes in the United States during the 1990s. Ask them to use complete sentences.
Below Expectations	• no change is correct or comprehensible	• few or no correct responses • responses are incomprehensible	• no correct response • no comprehensible explanations • many errors
Meets Expectations	• some changes are correct and comprehensible	• a few correct responses • responses are mostly comprehensible	• some correct responses • some comprehensible explanations • some errors
Above Expectations	• all changes are correct and comprehensible	• all responses are correct • all responses are comprehensible	• all responses are correct • all explanations are comprehensible • few errors

Use with Chapter 14, Lesson 1

Build Background

Access Prior Knowledge

Ask students to work in groups to list names, places, and events they know about the presidency of George W. Bush. Make a concept web by drawing a circle around the name *George W. Bush* and writing students' responses around it. During the discussion, try to connect students' ideas to lesson themes, including the election between George W. Bush and Al Gore, the events of September 11, and the 2004 and 2005 hurricanes.

- Before **Introduce**, p. 572
- 25 minutes

Lesson Vocabulary

Explain the word **hijack** using the vocabulary card for the lesson. Show students the correct spelling of the past tense, *hijacked*. Have students write two sentences using the word—one in the past tense and one in the present tense. Ask them to read their sentences aloud to a partner. Then have students trade, and read the partner's sentences aloud.

Additional Vocabulary Explain the words in the margin and provide examples of their uses. For example, point out that the word *call* has multiple meanings; in this lesson *to call* means to decide, so *The election was too close to call* means that the number of votes on each side are almost equal.

acts	field
call	hurricane
candidates	in favor
century	terrorist
damage	towers

Cognates As students read the lesson, you may want to point out cognates such as: **election/elección, hurricane/huracán, terrorist/terrorista**.

Build Fluency

Read aloud the following rhyme and point out the words that sound alike. Have students repeat it several times to develop oral language skills. Return to the rhyme throughout the lesson to help develop vocabulary, summarizing skills, and lesson content.

> The 2000 election was too close to call.
> A hundred million people voted in all.
> The Supreme Court ruled that George Bush had won.
> Counting the votes was finally done!
>
> On September 11 of the next year,
> Terrorists made people feel great fear:
> They **hijacked** planes with innocent people inside,
> Crashed into buildings, and 3,000 people died.
> The United States blamed the Taliban and went to war.
> It worried about security more than ever before.

Success for English Learners

Scaffolding the Content

Preview the Lesson

Present the lesson page by page. First show the photograph or illustration. Then ask questions that can be answered using headings or captions. For example, on page 572, show the photograph and ask: *What is the name of this person? What is the job he is starting in the photograph? When did he begin this job?* As you review pages, write lesson topics on the board and explain that students will learn about challenges the United States faced at the beginning of the twenty-first century.

- During **Teach**, pp. 572–575
- 30 minutes

Modify Instruction

Review the following summary of challenges the United States faced at the beginning of the twenty-first century. Help students take notes on the blackline master page. Then have students put a check mark next to the three most important ideas from the lesson. Finally, have students explain why they think a specific idea is important.

A New President

1. **Presidential Race** (2000) Republican Texas Governor George W. Bush ran against Democratic Vice President Al Gore. There were over 100 million votes. In the state of Florida, it was too close to call a winner. Finally, the Supreme Court decided Bush was the winner. He became the 43rd president on January 20, 2001.

Modern Challenges

1. **Terrorist Attack** On September 11, 2001, terrorists hijacked four American planes. Two planes flew into the towers of the World Trade Center in New York City, and one plane hit the Pentagon in Washington, D.C. The fourth plane crashed into an empty field. Nearly 3,000 people were killed.
2. **Afghanistan** In October 2001, the United States and its allies invaded Afghanistan and overthrew the Taliban government. The terrorists who attacked the United States had links to the Taliban government.
3. **Iraq** In 2003, the United States and its allies invaded Iraq. The leader of Iraq was Saddam Hussein. The United States and its allies continue to work to bring democracy and peace to Iraq, but the violence there continues.
4. **Reelection** In 2004, George W. Bush was reelected. Some Americans support the war in Iraq, but others do not.
5. **Hurricanes** In 2004 and 2005, several hurricanes damaged the southern coast. In 2004, four hurricanes hit Florida. In 2005, Hurricane Katrina hit the Gulf Coast. Hurricane Katrina was one of the worst natural disasters in United States history. Later that year, Hurricane Rita further damaged the Gulf Coast.

Extend

Have students refer to the blackline master to summarize the information into a few sentences. After they complete drafts, collect them. Read drafts aloud without identifying the writers. Ask questions about main ideas that need to be added and details that should be removed.

- After **Teach**, pp. 572–575
- 10 minutes

Name _____ Date _____

DIRECTIONS Listen to your teacher. Take notes as your teacher talks about things that happened during the early twenty-first century. Then work with a partner to place a check (✔) by the three most important ideas.

Topic	Details	Most Important Ideas
Presidential Race		
Terrorist Attack		
Afghanistan		
Iraq		
Reelection		
Hurricanes		

School-Home Connection Encourage students to take this page home to share with family members. They can use their notes to tell about the United States during the early twenty-first century.

Unit 6, Chapter 14, Lesson 1

Success for English Learners ■ 237

Apply and Assess

Write a Diary Entry

- During **Close**, p. 575
- 35 minutes

Help students identify images, feelings, and thoughts they felt when they heard about the events of September 11, 2001. Post pieces of chart paper labeled *images*, *feelings*, and *actions*. Ask students to work in groups to list things they heard about the events of September 11. Have each group record responses in all three categories. Discuss and clarify responses on each chart, and record each on the board using correct spelling and phrasing.

Write the beginning of a diary entry on the board. Tell students they should follow the form of the entry as they write their own, and remind them to use words and phrases from the board. Allow beginning students to copy the model and add one or two sentences to it. Have intermediate students copy or paraphrase it and add a few sentences. Ask advanced students to use the same form but to write their ideas using original language.

Informal Lesson Assessment

	Beginning	Intermediate	Advanced
Task	Provide true/false statements about challenges the United States faced at the start of the twenty-first century. Have students identify each as true or false.	Provide true/false statements about challenges the United States faced at the start of the twenty-first century. Have students identify each as true or false and to correct false statements.	Provide true/false statements about challenges the United States faced at the start of the twenty-first century. Have students identify each as true or false and rewrite false statements to make them true.
Below Expectations	• no trait correctly identified	• few or no correct responses • responses are incomprehensible	• no correct response • no comprehensible explanations • many errors
Meets Expectations	• some traits correctly identified	• a few correct responses • responses are mostly comprehensible	• some correct responses • some comprehensible explanations • some errors
Above Expectations	• all traits correctly identified	• all responses are correct • all responses are comprehensible	• all responses are correct • all explanations are comprehensible • few errors

Use with Chapter 14, Lesson 2

Build Background

Access Prior Knowledge

Ask students to work in pairs to list as many kinds of shoes as possible. Give them two or three minutes. Next, ask them to: 1) circle the least expensive kind of shoe; 2) underline the most expensive kind of shoe; and 3) put a star by the kind of shoe that lasts the longest. Review responses aloud, with students providing reasons why they think a shoe is expensive, inexpensive, or high quality. Explain that countries that sell many kinds of shoes generally have a free enterprise system. This means that businesses decide what goods to sell and how much money to charge because of what consumers want.

- Before **Introduce**, p. 576
- 25 minutes

Lesson Vocabulary

Explain the vocabulary words by giving brief definitions and examples. Write hints for each word on index cards. Hints can include descriptions or paraphrased definitions, such as: *In this system, people control businesses.* Then form two teams. Ask for a volunteer from each team. Draw the top card, and read it aloud. Let each volunteer try to identify the word described on the card. Confirm the correct answer and give each team with the correct answer a point. If neither volunteer answers correctly, ask for two additional volunteers until the correct word is identified. Continue until all students have a turn.

Additional Vocabulary Explain the words in the margin and provide examples of their uses. Review familiar terms and explain how they relate to the concept of economic systems, such as free enterprise. *Rationing*, for example, means limiting goods. It relates to economic systems because it is one of many ways to divide goods among people and businesses.

barter	produce
business	rationing
enterprise	resource
goods	scarce
human	sharing
increase	

Cognates As students read the lesson, you may want to point out cognates such as: **depend/depender, produce/producir, resource/recurso.**

Build Fluency

Read aloud the following rhyme and point out the words that sound alike. Have students repeat it several times to develop oral language skills. Return to the rhyme throughout the lesson to help develop vocabulary, summarizing skills, and lesson content.

> **Free enterprise** lets people decide
> What price to pay and which products to buy.
> You need resources for a business to run.
> You need **capital goods**, tools, and workers to get the job done.
> When a good has a little supply, the price gets high.
> If the supply increases, the high price stops, or ceases.
> When demand rises, so do the prices.
> When demand slows, the prices get low.

Success for English Learners ■ 239

Scaffolding the Content

Preview the Lesson

Conduct a picture walk of the lesson with students and preview headings and captions. Ask students to use this information to identify: 1) a specific type of good they will learn about in this lesson; 2) two types of economies they will read about; 3) two things that affect prices; and 4) whether different regions work separately or together to produce and sell goods and services. Review answers and briefly explain key words and concepts. Tell students that in this lesson they will learn how goods that people want control free enterprise systems.

- During **Teach**, pp. 576–581
- 30 minutes

Modify Instruction

Review the following points and ask the questions at the end of each section. Help students record information on the blackline master page. Then help students summarize each answer and record the summary in the table.

The Free Enterprise System

1 Companies need human resources, or workers. They also need natural resources, like water, minerals, and fuel. Finally, they need capital goods, such as buildings, technology, and tools to produce goods and services. Ask: *What three kinds of resources do businesses need?*

Using Scarce Resources

1 There are not enough resources for everyone, so resources are divided in many ways: paying prices, sharing equally, rationing, bartering, first-come-first serve, or having a lottery. In a market economy, as the United States has, people or businesses pay a price for resources. In a command economy, the government decides who receives resources. Ask: *How are resources divided?*

2 Prices are based on supply and demand. When demand is high, prices are usually high. When demand is low, prices are low. If supply is high, prices are usually low. If supply is low, prices are usually higher. Companies can lower prices so more people will want their product. They can also try to make better quality products than competitors. Ask: *How do business owners decide on prices?*

3 Productive businesses are those that produce more. Education helps people produce more. Capital goods, like computers, help companies produce more. Specialization, or when one person does only one main task, helps companies produce more. Ask: *What makes businesses productive?*

4 No place can produce everything people want, and no place has all natural resources. Some places, for example, cannot produce food, so they depend on those that can. Ask: *Why are regions interdependent?*

Extend

Have students recall the different types of shoes, and their respective qualities, they listed in "Access Prior Knowledge." Then ask students: *How do business owners decide on the price of shoes? Why are some shoes more expensive than others?* Review lesson concepts as necessary so that students can understand the concept of supply and demand as it relates to shoes.

- After **Teach**, pp. 576–581
- 10 minutes

Name _____ Date _____

DIRECTIONS Listen to your teacher. Take notes as your teacher discusses important parts of a free enterprise system. Then write a summary of each answer in the column on the right.

Question and Answer	Summary
1. What three kinds of resources do businesses need?	
2. How are resources divided?	
3. How do business owners decide on prices?	
4. What makes businesses productive?	
5. Why are regions interdependent?	

School-Home Connection Encourage students to take this page home to share with family members. They can use their notes to tell about free enterprise systems used in countries like the United States.

Unit 6, Chapter 14, Lesson 2 — Success for English Learners

Apply and Assess

Make a Poster

Review important aspects of producing goods, such as quality, price, and productivity. Have students brainstorm images they can include in a poster about producing and selling goods in a free enterprise system. Ask students to share their responses aloud, and list them on the board for reference as students work.

• During **Close**, p. 581
• 25 minutes

Help groups determine tasks for students of various proficiencies. Beginning students may draw pictures and record words on the poster. Intermediate students can write descriptive words and phrases and draw pictures as well. Advanced students can present the poster aloud to the class and write longer definitions or explanations for their posters.

Informal Lesson Assessment

	Beginning	Intermediate	Advanced
Task	Provide descriptions of various aspects of the free enterprise system in the United States. Have students label each aspect using key words or lesson vocabulary.	Provide descriptions of various aspects of the free enterprise system in the United States. Have students describe them using phrases and brief sentences.	Provide brief questions about aspects of the free enterprise system of the United States. Ask students to respond using complete sentences.
Below Expectations	• no aspect correctly identified	• few or no correct responses • responses are incomprehensible	• no correct response • no comprehensible explanations • many errors
Meets Expectations	• some aspects correctly identified	• a few correct responses • responses are mostly comprehensible	• some correct responses • some comprehensible explanations • some errors
Above Expectations	• all aspects correctly identified	• all responses are correct • all responses are comprehensible	• all responses are correct • all explanations are comprehensible • few errors

Build Background

Use with Chapter 14, Lesson 3

Access Prior Knowledge

Write *Colonial Times* and *Industrial Revolution* on the board. Have student pairs name one or two important crops the colonists grew to earn money during the colonial times. Next, have them list products that people manufactured to earn money during the Industrial Revolution. Discuss responses. Explain that in the past, the economy of the United States was based on growing or making goods. Today the United States' economy is based on providing services. Ask volunteers for examples of services.

- Before **Introduce**, p. 584
- 20 minutes

Lesson Vocabulary

Examine the roots of each vocabulary word. Write **service industry** on the board. Ask: *Who remembers the meaning of* industry? Confirm that *industry* is the buying and selling of a good or product, so *service industry* is the buying and selling of services. Next write **globalization** on the board. Underline *global*. Explain that *global* describes things that involve the world—they do not just involve a city, region, or country. Say: Globalization *means the development of a global economy.* Ask students to create a visual for each word.

Additional Vocabulary Explain the words in the margin and provide examples of their uses. For example, write the terms *international* and *interdependent* on the board. Explain that the prefix *inter-* means between. Ask: *What does international mean?* Confirm that it means between nations.

Cognates As students read the lesson, you may want to point out cognates such as: **agriculture/agricultura, global/global, international/internacional.**

age
agriculture
exact
high-tech
interdependent
international
manufacturing

Build Fluency

Read aloud the following rhyme and point out the words that sound alike. Have students repeat it several times to develop oral language skills. Return to the rhyme throughout the lesson to help develop vocabulary, summarizing skills, and lesson content.

> Today's economy is based on things people do for us,
> Like cooking, teaching, or driving a bus.
> People made money selling crops and goods before,
> But today, **service industries** earn much more.
> The high-tech industry makes the economy grow
> And increases information that people know
> Free trade agreements limit the amount of tax.
> This helps nations interact.

Success for English Learners ■ 243

Scaffolding the Content

Preview the Lesson

On the board, write *service industry, information age,* and *globalization,* the three main lesson topics. Point out the lesson illustrations and read the captions. As you do so, ask students to point to or state the related topic on the board. Explain how each image shows a change in the economy of the United States from 100 years ago. For example, as you discuss the illustration on page 585, explain that in the past, most people worked to make or grow products, but today, most people, like the veterinarian shown, work to provide services rather than goods.

• During **Teach**, pp. 584–587
• 30 minutes

Modify Instruction

Review the following points. Have students take notes on a separate sheet of paper. Then help them summarize how each topic reflects changes in the economy of the United States. Have students record summaries on the blackline master page.

Service Industries

In the past, more people in the United States worked to make goods. Today, more people work to provide services. Service industries give services, rather than goods, to people. Service jobs include being a doctor, lawyer, teacher, restaurant worker, and mechanic.

The Information Age

The 1970s was the beginning of the Information Age. Since then, people have more information than ever before. High-tech, or computer and electronic, industries have become very important to the American economy. One example is global positioning systems, also called GPS. These systems help people to find an exact location on Earth.

Free Trade Agreements

The United States depends on other countries for some goods and services. To have more international trade, some countries have signed free-trade agreements. In a free-trade agreement, countries agree not to charge tariffs, or taxes, on goods they buy and sell to each other. In 1994, Mexico, Canada, and the United States began the North American Free Trade Agreement, known as NAFTA. Trade between these countries increased.

Globalization

International trade helps the economy of the United States. Many United States companies have offices and factories in other countries. In addition, foreign companies have businesses in the United States. Nations of the world have experienced globalization, or the development of a global economy. Nations depend on each other for goods and services.

Extend

Play *What am I?* Divide the class into two teams. Make statements about key terms and concepts in the lesson, for example: *I find exact locations on Earth.* Ask students to raise their hands before guessing. Call on students to answer. The team that answers correctly first gets a point. At the end, the team with the most points wins.

• After **Teach**, pp. 585–587
• 10 minutes

Name _____ Date _____

DIRECTIONS Take notes as your teacher describes ways the United States economy has changed over the past 100 years. Summarize points under each topic that explain these changes.

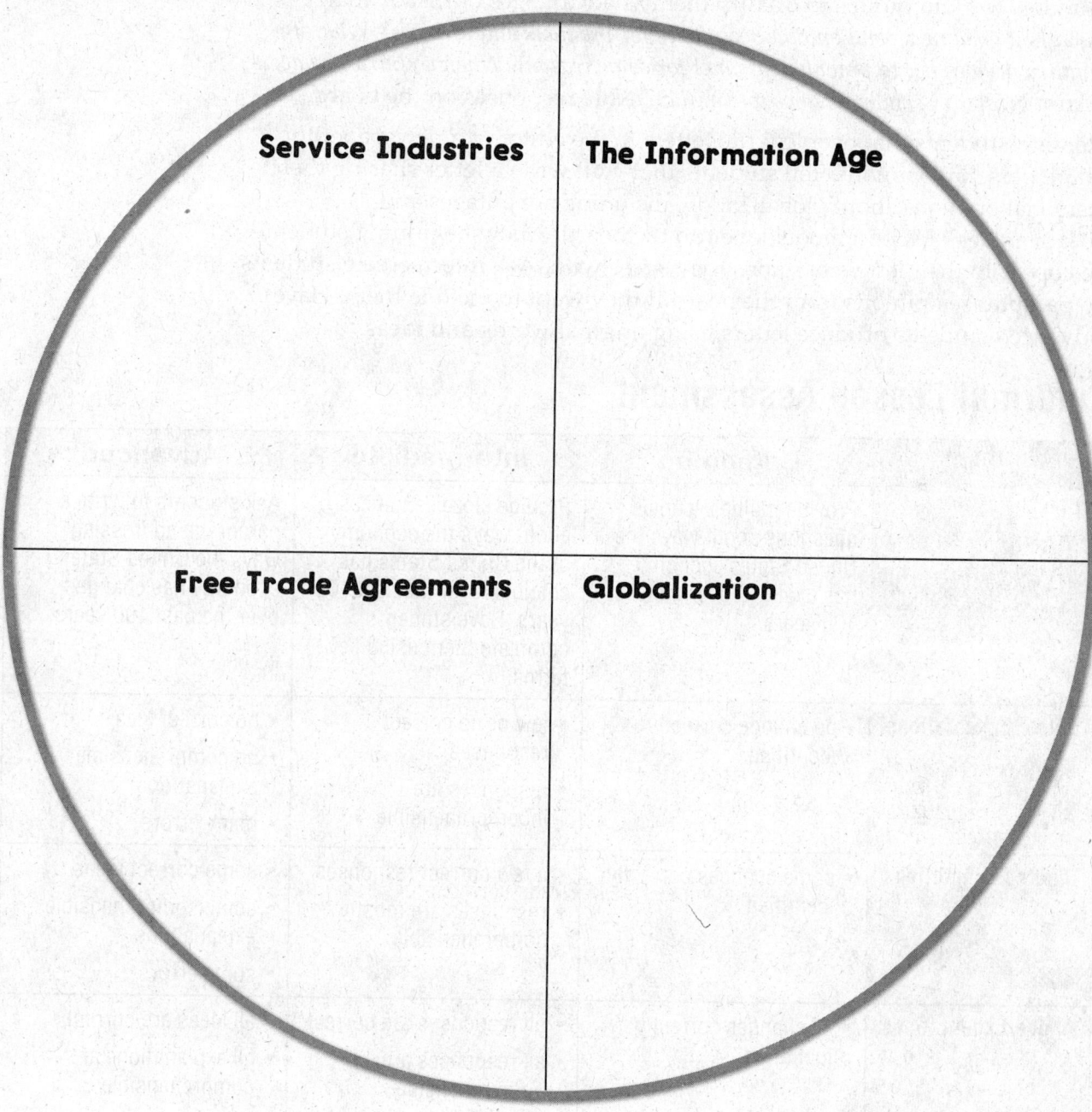

School-Home Connection Encourage students to take this page home to share with family members. They can use their notes to tell about changes in the economy of the United States over the last 100 years.

Unit 6, Chapter 14, Lesson 3

Apply and Assess

Write a Descriptive Letter

• During **Close**, p. 587
• 30 minutes

On the board, write a list of the effects of globalization, such as interdependence between countries and jobs in foreign countries. Have students work in groups to classify them as advantages or disadvantages. Ask: *Is it good to depend on other countries for products and services? What if a country decides not to provide a product for some reason? When countries trade, is there a greater or smaller chance for conflict?* Note responses on the board.

Remind students that people write letters to the editor of a newspaper to share personal opinions. Tell students they will write a letter sharing their personal opinions about globalization, including advantages and disadvantages. Write a model letter on the board. Allow beginning students to copy into their letters opinions they agree with. Ask intermediate students to paraphrase opinions from the board if they want to include them. Have advanced students produce letters using original words and ideas.

Informal Lesson Assessment

	Beginning	Intermediate	Advanced
Task	Provide multiple-choice questions about ways the United States economy has changed over the past 100 years.	Provide cloze sentences about ways the economy of the United States has changed over the past 100 years. Have students complete them using key terms.	Ask students to write a paragraph addressing ways the United States economy has changed over the past 100 years.
Below Expectations	• no change correctly identified	• few or no correct responses • responses are incomprehensible	• no correct idea • no comprehensible explanations • many errors
Meets Expectations	• some changes correctly identified	• a few correct responses • responses are mostly comprehensible	• some correct ideas • some comprehensible explanations • some errors
Above Expectations	• all changes correctly identified	• all responses are correct • all responses are comprehensible	• all ideas are correct • all explanations are comprehensible • few errors

Use with Chapter 14, Lesson 4

Build Background

Access Prior Knowledge

Ask students to volunteer the names of undeveloped places they have visited, such as rural areas, mountains, and forests. Then have them volunteer the names of developed places they have visited, where there are businesses, houses, and busy streets. Have partners tell a few characteristics of each place. Then ask: *Which place has more people, the country or the city? Which has more plants and animals? Which is cleaner?* Explain that when a community develops, its environment changes.

- Before **Introduce**, p. 590
- 25 minutes

Lesson Vocabulary

Read the definition for the word **sprawl** from the vocabulary card. Have students imagine what their community might have looked like before settlers developed the land. Ask: *What would you see, hear, and smell before there were buildings and homes here?* Next tell students to recall the sights, sounds, and smells of nearby shopping centers and busy streets in the community today. Then instruct students to draw three squares. The first should have a paraphrased definition of *sprawl*. The second should have a picture that represents the word. The third should have a sentence using the word in context. Allow time for students to share their vocabulary squares with classmates.

Additional Vocabulary Explain the words in the margin and provide examples of their uses. Explain familiar words in relation to environment and growth, for example, say: *Suburbs are areas outside of cities where people live. They are built during times of growth.*

Cognates As students read the lesson, you may want to point out cognates such as: **cooperation/cooperación, resource/recurso, suburb/suburbio.**

bridges	nonrenewable
environment	pollution
harmed	renewable
highways	shopping mall
mussels	suburbs

Build Fluency

Read aloud the following rhyme and point out the words that sound alike. Have students repeat it several times to develop oral language skills. Return to the rhyme throughout the lesson to help develop vocabulary, summarizing skills, and lesson content.

> What happened in the United States
> When the population rose?
> Well, environments always change
> When a community grows.
>
> Growth changes the land
> With each new bridge, road, and mine.
> We build things to make our lives easy,
> But they often leave damage behind.
> **Sprawl** brings the environment new dangers.
> It's not only industries and people
> That development changes.

Success for English Learners

Scaffolding the Content

Preview the Lesson

Read the summary on page 593 aloud or display it on an overhead projector. Then ask questions students may answer using information in the summary, for example: *What is one type of change we will learn about?* Demonstrate how to glean answers from the summary as needed. Tell students they will learn how growth of population and industry in the United States created challenges.

• During **Teach**, pp. 590–593
• 30 minutes

Modify Instruction

Present the following summary. Give students time to find each heading on the blackline master page. Guide them in taking notes on each section. Then have them work in pairs to summarize the information.

Growth
- In 1990, about 248 million people lived in the United States. In 2000, about 281 million people lived in the United States.
- Population centers of the United States are crowded. However, some places in the United States have very few people.
- Since 1980, more than 10 million acres of land were developed to create suburbs.

Growth Harms the Environment
- Growth means people need more water and electricity. Growth can cause problems like pollution.
- People changed the environment of North America by building bridges and highways. They mined natural resources. They changed the environment to make life easier.
- Highways help people travel, but the government builds them through forests or other land. This affects the plants that grow there and the animals that live there.
- Ships can travel all over the world from the Great Lakes. However, ships there pollute the lakes and harm plants and animals.
- Transportation can bring new species of plants and animals to an area. Ships carried zebra mussels to the Great Lakes. The mussels hurt fish and plants there.

Growth and Neighbors
- Many farmers use the Rio Grande River for irrigation. People in Colorado and New Mexico use so much water that people downriver in Mexico do not get enough water.
- The United States has agreed to make sure a certain amount of water reaches Mexico.
- Countries should conserve nonrenewable resources. Scientists are trying to develop affordable renewable resources.

Extend

Tell mixed-proficiency pairs to create flow charts showing the effects of development on the environment. For example, students can draw pictures to show how building a house destroys plant and animal habitats, or how automobiles pollute the air.

• After **Teach**, pp. 590–593
• 10 minutes

Name _____ Date _____

DIRECTIONS First, listen and take notes as your teacher reads the lesson summary. Next, work with a partner to write a summary about how growth in the United States has affected the environment.

Growth

Growth Harms The Environment

Growth and Neighbors

Summary

 School-Home Connection Encourage students to take this page home to share with family members. They can use their notes to tell about growth in the United States and changes to the environment.

Unit 6, Chapter 14, Lesson 4 — Success for English Learners

Apply and Assess

Create a Poster

- During **Close**, p. 593
- 30 minutes

As a class, brainstorm ways people help the environment. Lead students to name ways stated or implied in the lesson. Record suggestions on the board and supplement them with such ideas as: *picking up litter, walking or riding bicycles instead of driving cars,* and *making sure ships do not bring new species to places.*

Ask students to include images, labels, phrases, and sentences in their posters. Provide magazines that students may cut up for images and text, and allow them to draw pictures as well. Assign tasks according to students' proficiency. Have beginning students sketch and find pictures from magazines, as well as write labels. Ask intermediate students to write phrases to express important ideas on the poster. Have advanced students write definitions or sentences that express important points.

Informal Lesson Assessment

	Beginning	**Intermediate**	**Advanced**
Task	Have students list ways population growth and industrial growth have changed the environment. Ask them to use sketches and key words.	Have students list ways population growth and industrial growth have changed the environment. Ask them to use phrases and short sentences.	Have students describe ways population growth and industrial growth have changed the environment. Ask them to use complete sentences.
Below Expectations	• no item correctly identified	• few or no correct responses • responses are incomprehensible	• no correct idea • no comprehensible explanations • many errors
Meets Expectations	• some items correctly identified	• a few correct responses • responses are mostly comprehensible	• some correct ideas • some comprehensible explanations • some errors
Above Expectations	• all items correctly identified	• all responses are correct • all responses are comprehensible	• all ideas are correct • all explanations are comprehensible • few errors

Answer Key

 ## Chapter 1

Lesson 1 States and Regions, p. 4
Things that are true of all 50 states: part of the continent North America; part of the United States; states in the same region share similar history, culture, and land, so people live in similar ways; all states in the country have two neighbors—Canada and Mexico **Things that differ from state to state:** most states are contiguous, but Alaska and Hawaii are not; states are in different regions: the West, the Southwest, the Midwest, the South, and the Northeast; different regions have different land, history, and culture, so people live differently in states of different regions; states in the North are closer to Canada, but states in the South are closer to Mexico

Lesson 2 The Land, p. 8
Landform Regions Location: Across the United States; Description: landforms are physical features like plains, mountains, plateaus, hills, and valleys; a landform region is an area of land where there is a lot of a particular landform **The Coastal Plain** Location: along the Atlantic Coast from Massachusetts to Mexico; Description: flat and low land **The Appalachians** Location: from New Jersey to Alabama; Description: higher than the Coastal Plain and has hills and valleys; old mountains with worn down peaks; covered with trees **The Interior Plains** Location: east and west of the Mississippi River from the Great Lakes to the Gulf of Mexico; Description: east of the river—flat and rolling land covered with grasses; west of the river—flat land with few rivers and trees. **The Rocky Mountains and Beyond** Location: from Alaska to Mexico; Description: new mountains with jagged peaks; the Great Basin west of the mountains—desert area shaped like a bowl with low land in the middle and high land all around it **More Mountains and Valleys** Location: near the Pacific Coast between the Rocky Mountains and the Sierra Nevada; Description: Central Valley—thick grass and many streams; Coast Range—rocky and rugged mountains

Lesson 3 Bodies of Water, p. 12
1. River; 2. Inlet; 3. Inlet; 4. River; 5. River; 6. Lake; 7. River; 8. Lake; 9. Inlet; 10. River; 11. River; 12. Gulf; 13. River; 14. Gulf

Lesson 4 Climate and Vegetation, p. 16
Places close to the equator: warmer; **Places far from the equator:** cooler; **Places close to the ocean or large bodies of water:** in the winter, water warms places, in the summer, water cools places; **Places far from the ocean or large bodies of water:** winter is colder and summer is hotter without water; **Grassland Vegetation Region:** dry climate, grasses can grow but trees cannot, in part of Central Plains and all of the Great Plains; **Forest Vegetation Region:** many trees grow in eastern and northwestern United States; **Tundra Vegetation Region:** cold, dry climate, water is frozen all year, mosses and herbs grow; **Desert Vegetation Region:** dry climate without a lot of water; grasses, bushes, and cactuses grow.

Lesson 5 People and the Environment, p. 20
Physical Features and Human Features Examples: Physical Features—climate, water, landforms; Human Features—buildings, roads; Differences: a physical feature is natural; people build a human feature **Uses of Land and Uses of Natural Resources** Examples: Uses of Land—farming, mining; Uses of Natural Resources—drinking water, make paper products, heat homes; Differences: uses of land is how people use the land, and uses of resources involve how people use things that are grown on the land or found inside it **Renewable Resources and Non-renewable Resources** Examples: Renewable Resources—water, trees; Non-renewable Resources—oil, gas; Differences: renewable resources can be manufactured or made by nature quickly, non-renewable resources cannot be manufactured, and take thousands of years for nature to replace

 ## Chapter 2

Lesson 1 Early People, p. 24
Time Period—(Early people) 14,000 B.C.–8,000 B.C.; (Olmec) 1500 B.C.–A.D. 300; (Maya) A.D. 300–1500; (Mound Builders) 1000 B.C.–A.D. 200; (Puebloans) not included **Location**—(Early people) from Asia to North America; (Olmec) southern Mexico; (Maya) southern Mexico, Guatemala, and northern Belize; (Mound Builders) east and west of the Mississippi River; (Puebloans) the Four Corners (Utah, Colorado, Arizona, and New Mexico) **Achievements and Other Facts**—(Early people) the bow and arrow, and learning to farm and stay in one place; (Olmec) used rivers to travel and trade, had a writing system, a number system,

and a 365-day calendar; (Maya) had a writing system based on hieroglyphs, had a counting system with the number zero, had social classes; (Mound Builders) used mounds to bury their dead; (Puebloans) their houses were built against canyon walls or in caves

Lesson 2 The Eastern Woodlands, p. 28
Cause 1: Effects 5, 6, and 9 **Cause 2:** Effects 2 and 4
Cause 3: Effect 10 **Cause 4:** Effects 3, 7, and 8
Cause 5: Effects 2 and 4 **Cause 6:** Effect 1
Cause 7: Effects 3 and 4

Lesson 3 The Plains, p. 32
Life on the Plains Location: between the Mississippi River and Rocky Mountains; Importance of buffalo: Buffalo was their main resource. They used it for food, clothing, bags, cord for rope, needles, and other tools. **Farmers and Hunters** Location: the eastern part of the Plains and the valleys of the Missouri River and Platte River; Names of Tribes: Mandan, Pawnee, Sioux; Homes: lodges made of earth, sometimes covered with soil and grass **A Nomadic Society** Location: the western part of the Great Plains; Names of Tribes: Kiowa, Cheyenne, Crow; Homes: tepees made of wooden poles and animal skins **Plains Cultures** Government: Lakota formed seven groups that made their own choices; Cheyenne had council of chiefs with representatives from ten groups. Beliefs and Traditions: Plains peoples had many of the same traditions and beliefs; many of them did the Sun Dance to keep buffalo strong.

Lesson 4 The Southwest and the West, p. 36
Navajo, desert, hot, dry 1. clay—homes; 2. wood—homes 3. clay—pottery; Shoshone, desert, little food or water 1. small animals—food 2. buffalo—food; 3. dry brush—homes; Nez Perce, mountains, streams 1. salmon—food; 2. streams and rivers—food and water; 3. movable shelters—homes; Chumash, mild climate, near ocean 1. fish—food 2. acorns—food 3. many plants—homes

Lesson 5 The Northwest and the Arctic, p. 40
1. Northwest 2. Arctic 3. Northwest 4. Arctic 5. Arctic 6. Northwest, Sub-Arctic 7. Sub-Arctic 8. Northwest, Arctic, Sub-Arctic 9. Northwest, Arctic, Sub-Arctic 10. Northwest

Chapter 3

Lesson 1 Exploration and Technology, p. 45
I. A Rush of New Ideas—Marco Polo's travels to China created interest in other places; the printing press helped people to make more books; travel was difficult, because people did not have accurate maps or the right technology. **II. The World Awaits**—A. Prince Henry and Navigation: Prince Henry started a school for navigation in Portugal; sailors learned to sail the caravel; people made better maps and improved navigation tools like the compass; people went on expeditions and looked for a sea route to Asia; B. Limited Knowledge: Europeans knew about Asia and Africa, which were divided into empires, or lands ruled by a nation that conquered them; Europeans did not know the Vikings found other continents. **III. The Business of Exploring**—Columbus: Columbus wanted to reach Asia by sailing west, but to do this he needed money for supplies and ships; The Reconquista: King Ferdinand and Queen Isabella wanted all of Spain to be Catholic; Muslims and Jews had to leave Spain during the Reconquista movement; after this, Spain paid for Columbus' voyage. **IV. Two Worlds Meet**—In 1492, Columbus and his crew sailed on three ships, the Niña, the Pinta, and the Santa María; Columbus finally reached land he believed to be Asia; Columbus and his crew were heroes when they returned to Spain.

Lesson 2 A Changing World, p. 49
Cabot: land and wealth for the king of England; long, slow journey and claimed wrong land; reached present-day Newfoundland but thought it was Asia; **Vespucci:** to find out if Cabot and Columbus reached Asia or a different continent; learned that this was a new continent, the Americas, and a new world map was published; the continent was named America after Amerigo Vespucci; **Balboa:** to find gold; found the Pacific Ocean and proved the land Columbus and Cabot reached could not be Asia; **Magellan:** to find a trade route to Asia; long journey, illness, hunger, death of sailors and Magellan; some of his sailors went all the way around the world; their claims led to a treaty between Spain and Portugal.

Lesson 3 Spanish Explorations, p. 53
Juan Ponce de León: to find the Fountain of Youth; he found Florida and many other lands; **Hernando Cortés:** to find gold; he destroyed the Aztec capital, Tenochtitlán, and built Mexico City for Spain; **Francisco Vásquez de Coronado:** to find cities of gold; he claimed many lands in the southwestern United States for Spain; **Hernando de Soto:** to have wealth and glory; he and his men were the first Europeans to see the Mississippi River, and they claimed many lands in the Southwest for Spain; **Missionaries:** to convert Native Americans to the Catholic religion; some Native Americans changed the way they lived and worshipped

Lesson 4 Other Nations Explore, p. 57
Giovanni da Verrazano: present-day North Carolina to Newfoundland; he looked for the Northwest Passage, a waterway across North America to give Europeans access to Asia, for the king of France; he did not find it; **Jacques Cartier:** present-day Canada; he looked for the Northwest Passage for the king of France as well; he claimed land in Canada for France, but he did not find the Northwest Passage; **Henry Hudson:** what is now New York; he claimed the Hudson River valley for the Dutch and the Hudson Bay for the English, because his voyages were paid for by companies in these countries

Chapter 4

Lesson 1 The Spanish Colonies, p. 61
New Spain—Spain set up colonies in North America to control the land it claimed; other Europeans and Native Americans also believed they had claims to many of these lands; **Slavery in the Americas**—The first settlers needed workers to farm on plantations and mine gold and silver; they made Native Americans into slaves and later brought slaves from Africa; some colonists, like Bartolome de Las Casas wanted better treatment for slaves; **Settling the Borderlands**—A. Forts: Forts were built in borderlands so Spain could protect them; in St. Augustine, Florida, the first permanent European settlement was built; leaders of these colonies were chosen by the king of Spain; B. Missions: Spain built religions settlements called missions to convert Native Americans to the Catholic religion; some of them learned new ways of life from missions, but others were forced to work there, and many fought against the work of the missions; C. Haciendas: Ranchers built haciendas in the borderlands; haciendas were houses on large areas of land for raising crops and animals; the Spanish and the animals they brought with them changed the lives of Native Americans

Lesson 2 The Virginia Colony, p. 65
1) England wants a colony in North America. 2) Settlers go to Roanoke Island; 3) Captain John Smith helps Jamestown survive; 4) Tobacco brings wealth to Virginia; 5) Virginia had indentured servants and slavery began; 6) The colonists set up a legislature; 7) The Powhatan War takes place; 8) The king of England makes Virginia a royal colony

Lesson 3 The Plymouth Colony, p. 69
1. **The Pilgrims' Journey:** Pilgrims left England on the *Mayflower* to New England in 1620; some people left for religious freedom, some thought they would make money;
2. **The Mayflower Compact:** The Pilgrims made Plymouth their new home; they signed the Mayflower Compact which created fair laws for people; they made self-rule and majority rule; William Bradford became their leader;
3. **Building a Colony:** The first winter was hard; Pilgrims got help from Native Americans; they learned where to fish and how to plant squash, corn, and pumpkins; they lived in peace;
4. **Plymouth Grows:** William Bradford continued to lead them; as people worked hard Plymouth grew; more people arrived to the colony and problems began to develop between Native Americans and Pilgrims

Lesson 4 The French and the Dutch, p. 73
I. New France France claimed land in the northeast and Canada; not many people from France wanted to come to the Americas, so the French built only two settlements, Montreal and Quebec; II. New Netherland The Dutch settled lands in present-day New York and New Jersey; Peter Minuit became their governor; the Dutch and Algonquian worked closely together, but later had many conflicts; III. Exploring New France—A. Wars Over Fur: The Dutch and Iroquois fought the French and the Huron, and the fighting almost destroyed the French fur trade and the Huron population. B. Explorers: The king of France sent explorers to find the Northwest Passage. 1. Marquette and Joliet found the Mississippi River with the help of Native Americans; they did not find the Northwest Passage 2. La Salle claimed land near the Mississippi for France; he named it Louisiana after King Louis XIV. IV. Louisiana—The king made Louisiana a proprietary colony, so he gave it to one person to rule; his name was John Law. A. New Orleans: The city of New Orleans was founded in 1717, and it became the capital of Louisiana after a few years. B. Growth of New France: New France did not grow fast because it did not attract a big enough population.

Chapter 5

Lesson 1 The New England Colonies, p. 77
The Puritans started the Massachusetts colony: began on Atlantic coast, Puritans received products from England; Puritans left England to begin pure Church of England; lifestyle—strict; church every Sunday, people worked hard; education—important to read the Bible. **New colonies began near the Massachusetts colony:** Puritans expelled colonists who did not follow rules; Roger William was expelled because he wanted church and government to be separate; Anne Hutchison was expelled because she questioned the teachings of ministers; they formed Rhode Island colony. **Native Americans already lived in locations where colonists settled:** Colonists—settled where Native Americans lived; 1675—King Philip's War, Metacomet led Native Americans in a war with colonists; British called Metacomet, King Philip; many colonists and Native Americans were killed. **Geography affected the economy through products colonists sold:** New England colonists—sold cows, sheep, fish, whale oil, and lumber; little farming—rocky soil; raised sheep and cows; caught fish and whales (oil to light lamps); New England forests—trees for homes, churches, and ships. **Geography affected trade:** New England colonies led trade, on the Atlantic coast; colonists could trade only with England or English colonies; triangular trade routes—from the New England colonies to colonies in Africa to England; Middle Passage—journey from Africa to colonies where many enslaved Africans suffered and died.

Lesson 2 The Middle Colonies, p. 81
New York and New Jersey were formed from New Netherland: Middle Colonies: New York, New Jersey, Delaware, and Pennsylvania—in the middle of the Southern and New England colonies; King Charles II of England wanted control; settlers refused to fight, so England took power from Peter Stuyvesant; The Duke of York—split New Netherland into New Jersey and New York. **Middle Colonies had diversity:** Quakers—New Jersey, wanted to practice religion safely; believed all people are equal; did not believe in war; William Penn—proprietor of the Pennsylvania colony, gave people freedom of speech, freedom of religion, and the right to trial by jury; immigrants from European countries settled there; some free Africans lived there, but most Africans there were enslaved. **Social activities were different in the city and country:** Religion—important part of life; 1720s—the Great Awakening; in the country—people met after religious services, had barn raisings; cities—dances, plays, and concerts; Philadelphia—biggest city. **People needed to earn money in different ways in the Middle Colonies:** main crops—wheat, corn, and rye; used to make bread, so the Middle Colonies was also called the Breadbasket Colonies; farmers—sold crops and livestock to merchants, merchants took products to port cities, products shipped to England and other colonies; jobs—farming, shipping, skilled trades like blacksmiths and carpenters, learned by being apprentices; women worked at home.

Lesson 3 The Southern Colonies, p. 85
1. Indigo was a cash crop: **South Carolina** 2. Tobacco was the main cash crop: **Maryland, Virginia** 3. The first settlers were English debtors: **Georgia** 4. People moved West to the backcountry: **The South** 5. The economy depended on plantations: **The South** 6. This colony was controlled by the king: **Virginia** 7. This colony was controlled by the Calverts: **Maryland** 8. These colonies began as one: **North Carolina, South Carolina** 9. Rice was a cash crop: **South Carolina, Georgia** 10. Enslaved people worked on plantations: **The South** 11. Corn was a cash crop: **North Carolina** 12. Shipbuilding was an industry: **Maryland** 13. There was a center for shipping forest goods: **North Carolina** 14. Planters paid brokers to buy and sell things: **The South**

Chapter 6

Lesson 1 Fighting for Control, p. 90
1. Both Britain and France claimed the Ohio Valley; 2. The French and Indian War began with the colonists fighting against the French and their Native American allies; 3. The colonists and the British defeated the French; 4. The colonists became upset with Britain.

Lesson 2 Colonists Speak Out, p. 94
Britain taxes tea—7; Parliament passes the Stamp Act—2; Colonists and British soldiers fight—8; Colonists write letters—6; Colonists speak out against the Stamp Act, saying they did not want to be taxed without representation—3; Parliament repeals, or takes back, the Stamp Act—5; Colonists boycott products from England—4; Britain needs money—1

Lesson 3 Disagreements Grow, p. 98
1. **Causes:** the Tea Act, colonists did not want to pay tax on tea; **Effects:** colonists made local tea; colonists destroyed British tea through the Boston Tea Party; 2. **Causes:** the British passed laws that closed the Boston Harbor and made the colonists provide British soldiers food and a place to live; **Effects:** colonists had the First Continental Congress and signed a petition of their rights; the Continental Congress decided to form an army and stop most trade with England; 3. **Causes:** British learned that two leaders of the Sons of Liberty were in Lexington, and that Minutemen had weapons in Concord; British planned a secret march to arrest the leaders and take weapons; **Effects:** Paul Revere learned the secret and warned the leaders; British did not find leaders or weapons, but there was fighting.

Lesson 4 The Road to War, p. 102
May 1775—**Event:** the Second Continental Congress meets; **Result:** the Second Continental Congress decided to prepare for war with Britain, formed a full-time continental army, named George Washington the commander in chief of the army, printed money called continentals. June 1775—**Event:** the Battle of Bunker Hill; **Result:** British soldiers lost many more soldiers, but they won because colonial troops ran out of ammunition. July 1775—**Event:** colonial leaders sent an Olive Branch Petition for peace to King George III; **Result:** King George III was angry about the Battle of Bunker Hill and rejected the petition for peace.

Lesson 5 Declaring Independence, p. 106
The People—Thomas Paine: wrote *Common Sense*; after this book, many wanted to form their own country; Richard Henry: asked the Second Continental Congress for a resolution of independence from Britain; Thomas Jefferson: wrote most of the Declaration of Independence; John Hancock and others signed it; Abigail Adams: Jefferson's wife, asked him to remember women, as only free, white men could vote then; Native Americans, African Americans, and women: did not have the same rights as white men for many years. **The Ideas**—Preamble of the Declaration of Independence: why the colonists had the right to form a new nation; colonists' ideas about government: the right to live, be free, and seek happiness; longest part of the declaration: grievances, or complaints, against the king and Parliament; colonies: should be free and independent states; ideas in the declaration: dangerous, because involved treason; treason—acting against the government; **The New Government**—Second Continental Congress: accepted the Declaration of Independence on July 4, 1776; new government: 13 colonies could work together without controlling each other; Articles of Confederation: plan for states to work together; Congress: each state had one delegate and one vote in the Congress; national government could declare war and make treaties but could not control trade or collect taxes; this government led the states during the Revolutionary War.

 Chapter 7

Lesson 1 Americans and the Revolution, p. 110
A. **Personal Hardships**—some colonists were Patriots and supported independence; other colonists were Loyalists and supported Britain; families, friendships, and churches were divided; British soldiers robbed and destroyed homes and crops; B. **Economic Hardships**—British stopped imports; shortage of imports, inflation (higher prices), people needed more money to buy products; profiteering: some people charged extra-high prices for products; hoarding: collecting large amounts of goods; laws: states passed laws against profiteering and hoarding C. **Women**—life changed: husbands left home to fight in the war; ran farms and businesses; raised money and collected clothing for soldiers; Martha Washington: followed husband and cooked food, washed clothes, and brought water to soldiers during battles; some women fought in battles. D. **African Americans**—enslaved Africans like James Armistead helped the Continental Army in return for their freedom; other enslaved Africans fought for the British for freedom; some free Africans like Peter Salem fought for the colonists E. **Western Settlers**—wanted to be neutral; did not want the British in western lands, so many joined the war. F. **Native Americans**—remained neutral at first, later became divided; many groups sided with the British to keep settlers from moving west, like the Mohawk tribe; some fought for the Americans, like the Oneida tribe

Lesson 2 Fighting for Independence, p. 114
Spring 1776—Event: The Battle of Long Island; Effect or Result: Patriots were outnumbered and suffered big losses Christmas 1776—Event: The Battle of Trenton; Effect or Result: Americans had hope after defeating the Hessians September 1777—Event: The Battle of Saratoga; Effect or Result: Americans captured British cannons and supplies, and the British surrendered; this was a turning point, and it seemed possible that the Americans might win the war Winter 1777—Event: The winter at Valley Forge; Effect or Result: American troops had little food, old and torn clothes; Marquis de Lafayette and Friedrich Wilhelm von Steuben helped the troops become stronger

Lesson 3 Winning Independence, p. 118
The British moved to the South—2; The British had a victory at Guilford Courthouse—6; Cornwallis surrendered at Yorktown—8; The French and Americans surrounded Cornwallis at Yorktown—7; Washington retired—10; The Treaty of Paris ended the war—9; Nathan Hale, John Paul Jones, Molly Pitcher, and Tadeusz Kosciuszko became Revolutionary War heroes—1; Benedict Arnold became a traitor—4; The Battle of Cowpens was fought in the South—5; The British took Savannah in Georgia and Charles Town in South Carolina—3

Lesson 4 Effects of the War, p. 122
New Ideas—states: needed constitutions; Declaration of Independence: gave people rights to life and liberty, but state constitutions did not give some rights to women and African Americans; Quakers: began the first abolitionist group; Elizabeth Freeman: sued to be free and won; Massachusetts: abolished slavery, and other northern states followed; Western Settlements—after the war the United States did not have enough money; soldiers were paid with land in the west; other settlers bought land in the west from Congress. Battles for Land—Native Americans got no more help from the British, it was difficult to stop settlers from moving onto their land; they united to fight against settlers; Michikinikwa was one leader who commanded a group of warriors; in the early 1790s, Native Americans had victories in Indiana and Ohio; Treaty of Greenville: in 1795, Native Americans gave up most of their land in the Northwest Territory; the Seneca sold their land. The Northwest Territory—land north of the Ohio River; land ordinance: laws passed in 1785 explained how land would be measured and sold; divisions: townships and sections; Northwest Ordinance: a plan for governing the territory, regions with over 60,000 residents could become states, also promised freedom of religion and banned slavery.

Chapter 8

Lesson 1 The Constitutional Convention, p. 127
Where: Pennsylvania State House in Philadelphia; When: May to September, 1787; Who: 1. George Washington 2. Benjamin Franklin 3. James Madison 4. Edmund Randolph 5. William Patterson 6. Gouverneur Morris; Why: Shay's Rebellion— the rebellion made people think the national government could not protect them; each state had a governor, but people wanted a national leader; What: 1. Relationship between states and federal government—some delegates wanted the federal government to have more power, but others wanted the states to have power; the delegates decided that the states and national government should share power in the new federal system. 2. Law—the Constitution would become the supreme law of the land. 3. Representation—delegates wanted the people to choose their representatives; delegates had different ideas, but they compromised so Congress would have two houses; in one house, each state would get one representative, in the other house, states with a larger population would get more representatives. 4. Slavery—delegates disagreed on how to count slaves in the population; they decided to count three-fifths of the total number of slaves in each state.

Lesson 2 Three Branches of Government, p. 131
The Preamble: explains the purpose of the Constitution, and that it is based on principles of individual liberty, justice, and peace; The Legislative Branch: makes laws to manage conflict, raise an army, declare war, make money, and control trade; Congress is made up of two houses, the Senate and the House of Representatives; both houses can propose bills; Congress can impeach the president; The Executive Branch: enforces laws; led by the president; the president can veto bills passed by Congress, but Congress can override the veto with a two-thirds vote; The Judicial Branch: decides cases that involve the Constitution, treaties, and national laws; highest court is the Supreme Court; the Supreme Court can strike down laws that go against the Constitution.

Lesson 3 The Bill of Rights, p. 135
1787—the Constitution was completed, but to become law, nine states had to ratify it; 1788—the Constitution was ratified; 1789—George Washington became the first president and made the State Department, Treasury Department, and War Department; the heads of the departments

became the first Cabinet; **1791**—the Bill of Rights was added to the Constitution; the rights are called Amendments; the **First Amendment**—protects freedom of religion, speech, and press; the **Second Amendment**—gives people the right to have weapons; the **Third Amendment**—does not allow the government to make people house soldiers; the **Fourth Amendment**—protects citizens from unfair searches; the **Fifth through Eighth Amendments**—give people right of due process of law and public trial by jury; the **Tenth Amendment**—states that the national government can only do what is in the Constitution; all other authority, or reserved powers, belong to the states or the people; **1797**—John Adams became the second president; **1800**—the capital was moved to Washington, D.C.

Lesson 4 A Constitutional Democracy, p. 139

Constitution: <u>Powers</u>—describes powers of the three branches of the federal government; ensures checks and balances; each branch can block power of the others. <u>One or Two Conclusions</u>—Power in the three branches of government stay balanced because of the Constitution. **Federal Government:** <u>Powers</u>—takes care of things that affect the entire country like training the military, protecting the environment, and helping children, elderly, and people who are ill. <u>One or Two Conclusions</u>—the federal government controls issues like protecting the country, keeping the country clean, and monitoring public health. **State Government:** <u>Powers</u>—states can build and manage state highways, parks, public schools, and colleges and universities; they help people who cannot pay for food, homes, and medical care; states cannot print money, make an army, or make a treaty with another country. <u>One or Two Conclusions</u>—States have a lot of power to build and manage transportation, education, and other programs that meet people's needs; states cannot make money, armies, or do other things that could affect other states or the unity of the country. **Local Government:** <u>Powers</u>—collect taxes within counties or cities; run legislative, executive, and judicial branches of government. <u>One or Two Conclusions</u>—Local governments have the same branches of government and other systems, like collecting taxes. **Citizens:** <u>Powers</u>—making choices about government by voting; acting with civic virtue; citizens have to obey, or follow laws; some people are born citizens; other people can become citizens through naturalization. <u>One or Two Conclusions</u>—People control the government by voting, and people must help the government keep the country healthy by acting with civic virtue.

Chapter 9

Lesson 1 Exploring the West, p. 143

1700s and 1800s: <u>Event:</u> many immigrants came to the United States; <u>Details:</u> from England, Scotland, Ireland, Germany, and other countries; hard times in home countries; wanted to find land or make money; **1801:** <u>Event:</u> Thomas Jefferson became the third President; <u>Details:</u> he wanted a port near the Gulf of Mexico where American farmers could ship their goods; sent representatives to France to ask Napoleon Bonaparte to sell New Orleans and part of Florida; **1803:** <u>Event:</u> Ohio became the sixteenth state; <u>Event:</u> Napoleon sold Louisiana to the United States in the Louisiana Purchase; <u>Details:</u> cost $15 million; doubled the size of the United States; **1804:** <u>Event:</u> Jefferson set up a trip to learn about the resources in Louisiana; <u>Details:</u> chose Meriwether Lewis to lead the trip; Lewis chose his friend William Clark to help him; group called the Corps of Discovery; left from St. Louis, Missouri on the Missouri River; winter in a Mandan Indian village; help from York, an enslaved hunter and fisherman, and Sacagawea, a Shoshone Indian; **1805:** <u>Event:</u> Lewis and Clark expedition traveled across the Rocky Mountains; <u>Details:</u> they reached the Pacific Ocean; **1806:** <u>Event:</u> Lewis and Clark returned home; <u>Details:</u> brought back seeds, plants, and animals; mapped mountains and rivers; frontier pushed farther west; Jefferson was proud; Event: Zebulon Pike went to explore part of the Louisiana Purchase; <u>Details:</u> went to Spanish lands by accident and was arrested; reported that people in Spanish territories needed goods; American traders began to sell goods there

Lesson 2 Expanding Borders, p. 147

1. The British army forced American sailors to work on British ships; 2. Chief Tecumseh united Native Americans to defend their land; 3. In 1812, President Madison asked Congress to declare war on Britain; Britain had strongest navy in the world; 4. Americans won at Lake Erie and at the Battle of the Thames; in 1814 the British fired on Americans in Fort McHenry for hours, but the Americans did not give up; Francis Scott Key wrote "The Star Spangled Banner," the national anthem; 5. The British burned the White House and the Capitol, in Washington, D.C.; 6. The British lost the Battle of New Orleans to Andrew Jackson and his troops; neither side knew that a peace treaty was signed two weeks earlier in Europe; 7. After the war, President James Monroe wrote the Monroe Doctrine which says Europe cannot form colonies in America; 8. In 1828, Andrew Jackson was elected president; he was a "common man" from a new state, Tennessee; in this election,

Answer Key

all white men could vote, not only those who owned land; 9. In 1830, Jackson signed the Indian Removal Act forcing the Cherokee and other tribes to go west of the Mississippi River; in 1838, President Martin Van Buren forced the remaining Cherokee to walk 800 miles to the Indian Territory in bad weather; one of every four Cherokee died during this trip; it is called the Trail of Tears.

Lesson 3 From Ocean to Ocean, p. 151
Texas Independence: 1821—Mexico became independent from Spain; many Americans went there for land; Santa Anna was dictator of Mexico; he sent troops to the Alamo; pioneers held off Santa Anna's army for 13 days; Mexico won; Sam Houston led Texan army; 1836—the Texan army captured Santa Anna; he gave Texas independence for his freedom; 1845—Texas became a state; Conclusion: It took a long time and lot of work for Texas to become a state. **Trails West:** Oregon Trail began in Missouri at Independence; pioneers traveled this trail in covered wagons; difficult and dangerous; people traveled in spring to avoid storms; people walked because wagons were full of supplies; Mormon Trail was used by Mormons, or members of the Church of Jesus Christ of Latter Day Saints; in 1846 Brigham Young led settlers from Illinois to Utah. Conclusion: Trails helped the United States grow because people used them to travel west. **Expanding Borders:** Manifest destiny was the belief that the United States was meant to stretch from the Atlantic Ocean to the Pacific Ocean; in 1846 war on Mexico over the border between Texas and Mexico; Treaty of Guadalupe Hidalgo—Mexico sold the Mexican Cession to the United States (California, Nevada, Utah, and parts of New Mexico, Arizona, Colorado, and Wyoming). Conclusion: The United States gained a lot of territory in the west after the war with Mexico. **The California Gold Rush:** 90,000 people from other states and countries rushed to California in 1849 for gold; they were called the forty-niners; California became a state in 1850. Conclusion: Gold brought many people to the West.

Lesson 4 New Ideas and Inventions, p. 155
National Road—to ship things over mountains from Maryland to West Virginia; Congress voted for it in 1818; it connected Maryland to West Virginia. **Canals**—to connect waterways without obstacles and move boats by a system of locks; **Steam Engines**—to power boats, invented in Britain, but used in 1807 by American inventor Robert Fulton; steamboats could travel upstream faster than other boats. **Railroad Engines**—to power locomotives, or railroad engines; Peter Cooper built first locomotive; Railroads grew quickly and made it easier for people and goods to travel. **Cotton Gin**—to remove seeds from cotton; invented by Eli Whitney; made it necessary for plantation owners to have more slaves. **Interchangeable Parts**—parts made by machine that can be mass produced; invented by Whitney; led to mass production. **Mechanical Reaper**—to harvest grain; invented by Cyrus McCormick; farmers could cut the same amount of wheat in one day as they earlier could in two weeks. **Steel Plow**—to cut through heavy soil; invented by John Deere; helped farmers. **The Industrial Revolution**—Inventions: people used machines instead of hands to make goods quickly and cheaply; began in Britain with textiles, or cloth

Chapter 10

Lesson 1 The North and the South, p. 160
Slavery—Northern States: different industries, jobs in factories, small farms, slavery was outlawed; Southern States: plantations depended on the work of enslaved Africans; slavery became stronger when plantation owners made money, slave states below Mason-Dixon line; **New States**—Northern States: Missouri Compromise: Maine admitted as a free state and Missouri as a slave state at the same time to keep balance in the Senate; Compromise of 1850: California joined as free state, Utah and Mexico decided whether to allow slavery; Kansas-Nebraska Act: in 1854, Congress allowed people in Kansas and Nebraska to choose whether to allow slavery, so people from free states and slave states moved to Kansas; Kansas became a free state; Southern States: Missouri Compromise: Missouri admitted as a slave state and Maine as a free state at the same time to keep balance in the Senate; Kansas-Nebraska Act: people moved from slave states (and free states) to Kansas to vote to make it a slave state, but it became a free state; **Trade**—Northern States: wanted a tariff on European goods so factories in Northern states could sell their products more cheaply; Southern States: did not want a tariff on European goods, because wealthy people liked to buy European products and did not want them to be more expensive; **Government**—Northern States: many Northern people liked President Andrew Jackson's ideas that the federal government could set tariffs; in 1882, Congress passed a tariff on European products; Southern States: many Southern people liked the ideas of Vice President Calhoun; he believed in state's rights and thought states should decide about tariffs.

Lesson 2 Resisting Slavery, p. 164

1. Dred Scott; enslaved Africans; his owner died, and he tried to win his freedom in court; the Supreme Court did not give him his freedom; 2. William Lloyd Garrison; white Northerners; founded American Antislavery Society; 3. Elizabeth Cady Stanton and Lucretia Mott; women; in 1848 wrote the *Declaration of Rights and Sentiments*; this called for the equity of all Americans; 4. Harriet Beecher Stowe; women; wrote *Uncle Tom's Cabin*. This book told how enslaved workers were mistreated; Northerners stopped ignoring slavery; 5. Samuel Cornish and John Russworm; free African Americans; in 1827 started the first newspaper owned by African Americans called *Freedom's Journal*; 6. Frederick Douglass; free African Americans; escaped slavery and became famous for writing and speaking against slavery; 7. Isabella Van Wagener (Sojourner Truth); free African Americans; escaped slavery; preached and spoke out against slavery; 8. Harriet Tubman; supporter of the Underground Railroad; was a famous African American, escaped slavery, and worked as a conductor along the Underground Railroad

Lesson 3 The Nation Divides, p. 168

1846—Abraham Lincoln elected to Congress; this was an important year for Abraham Lincoln. **1858**—Lincoln ran for Senate against Stephen A. Douglas; Douglas thought states should form laws about slavery; Lincoln wanted to stop slavery from spreading to the West; Lincoln lost the election, but became well known after debates with Douglas; The election of 1858 made Lincoln famous. **1858**—John Brown led a raid on a government building full of guns; Brown wanted to give guns to enslaved people; raiders were either killed or captured; John Brown's Raid divided the Union even more. **1860**—Abraham Lincoln won the election for president; Lincoln was Republican; Democratic party had two branches; Northern Democrats thought states should make their own laws about slavery; Southern Democrats wanted to protect slavery; Southern states wanted to secede when Lincoln won; Southerners did not want a leader who opposed slavery. **1861**—Alabama, Florida, Georgia, Louisiana, Mississippi, and Texas seceded from the Union; South Carolina was the first state to secede one year earlier, President Lincoln said he would not use military force against them; Union soldiers were attacked at Fort Sumter, and Lincoln prepared to fight the Confederacy; Lincoln did not want a war, but he was forced to prepare for one.

Lesson 4 The War Begins, p. 172

1. Union and Confederate states planned strategies; the Union strategy was to weaken the South, invade blockade ports to stop delivery of weapons and supplies from Europe to the South; Confederate strategy was to defend their lands, make a long war so Northerners would get tired; they expected help from Britain and France; **Generalization:** Both sides planned strategies to win the war. 2. The Union and Confederate states fought battles; Battle of Bull Run (Battle of Manassas) was fought in Virginia, first major battle of the Civil War; Thomas Jackson (Stonewall Jackson) led Confederate soldiers to victory; Battle of Antietam was in Maryland; General Robert E. Lee led Confederate soldiers; neither side won; many soldiers from both sides were killed; **Generalization:** Many soldiers were killed in battles when the war began. 3. Lincoln wrote the Emancipation Proclamation; Lincoln did not plan to stop slavery, he went to war to keep the country united; realized later war could help end slavery; issued the Emancipation Proclamation that freed enslaved people in areas fighting against the Union; enslaved people in border states and Union were not yet freed; **Generalization:** When the war began, Lincoln realized the war could help end slavery. 4. Women helped in the war; they found ways to help soldiers but could not join the military; Dorothea Dix and Clara Barton were nurses for the Union; Sally Tompkins ran a hospital for Confederate soldiers; Belle Boyd spied for the Confederacy; **Generalization:** Women helped the Union and Confederate armies in many ways. 5. African Americans fought in the war; 180,000 African Americans in the Union army; victims of prejudice from North and South; Robert Gould Shaw was famous leader of African American regiment; **Generalization:** Many African Americans fought in the Civil War of the United States.

Lesson 5 Toward a Union Victory, p. 176

Ulysses S. Grant: general who led Union soldiers; helped the Union win, because he was strong like the Confederate leader, Lee; **The Battle of Gettysburg:** turning point for the Union soldiers; seemed they would win; many soldiers were killed and wounded; **The Gettysburg Address:** speech by President Lincoln; given after the Battle of Gettysburg on November 18, 1863; became a famous speech, about liberty, equality, and honoring soldiers who died defending their ideals; **Sherman's March:** Union General William Tecumseh Sherman marched from Chattanooga, Tennessee to Atlanta, Georgia; March to the Sea was when Sherman's men went from Atlanta toward Savannah, burned homes and stores, destroyed crops, and tore up railroads;

Lee's Surrender: Lee ran out of men and supplies in the North; Grant and Lee met at Appomattox Court House; Lee surrendered; Civil War was over; states were still united; more than 600,000 soldiers had died; South in ruins; John Wilkes Booth, a Confederate supporter, assassinated Lincoln; **Generalization about the Union victory:** Many factors contributed to the victory of the Union, and the country suffered during and after the war.

Chapter 11
Unit 5

Lesson 1 Reconstruction, p. 180
New Presidents: Lincoln—did not want to punish the South; Vice President Andrew Johnson—president after Lincoln was assassinated; ended slavery everywhere in 1865; allowed most Confederates to become full citizens; Grant—wanted to punish Southern states; Rutherford B. Hayes—ended Reconstruction in 1877; **Political Changes:** Congress—punished Confederate states; put them under military rule; made each state write new constitutions that allowed African American men to vote; President Johnson tried to limit this plan; Congress impeached him and he was found not guilty. **Changes in Law:** African Americans—voted and elected African American leaders; secret societies like the Ku Klux Klan used violence to keep African American men from voting; Southerners passed laws that stopped African American men from voting, created segregation; Reconstruction ended—African Americans had few rights; **Economic Changes:** the economy in the South—in ruins; Freedmen's Bureau helped needy people in the South; many former enslaved people worked on plantations; paid through sharecropping; taxes in the South were very high to repair structures damaged in war; **Generalization:** Reconstruction was a difficult time for Southerners. They needed to build new buildings, a new government, and a new economy.

Lesson 2 The Last Frontier, p. 184
Q: Why did mining bring people West? Silver—prospectors went to Nevada in 1859; set up mining camps; towns grew around the camps; business owners sold products miners needed; this caused a boom, or quick growth **Q: Why did cattle trails bring people West?** Ranchers—wanted to sell meat to people in the East; made cattle trails and took trains; "cow towns" developed along the railroad; American cattle drivers learned from Mexican and African American cowhands about moving cattle; Nat Love—famous African American cowhand **Q: What happened to Native Americans as settlers came West?** Native Americans—lost buffalo and land; some tribes signed treaties for reservations; other tribes were forced on reservations including the Sioux, Nez Perce, and Apache **Q: Why did the Homestead Act bring people West?** 1862—Congress passed the Homestead Act; law gave land to people who lived there for five or more years; many Americans and 100,000 immigrants from Europe rushed to get this land; they were homesteaders and had difficult lives; they built houses from sod, or dirt **Generalization:** Mining, ranching, and the Homestead Act brought people West.

Lesson 3 New Industries, p. 188
1. Transcontinental Railroad: 1869—railroad across the entire country; people could sell goods and travel through the entire country, cities grew; **2. Steel:** 1872—Andrew Carnegie learned to make steel in Britain; built steel mill in Pennsylvania; steel was used for many things, like to make stronger trains and build skyscrapers; many people moved to cities for jobs; **3. Oil:** 1863—John D. Rockefeller set up oil refineries; he made kerosene to light lamps; made one very successful business, the Standard Oil Company; other oil companies could not compete; **4. Electric Light and Power:** 1874—Thomas Alva Edison opened a laboratory for inventions; had a team of inventors; best-known invention was a type of electric lightbulb; 1882—Edison set up the first central electrical power station; Lewis Lattimer was a famous African American engineer who directed the station; **5. Telephone:** 1876—Alexander Graham Bell designed a new telephone; Bell began the first telephone company in the country; people spoke over long distances **6. Unions:** owners of railroads, mills, and factories became rich; workers had little money, worked long hours, and dangerous jobs; labor unions organized strikes that forced employers to make changes; **How They Changed Life in the United States**—Industries and inventions of the 1800s improved the economy, working conditions, communication, and daily life in the United States.

Lesson 4 Cities and Immigration, p. 192
Challenge #1: It was difficult for immigrants to find jobs; sometimes children had to work full-time to support their family. **Challenge #2:** Some immigrants lived in poverty; many lived in crowded apartments called tenements without clean water. **Challenge #3:** Some immigrants had health problems because of dirty water and garbage in the streets. **Challenge #4:** Many Americans did not want immigrants in the United States; they felt that immigrants took jobs from Americans and were not educated enough. **Challenge #5:** Many immigrants did not know English; their children needed to teach them the language. **Generalizations:** 1) Life was difficult for immigrants. 2) Immigrants lived in poor conditions.

Chapter 12

Lesson 1 A New Role in the World, p. 197

1867: Alaska—bought from Russia, $7.2 million; 1893: Hawaii—was independent country, the queen changed laws that affected American sugar farmer, Americans imprisoned the queen; 1898: The United States annexed Hawaii; the United States declared war on Spain, because American ship *Maine* exploded; the Spanish-American War ended, and Spain gave the United States control of Spanish Cuba, Puerto Rico, the Philippines, and Guam; 1900: President William McKinley was assassinated, and Vice President Theodore Roosevelt became President; 1904: Roosevelt began the Panama Canal to connect the Atlantic and Pacific Oceans; President Roosevelt was supported by progressives; 1909: W.E.B. DuBois and other leaders formed the National Association for the Advancement of Colored People (NAACP); the NAACP worked to make fair laws for African Americans; 1959: Alaska became the 49th state of the United States; Hawaii became the 50th state.

Lesson 2 World War I, p. 201

Causes of World War I—Details: 1914—A Serbian rebel killed Archduke Francis Ferdinand of Austria-Hungary; Allies backed Serbia; Central Powers backed Austria-Hungary; Allied Powers (Allies)—Britain, France, Russia, Italy, and Serbia; Central Powers—Austria-Hungary, the Ottoman Empire, and Bulgaria; 1917—United States joined the Allies; Summary: World War I began, because a Serbian rebel killed Archduke Francis Ferdinand of Austria-Hungary. Many countries fought on the side of the Allies and Central Powers; **Fighting the War—Details:** United States had a small army; Congress made men ages 21 to 30 sign up for a military draft; trench warfare—digging trenches for protection and trying to reach "no man's land" between the trenches; new machine guns, tanks, poison gas, and airplanes; millions died; about 26,000 were Americans; Summary: Congress made a military draft to make the army bigger. Trench warfare and new weapons resulted in the deaths of millions; **The War at Home—Details:** Workers left their jobs to fight the war; to fill jobs, businesses increased pay, hired more women and African Americans; about 500,000 African Americans moved north to work in factories; families grew vegetables to send to soldiers. Summary: Workers left to fight in the war, so businesses hired more women and African Americans. Families supported soldiers by growing vegetables to send to soldiers; **The Effects of the War—Details:** American troops gave the Allies a boost; 1918— Germany surrendered; Treaty of Versailles—the League of Nations was begun to help nations solve problems; the United States did not join; 1920—women were given suffrage, the right to vote; Summary: Americans gave the Allies a boost, and Germany surrendered in 1918. The League of Nations and women's suffrage were results of events during the war.

Lesson 3 Good Times and Hard Times, p. 205

The Good Times: factories make vacuums, refrigerators, radios, assembly line Summary: After World War I, factories made new consumer goods. **New Art Forms:** jazz age begins; Louis Armstrong and Duke Ellington musicians and perform in Harlem; people listen to radio and watch movies Summary: Jazz music became popular, and people enjoyed pastimes such as listening to the radio and watching movies. **The End of Good Times:** people can buy shares of a business in the stock market; lots of people sold stocks in 1929, and the market crashed; economy collapsed Summary: In 1929, the stock market crashed, causing the economy to collapse. **The Hard Times:** companies lost money, cut jobs; banks ran out of money and closed; people lost money and went hungry; Midwest had Dust Bowl Summary: Factories closed, and people lost their jobs and money. The Midwest suffered the Dust Bowl. **The New Deal:** Franklin Delano Roosevelt became President; he formed The New Deal to help economy: Social Security, Tennessee Valley Authority, Civilian Conservation Corp; plan didn't fully work, but gave people hope Summary: President Franklin Delano Roosevelt introduced the New Deal, a program that provided jobs and helped the economy. It didn't completely work, but it gave people hope.

Lesson 4 World War II, p. 209

1. Adolf Hitler became dictator of Germany. 2. Germany, Japan, and Italy began taking over countries. 3. In 1939, Germany invaded Poland. 4. A military draft began. 5. Japanese planes dropped bombs on military ships in Pearl Harbor, Hawaii. 6. The United States joined the Allies. 7. The government began rationing goods. 8. Roosevelt ordered American military to put Japanese Americans in internment camps. 9. General Dwight D. Eisenhower led American troops invading Morocco. 10. The Allies defeated German troops in France on D-Day. 11. The war in Europe ended when the Allies accepted Germany's surrender. 12. America dropped atom bombs on the Japanese cities of Hiroshima and Nagasaki.

Lesson 5 The Effects of War, p. 213

The Holocaust: Hitler and the Nazis made concentration camps; Holocaust—murdered more than six million men, women, and children, mostly Jews; 1945—Allies brought Nazi leaders to trial; most important trials in Nuremburg, Germany; **The United Nations:** World War II—20 million soldiers died, 30 million civilians died; April 1945—50 countries met in San Francisco to form the United Nations to keep world peace; now UN is in New York; **Communism Expands:** The Soviet Union—on Allies' side in World War II; communist—government owned industries and property; Soviet Union pushed Nazis back into Germany and set up communist governments in the countries it marched through; eastern Europe—controlled by the Soviet Union; **The Berlin Airlift:** The United States, Britain, and France controlled West Germany; Soviet Union—controlled East Germany, so East Germany had a communist government; part of Berlin was in the east and part in the west; 1948—Soviets blockaded Berlin, so the Allies could not travel from Berlin to West Germany; Allies started the Berlin Airlift to get supplies into West Berlin; 1949—the Soviets ended the blockade.

Chapter 13

Lesson 1 The 1950s, p. 217

What happened in the Korean War? In 1950, the United States helped South Korea defend itself against an invasion by North Korea. The Soviet Union and China helped communist North Korea, and eventually a ceasefire was called. *What happened when the economy grew in the 1950s?* After rations were used in World War II, people bought many products and homes. Suburbs, or communities outside of cities formed, and Americans had more children. *Why was television important during the 1950s?* Television was the most popular pastime in the 1950s. Television was used in Dwight D. Eisenhower's presidential campaign and in the trial of Senator Joseph McCarthy. *Why did the United States and the Soviet Union compete?* During the Cold War, the United States and Soviet Union had an arms race to buy more weapons and competed to make progress in exploring space. As a result, the first space satellite, called Sputnik, was launched by the Soviet Union in 1957.

Lesson 2 The 1960s, p. 221

John F. Kennedy (elected in 1960) 1. Peace Corps: a program that sends American teachers, health educators, and engineers to developing countries. **2.** Space Exploration: 1961—President Kennedy asked Congress to give money for space exploration; the Soviet Union and the United States put men in space. **3.** Cuban Missile Crisis: 1962—President Kennedy ordered a blockade to prevent the shipment of Soviet missiles to Cuba, and Nikita Khrushchev took the missiles out of Cuba. **Lyndon B. Johnson (became President in 1963 after Kennedy was assassinated) 1.** Programs: Great Society—plan to make life better for Americans; Head Start—education for young children before school; Medicaid—free health care for the poor; Medicare—health insurance for older Americans. **2.** Man on the Moon: 1962—John Glenn was the first American to orbit the earth; in 1969—Neil Armstrong and Buzz Aldrin, Jr. were the first people to walk on the moon. **3.** The Vietnam War: 1964—President Johnson sent American soldiers to South Vietnam to help defend the country from communist North Vietnamese. In 1973, President Nixon ordered a cease fire. **Summary of Events in the 1960s:** During the 1960s important programs were developed, such as the Peace Corps by President Kennedy and Head Start and Medicaid by President Johnson. Americans Neil Armstrong and Buzz Aldrin, Jr. were the first men to walk on the moon in 1969. There were major conflicts including the Cuban Missile Crisis that ended peacefully in 1962 and the Vietnam War that divided the country and lasted from 1964 until 1973.

Lesson 3 Equal Rights for All, p. 225

Segregation in Schools—Details: Linda Brown—her family fought segregation in schools and won in 1954; Thurgood Marshall—the lawyer who argued this case to the Supreme Court. Summary: The family of Linda Brown fought segregation in public schools and won in 1954. **Segregation on City Buses—**Details: 1955—Rosa Parks refused to move to the back of the bus and was arrested; thousands of African Americans boycotted city buses; city buses needed their business; segregated seating on city buses was outlawed; Summary: After Rosa Parks was arrested for refusing to sit in the back of a city bus, African Americans boycotted city buses and segregated seating on city buses was outlawed; **Civil Rights Act of 1964—**Details: Many places segregated African Americans and whites; Martin Luther King, Jr.—African American leader who wanted to make changes using nonviolence; Civil Rights Act of 1964—gives all Americans the right to use public places and services, says employers cannot refuse to hire people based on race, religion, national origin, or gender; main goal of the Civil Rights Movement—to get full civil rights for all minorities under the Constitution; Summary: The main goal of the Civil Rights movement was getting full civil rights for all minorities under the Constitution. The Civil Rights Act of 1964 gives all Americans the right to use public places and services, and forces employers to hire fairly; **Violence**—Details: The Civil Rights movement was violent; riots because of integration in schools; African American leader named Malcolm X—supported separation between races; Malcolm X was assassinated in 1964; Martin Luther King, Jr. was assassinated in 1968; Summary: The Civil Rights movement was violent due to riots and assassinations of important civil rights leaders like Martin Luther King, Jr. and Malcolm X; **Rights for All Minorities**—Details: Cesar Chavez—formed the United Farm Workers (UFW) for better wages and conditions for migrant farm workers; new laws said employers must treat men and women equally; Summary: People fought for rights for other minorities, including migrant farm workers and women in the workplace.

Lesson 4 The 1970s and 1980s, p. 229
What were actions of Richard M. Nixon during the 1970s? President Nixon—he and Soviet leader Leonid Breznev agreed on arms control; 1972, Nixon was reelected; during his campaign, people working for him broke into an office of the Democratic Party in the Watergate building; Nixon covered it up; he resigned after a scandal. **Who did Americans blame for the troubles in the 1970s?** Jimmy Carter—elected in 1976; before this, Arab leaders limited oil shipped to the United States, so high gas prices and inflation began; 1979—students in Iran took Americans hostage; Americans wanted Carter to stop the crisis; they blamed Carter for the economy. **What were actions of President Ronald Reagan during the 1980s?** Reagan—elected in 1980; cut taxes; economy got stronger, inflation declined; government had less tax money and had to borrow money to pay bills; this made a budget deficit, or shortage; built a stronger military; Soviet Union made more weapons. **What changes did Soviet leader Mikhail Gorbachev make in the 1980s?** Gorbachev—leader of the Soviet Union in 1985; agreed to limit missiles; gave the people more freedoms in the Soviet Union; November 1989—the Berlin Wall was removed, the next year Germany was reunited; 1991—Gorbachev outlawed the Communist party; little to reunite the 15 Soviet republics, so they declared independence.

Lesson 5 The 1990s, p. 233
President George H.W. Bush—Details: In 1988, George H.W. Bush was elected President; he was Vice President under Ronald Reagan; economy had a recession, or time of slow activity; millions of Americans lost jobs; people worried about the economy; Bush was popular after the Gulf War. Summary: Under President Bush, the country had a recession, and millions of people lost jobs. The President remained popular, because of the victory in the Gulf War. **The Persian Gulf War**—Details: In 1990, Saddam Hussein and Iraq invaded Kuwait (a producer of oil in the Middle East); President Bush—built a coalition of 33 nations; the United States attack was called Operation Desert Storm, or the Gulf War; the Allies won; General Colin L. Powell became a national hero; Summary: After Saddam Hussein led Iraq to invade Kuwait, the United States responded with Operation Desert Storm. The Allies won, and General Colin Powell became a hero. **President Bill Clinton**—Details: Bill Clinton was elected in 1992; millions of new jobs; unemployment dropped; the President and Congress balanced the national budget; President Clinton and Congress made a law that people could receive welfare for only two years; controversy—Clinton was impeached, or accused of crimes, including lying under oath; he was not convicted; Summary: Under President Clinton, there were millions of new jobs, unemployment was low, and the budget was balanced through cooperation of the President and Congress. Clinton was impeached for lying under oath, but he was not convicted. **Terrorism**—Details: In 1993, foreign terrorists set off a bomb at the World Trade Center in New York City; six people were killed and 1,000 wounded; 1995—an American citizen set off a bomb at a government building in Oklahoma; bombs exploded at two American embassies in Africa; the USS *Cole,* a United States Navy ship, was bombed near Yemen; Summary: In the United States, foreign terrorists set off a bomb at the World Trade Center, and an American citizen bombed a government building in Kansas. Abroad, bombs were set off at U.S. embassies in Africa and the USS *Cole* near Yemen.

Chapter 14

Lesson 1 New Challenges, p. 237

1. **Presidential Race:** In 2000; Republican George W. Bush ran against Democratic Al Gore; 100 million votes; in Florida, too close to call a winner; Supreme Court said Bush wins; January 20, 2001; George W. Bush—43rd President; 2. **Terrorist Attack:** September 11, 2001; terrorists hijacked four American planes and killed nearly 3,000 people; two planes hit the towers of the World Trade Center in New York City; one plane hit the Pentagon in Washington, D.C; one plane crashed into an empty field; 3. **Afghanistan:** October 2001; the United States and allies overthrew the Taliban government in Afghanistan; 4. **Iraq:** 2003; the United States and its allies invaded Iraq; leader of Iraq was Saddam Hussein; violence there continues; 5. **Reelection:** 2004; George W. Bush was reelected; Americans split on the war in Iraq; 6. **Hurricanes:** 2004 and 2005; four hurricanes hit Florida in 2004; Hurricane Katrina hit the Gulf Coast in 2005; Hurricane Katrina was one of the worst natural disasters in United States history.

Lesson 2 Our Nation's Economy, p. 241

1. **What three kinds of resources do businesses need?** human resources—workers; natural resources—water, minerals, fuel, and others; capital goods—buildings, technology, and tools to produce goods and services. Summary: Businesses need human resources, natural resources, and capital goods. 2. **How are resources divided?** not enough resources for everyone; paying prices, sharing equally, rationing, bartering, first-come-first serve, or having a lottery; market economy (as in United States)—people or businesses pay for resources; command economy—government decides who gets resources. Summary: In a market economy, people or businesses pay for resources, but in a command economy, the government decides who gets them. There are many ways to divide resources. 3. **How are prices determined?** big demand—big prices; small demand—small prices; high supply—lower prices; low supply—higher prices; companies can lower prices or make higher quality, so more people will want their product. Summary: Prices are determined by supply and demand. 4. **What makes businesses productive?** productive businesses—produce more; education, capital goods like computers, and specialization help companies produce more. Summary: Education, capital goods like computers, and specialization help companies produce more.

5. **Why are regions interdependent?** No place produces everything people want; no place has all natural resources; places depend on those that have what they do not. Summary: Places depend on each other for what they cannot produce.

Lesson 3, A Global Economy, p. 245

Service Industries: In the past, more people worked to make goods. Now, more people work to provide services like teaching, checking medical health, and repairing cars. **The Information Age:** Since the 1970s, people have access to more information than before. High-tech, or computer and electronic industries have become very important to the American economy. **Free Trade Agreements:** Free-trade agreements, or agreements not to charge tariffs, or taxes, on goods, increases trade between nations. One example is the North American Free Trade Agreement between Canada, the United States, and Mexico. **Globalization:** Nations of the world have experienced globalization, or growth to a global economy, and nations depend on each other for goods and services.

Lesson 4, Growth and the Environment, p. 249

Growth: 2000—population 281 million; population centers of the United States are crowded; since 1980, more than ten million acres of land and forest made into suburbs; **Growth Harms the Environment:** growth—pollution; more water and electricity are needed; environment of North America—changed by bridges and highways, mining natural resources; changed to make life easier; highways—help people travel, but they are built through forests or other land; affects plants and animals there; Great Lakes—ships can travel all over the world from them; ships pollute the lakes and harm plants and animals there; zebra mussels—foreign species that damaged fish and plants there; **Growth and Neighbors:** Rio Grande river—needed for irrigation; people in Colorado and New Mexico—use so much that people in Mexico do not get enough water; the United States agreed to limit use; countries should conserve nonrenewable resources; scientists making affordable renewable resources; **Summary:** When population of the United States grew, the environment changed. Land changed through building bridges, mines, and highways. Water bodies like the Great Lakes changed because of pollution and foreign species.